C000173264

ULTIMATE GIG

ULTIMATE GIG

Flexibility, Freedom, Rewards

BY

JOHN T. FLEMING
Ideas & Design Group, USA

WITH

LAUREN LAWLEY HEAD
Lawley Head Media, USA

United Kingdom – North America – Japan
India – Malaysia – China

Emerald Publishing Limited
Howard House, Wagon Lane, Bingley BD16 1WA, UK

First edition 2021

British Library Cataloguing in Publication Data
A catalogue record for this book is available from the British Library

ISBN: 978-1-83982-861-4 (Print)
ISBN: 978-1-83982-860-7 (Online)
ISBN: 978-1-83982-862-1 (Epub)

ISOQAR certified
Management System,
awarded to Emerald
for adherence to
Environmental
standard
ISO 14001:2004.

Certificate Number 1985
ISO 14001

INVESTOR IN PEOPLE

ABSTRACT

Author – John T. Fleming
Editor – Lauren Lawley Head
August 27, 2020

Context: The gig economy has become a popular subject in mature markets throughout the world, especially the United States. The words were even used by the United States Congress when recently addressing the different classification of workers impacted by COVID-19. The gig economy has become a new phenomenon attracting record numbers of people to the possibility of part-time work or work that offers flexibility in how and where the work is being done. Some gig workers turn gigs into a preferred way of earning full-time income.

Gigs are not new. Part-time work has always been a possibility for those who sought incremental work opportunities. What is different about the gig economy is its innovative use of technology in connecting gig workers with a source of product, service, or client, and a consumer who is interested in making a purchase. Many gig workers now find technology to be the enabler in turning underutilized assets such as homes, rooms, and cars into income-earning opportunities. The choices in how we work, when we work, and where we work from have never been greater!

Information relative to the gig economy, the definitions and understanding of gig economy, motivations for working a gig, selecting a gig, and working a gig can be difficult to find; therefore, *Ultimate Gig* can help to eliminate misunderstanding and confusion when seeking to better understand the gig economy.

Ultimate Gig	Title	Description
Dedication		Gig workers
Acknowledgments		Those who make this book possible
Preface		What the book is all about
Chapter 1	Welcome	Defining the gig economy and types of gigs
Chapter 2	Academic Perspective	Making sense of the gig economy
Chapter 3	Motivations	Why people from all walks of life work gigs
Chapter 4	Gigs Redefine Entrepreneurship	Gigs make microentrepreneurship easily available
Chapter 5	How Technology Is Shaping Gigs	The gig economy leverages technology effectively
Chapter 6	Direct Selling – The First Gig	The 100-year-plus channel of distribution is a gig
Chapter 7	Women and the Future of Gigs	We explain why women appear to be the future of gigs
Chapter 8	Defining the Ultimate Gig	Leverage your strengths and passions – your ultimate gig
Chapter 9	Maximizing the Potential of a Gig	The guidance all gig workers need
Chapter 10	A Perspective on Challenges	Identification of the obvious, solutions, resolutions
Chapter 11	Research Findings and Insights	The most current research and insights on gig economy
Chapter 12	Game Changers	Companies and individuals who are changing the game
Epilogue	Glimpse of the Future	A summary of the book, our experiences, future of work

This book is about better understanding the gig economy conversation. It is also about understanding one of the most significant labor revolutions in the past 100 years as to how work can be done. *Ultimate Gig* is about the value of microentrepreneurship and putting entrepreneurship tools into the hands of the masses, the crowd. This book will inspire, inform, and educate. It will help gig workers and potential gig workers better understand the incredible value of new choices that allow anyone – regardless of age or walk of life and irrespective of experience or inexperience – opportunities to leverage time and convert hours into meaningful and fulfilling work in a flexible manner.

DEDICATION

*Today, people of all ages and from all walks of life find it possible
to work in a new way. They are independent contractors using
various labels to describe their approach to working when they
wish and, often, from wherever they choose. These are not
contractors filling typical job functions. We are referring to a new
breed of workers.*

Ultimate Gig *is about the millions of people (approximately 60
million in the United States alone) who have embraced a new way
of working. Perhaps more so than any other type of worker, gig
workers have decided to bet on themselves. Gig workers
understand that their success will depend on the quality of the
service and products they provide to others.*

*We dedicate this book to the gig-providing companies and their
founders who envisioned work differently, and to the new army of
microentrepreneurs who bring positive change to their personal
lives and the lives of those they serve.*

TABLE OF CONTENTS

LIST OF FIGURES AND TABLES

ABOUT THE AUTHOR

John T. Fleming has always embraced a belief that being the first to do something different is always a choice. His parents, both educators, encouraged a belief that you accomplish what you think you can. This belief is foundational to everything John has accomplished from high school to engineering school, to working in the office of Mies Van der Rohe – the German architect recognized as being one of the "masters" of modern architecture, to direct selling entrepreneur, to an officer in one of the world's largest and most notable direct selling company's brands, to publisher and editor of a trade publication, to founder of Ideas & Design Group, LLC, to consultant, speaker, writer, student, researcher, advocate of microenterprise, and now author of this book.

John is also the author of *The One Course*, a course written to stress the importance of personal development beyond what is offered in our traditional educational system and served as a co-author with New York Times best-selling author Robert Kiyosaki (Rich Dad Poor Dad) on the book, *The Business of the 21st Century*.

John remains one of our country's strongest advocates for the selling profession, the gig economy, and the independent contractors who benefit from what gig-providing companies make possible. He consistently speaks and writes about "work" being redefined and the new choices which enable people from all walks of life, regardless of age, past experience or inexperience, the opportunity to learn basic skills associated with selling and/or serving customers, and the opportunity to engage in the free enterprise system. His recognition includes Direct Selling Association Hall of Fame, Direct Selling Education Foundation Circle of Honor and Direct Selling News Lifetime Achiever.

ABOUT THE EDITOR

Lauren Lawley Head became intrigued by the power of storytelling at an early age and has spent her career immersed in the craft.

She earned two degrees from the University of Missouri-Columbia, one in journalism and one in economics. After graduation, she combined the two in her work as a business reporter, covering retail, technology, and health care. She worked her way up through multiple newsrooms, developing a passion for interviewing entrepreneurs and sharing stories that inspire others to embrace innovation and positive change.

After a 20+ year career in journalism, Lauren took the entrepreneurial plunge herself, founding Lawley Head Media, LLC to help organizations, authors, and entrepreneurs use the power of their stories to create and launch new products, streamline content development, and implement effective marketing practices.

She is a former Senior Vice President of *SUCCESS* magazine, Publisher and Editor in Chief of *Direct Selling News,* and Editor for American City Business Journals' *Dallas Business Journal* and *Pittsburgh Business Times.*

PREFACE

Ultimate Gig is about helping people better understand what the gig economy is all about. Our research and thoughts have always been focused on why gigs fuel new values, such as the desire for more flexibility and freedom in how we work. There are solid reasons why a diverse population gravitates toward work that focuses more on flexibility and freedom and the potential rewards that can be achieved.

Traditional companies embraced the idea of flextime many years ago. Once considered a risky experiment, human resource professionals found ways to bolster their company culture by offering flexible work opportunities. The idea is no longer an experiment. A growing percentage of job applicants will not be interested in traditional nine-to-five working hours. Many employees now complete part of their job during set hours in the office and the remainder when and where they choose. In some cases, employees do not work in a fixed facility at all. This type of flexible work and those who perform it are often defined as "the alternative workforce."

COVID-19 increased the value of flexibility in how work is done. With states and countries enforcing stay-at-home orders, many businesses were forced to close their physical locations and adapt to find ways to allow people to work from their homes. The value of gig work increased as the unemployment rate soared very quickly from an all-time low to an all-time high in the United States. Some organizations even began to abandon an office-centric work environment altogether, as they found that the benefits of virtual working outweighed the disadvantages.

While the gig economy is considered a new phenomenon, the concept of gig work has been around for more than 100 years.

Direct selling companies, which utilize independent contractors to handle the primary responsibility of acquiring, selling, and serving customers, offer one of the first forms of gig work. In the traditional nine-to-five work culture, the direct selling opportunities created by such trailblazing brands as Amway, Avon, Mary Kay, and Tupperware stood out. When these companies began, they offered unique opportunities for people to earn money with immense flexibility and freedom in how they completed the work. These characteristics made direct selling very attractive to women, representing approximately 75% of direct selling participants.

Today, the growing number of gigs produces even more work choices and more flexibility. The opportunity to work following personal preferences has never been more numerous. Being limited to a single source of income no longer exists. An individual's ability to increase his or her income potential is only limited by the person's objectives and the number of hours available to embrace a new activity.

There are many types of gig opportunities, and nearly as many names used to describe them. You will learn about each as you continue to read. The gig economy has provided all ages and backgrounds with opportunities that are not linked to the qualifications you would typically find on a résumé.

This book will take you on a journey, one that is easy-to-read at times, and more academic in approach at other times. We tell a story based on personal and collective perspectives gained from many years of working as an independent contractor and in support of independent contractors. Our work began with natural curiosity, study, and ultimately the formal research we just completed.

This story is about the revolution taking place in how work is performed and the diverse motivations that have attracted more people to part-time work than perhaps any other time in history. We are focused on making sense out of the gig economy to benefit those who seek gigs and provide gigs. We think you will find the information we share to be very valuable to the objectives that caused you to acquire a book such as this one.

This book will inform, inspire, and motivate. It may serve to answer questions, and it may help confirm decisions that gig-providing companies are evaluating. It will provide insights and guidance to those working or seeking a gig. Parts of this book may serve as a teaching tool or a means to confirm your decision about engaging in a gig opportunity.

This book is about understanding the conversation and understanding one of the most significant revolutions in the past 100 years as to how work can be done. It is about the value of micro-entrepreneurship and putting entrepreneurial tools into the hands of the masses. It may trigger discussions that need to be scheduled, and it may trigger the reexamination of strategic plans. This book will help gig workers better understand the incredible value of new choices that allow anyone – regardless of age or walk of life and irrespective of experience or inexperience – to leverage time and convert hours into meaningful and fulfilling work.

Many of us have lived through times when, regardless of our experience or educational background, we could not leverage more hours into more possibilities because we could not find the flexibility we needed. Perhaps you have experienced a time when pre-defined work schedules did not fit within your life's constraints or conflicted with your chosen values, such as how you wished to care for your family. You may have experienced times when a flexible work arrangement would have served as a bridge between the last job and the next long-term opportunity you were pursuing. You may have determined you needed to work again after formally retiring because your retirement plan did not work as you had envisioned. Or you may have been looking for an entrepreneurial opportunity that offered minimal risk.

Today's gig-providing companies have created what past generations hoped to find: flexible work opportunities that can be engaged by the masses. The dreams of yesteryear have become today's realities and possibilities. This book is about the gig economy. We hope you enjoy the journey.

ACKNOWLEDGMENTS

We might readily agree that ideas fuel the evolution of wisdom and knowledge. This book is the result of ideas shared by a multitude of others who, perhaps, never realized the meaning to me of the thoughts they shared.

Capturing and recording ideas is hard work. As an architectural student, I learned quickly that every idea could not be transformed into real design and real plans that lead to the construction of actual structures. Therefore, writing a book on the gig economy phenomena was both a big and scary idea.

When I shared the idea with a couple of close friends, Kate Gardner and Alan Luce, they said, "Let's do this!" Alan Luce is a principal of Strategic Choice Partners and an attorney with many years of experience working within and in support of the direct selling model. He is a dear friend who I first met when he was chief legal officer at Tupperware Brands. Over the years, I have had many conversations with Alan relative to independent contractors and how best to support their efforts. Alan shared much insight into the topic and contributed specifically to the thoughts and insights shared in Chapter 6. Kate Gardner, principal of GardnerCo, LLC, is another exceptional friend. Kate was enthusiastic about this project from the beginning and facilitated the capturing of many of the testimonials sprinkled throughout the book. Kate also helped open many doors, introducing us to many others who became supportive of what we were doing.

Next, I knew I would need the input of a few academics. I called my friend, Dr. Greg Marshall, the Charles Harwood Professor of Marketing and Strategy at Rollins College's Crummer Graduate School of Business in Winter Park, Florida. I shared the idea of writing a book on the gig economy phenomenon and its impact on redefining work and the composition of the labor force. I asked Greg if he would be interested. When he also said, "Let's do this!" I knew that we were on to something that could be meaningful to everyone seeking to make sense of the gig economy, its impact on the marketplace, and, most importantly, the labor force. Greg wrote Chapter 2.

When Lauren Lawley Head, principal of Lawley Head Media, became interested in the role of *Ultimate Gig* Project Manager, I knew we had a core team that could do the work. Lauren is the ultimate project manager. She brings the poise, experience, and a very organized approach to the reporting and storytelling associated with this project. We were fortunate that Lauren, also a dear friend, was available to assume the role of editor and project leader. Lauren has read and reread every word of every chapter. The fine-tuning only ended when the manuscript was submitted to our publisher.

We are also very proud of the core team, including two graduate students, Christian Panier and Christina Schreiber of Rollins College's Crummer Graduate School of Business, who contributed to this work. Lauren worked with the graduate students weekly to ensure their experience with the project was a gratifying learning experience. There are so many details to be covered when writing a book and so many questions. Christian and Christina helped a lot, and we are grateful for their contributions and to Dr. Deborah Crown, Dean of the Crummer Graduate School of Business at Rollins College, for considering work on our project worthy of the time invested by two outstanding graduate students.

Our publisher, Emerald Publishing Limited, United Kingdom, is precisely the type of publisher we sought. I was introduced to Emerald Publishing and Senior Publisher Andrew Pert over a dinner suggested by Dr. Marshall. Emerald is a global publisher known for its focus on research. Emerald CEO Vicky Williams shares in a statement on the Emerald website: "At Emerald we're all guided by one thing which is to find and share research which challenges, disrupts and changes the world – little by little – for the better." I knew we had a story to tell from a unique perspective. The possibility of being in the Emerald community of outstanding writers and researchers kept us awake for a few nights. We are proud to be in the Emerald community.

We are also profoundly grateful to those who became sponsors of our efforts. The support of Robert Cavitt, CEO of Jenkon Inc., has been invaluable. His visionary leadership and willingness to participate served to inspire us to take on the project. I have known Robert for close to 20 years. Throughout the tenure of our friendship, I always found Robert to be very interested in sharing his wisdom or, as the expression goes, paying it forward. Robert always wants to make a personal contribution to the welfare of others, the education of others, and the future of others. I know Robert runs a very successful company; however, I never hear him talk that much about his success. He is always more comfortable talking about what the future will be like. His company is a technology company, so it was most fitting for Robert to become the primary contributor to the chapter on technology.

John Parks, of John A Parks Company, Inc. – Insurance Agency, a long-time friend, who has always been innovative in seeking and providing insurance products and services to support independent contractors also contributed to the ideas we explored relative to the new type of safety-net gig workers will need in the future to enhance and encourage participation in the gig economy as a gig worker.

Stephanie McVeigh, Founder, and CEO of Strategic Incentive Solutions, Inc., a travel incentive company based in Canada, brought to us insights relative to the importance of incentives in inspiring human behavior. We were grateful to be introduced to Stephanie by Kate Gardner.

Toward the end of our quest to identify needed support for the project, we were fortunate to meet Paul Beldham, CEO, and Karen Dworaczyk, Chief Revenue Officer, at PayQuicker. Good friend Kelly Thayer made the introduction. Both Karen and Paul have been a joy to work with. Our relationship will yield much more information and data as we continue our work long after publishing this book. Their contribution to the chapter on technology enlightened us to the importance of prompt compensation once work is done, which is also a part of the labor revolution we are experiencing.

In this book, we tell a story. It is based on personal and collective perspectives gained from many years of working as an independent contractor and in support of independent contractors. And it would not have been possible without the dozens of gig workers who were willing to share their personal stories and experiences with us. You will find glimpses of these conversations throughout the book, but the depth and breadth of their contributions are infused throughout our work.

As of this writing, our research is the most current and insightful conducted on the gig economy. In this book, we share highlights. We also acknowledge the importance of the contributions of Dr. Robert A. Peterson for encouraging us to conduct formal research to gain empirical data to support the ultimate gig project, and we did. Dr. Peterson is a professor at The University of Texas at Austin, where he holds the John T. Stuart III Chair in Business Administration. A former vice president of the university, he was recently honored by the government of Portugal when it named the first supercomputer in Portugal after him ("BOB"). Working with Dr. Peterson has been one of the great experiences of this project, and we are grateful for the time he gave us.

Others who contributed their time, insights, helped to arrange conferences, provided interviews, contributed to articles, and helped to connect our dots when we needed, included: Kerry Tassopoulos Esq., The Tassopoulos Law Firm, Yogi Shankar, Founder and CEO Prescriptive Insights, Inc., Vince Han, Founder, CEO Mobile Coach, Lori Bush, Cofounder, CEO of Solvasa Beauty, Inc., Janet Meeks, Author of *Gracious Leadership: Lead Like You Have Never Led Before*, Maria Locker, Founder, CEO, RevolutionHER, Milind Pant, CEO, Amway Corporation, Sheryl Adkins-Green, CMO, Mary Kay, Kevin Guest, Chairman, CEO, USANA Health Sciences, Cindy Droog, Amway Corporation, and Melissa Fields, USANA Health Sciences and Margaret Jones, Mary Kay. Our conversations with each provided value beyond their actual contributions.

There are also friends, new and enduring, who impacted our thinking. I remember listening to Dr. Keenan Yo Ho, Crummer

Graduate School of Business, Rollins College, speak on innovation and creativity. Dr. Yo Ho helped me to understand real innovation better. That understanding transferred to an even greater appreciation for the innovation gig providing companies bring to the subject of work and how it can be done. Stuart Johnson, Founder and CEO of SUCCESS Partners, a long-time dear friend, keeps me inspired simply through our conversations relative to what inspires others to do what they do. Stuart remains a positive source of information, education, and inspiration available through both the *SUCCESS* and Direct Selling News brands. Teresa Craighead, Publisher of Social Selling News, is another who serves to keep us informed and inspired through the work that they do. Brett Duncan and his team at Strategic Choice Partners, especially Brooke Hawkins, a talented graphic artist and digital asset builder, and Clark Diemer, Left Hook Videos, stepped up at the very beginning and said, we support you. We are indebted to them for their ongoing support of our website, video, and social media work. Bobbie Wasserman, principal and owner of Wave 2 Alliances, has always been there when I had a question or needed guidance on how to find the answer to a question. Marcia Allen, principal and owner of Marci Designs, helped us launch our first publication, the *Ultimate Gig Special Report*. It was Marci's very creative and unique approach to design and layout that made the *Ultimate Gig Special Report* interesting, appealing, and easy-to-read.

I also acknowledge the personal experience gained from being able to work with Cindy and Scott Monroe, founders of Thirty-One Gifts. During what became many years of association, I learned firsthand how owners of a direct selling company approached the founding and management of their business in a manner that always focused on strong principles and values and the people who represented the brand. Through the association with Thirty-One Gifts, I also met two extraordinary people: Janet Meeks, author and former chief executive of a large and well-respected medical complex, and Kerri Anderson, former Chief Financial Officer and Chief Executive Officer at Wendy's International. The working relationship and friendship impacted personal thinking about many things, this book included.

I would like to thank those who invited me to speak on the subject of gig economy when we first started our research: Kate Gardner and Bret Duncan, founders of theJuice networking breakfasts for executives; Al Bala and Landen Fredrick, the CEO and CSO of Mannatech Inc.; Peter Maddox, president of the Canadian Direct Selling Association; Joe Mariano and Melissa Brunton, president and vice president of the U.S. Direct Selling Association. Thanks also to Sonya Cooper Turner, a personal consultant and friend over many years, for your encouraging support. Brian Connolly and Larry Thompson, the conversations always mean more than you know. Larry, your invitations to speak at your Gig Summits provided opportunities to share research and gain the feedback of an audience. Your events definitely impacted my thinking.

Special acknowledgment is extended to family members who often wondered, "What in the world are they doing?" A project such as this requires work beyond traditional working hours. There are long days and some nights that turn into days. The sunrise is most amazing after a long night. Lauren's husband, David, is an invaluable support and creative sounding board. Their two sons, David and Alexander, are growing up alongside the gig economy. Seeing the world's possibilities and optimism through their eyes is inspiring, and getting to enjoy their smiles and laughter makes every day brighter.

Personally, I hope that my family – my wife, Joyce, my son John and his wife Nicole, my daughter Kassandra and her husband Mel, and our grandchildren Kennedy and Hunter – will one day realize their pop-pop gathered together a great group of people who researched and wrote about a subject beginning to change and revolutionize the way we work. My oldest granddaughter Kennedy will graduate from Southern Methodist University with one of her first degrees within a couple of years. I do not expect her to work in a traditional format. The format will be quite different. The youngest granddaughter, Hunter (10 years), is way too smart ever to be confined nine to five! It just will not happen, or at least that is my prediction.

My personal friends also mean a lot to me, more than they will ever know. It is through special friendships and the interaction that thoughts are formed, sometimes cultivated but always encouraging. I am now talking about those friends who I hold in a category far beyond friendship. I love that even though we do not physically see one another often, we always know what we mean to each other. Our conversations inspire me to think differently and always be full of gratitude for so many things that we experience. A few of us go back to first grade; others go back to times when we rode stick horses and played with whatever we could find. Remember marbles??? I doubt that you do. Bobby, Clem, Willie B., Willie D., Charles, Delores, Armenta, Vondell, Ralph, Elaine, Thomas, Jim T. all of these special friends have impacted my life and my way of thinking, and I am grateful. Joanne, my first cousin and retired educator, loves to write poems. They have always inspired me to capture thoughts in words.

My last acknowledgment is extended to everyone I have had to pleasure of interacting. Your stories and experiences helped to shape my experiences and the contributions I have attempted to make. I close with the last paragraph of the poem *Desiderata*.

> *And whether or not it is clear to you, no doubt the universe is unfolding as it should. Therefore be at peace with God, whatever you conceive Him to be. And whatever your labors and aspirations, in the noisy confusion of life, keep peace in your soul. With all its sham, drudgery and broken dreams, it is still a beautiful world. Be cheerful. Strive to be happy.*

> — Max Ehrmann © 1927

1

WELCOME TO THE GIG ECONOMY

The "gig economy" is a popular topic that has the trappings of a new phenomenon. The phrase is often used in the context of prominent online platforms, such as Uber, Fiverr, and TaskRabbit, which make it easier for clients and gig workers to find each other. These new kinds of technology platforms readily connect individuals in need of personal services with those who will provide them. Accompanied by economic shifts and changing attitudes, these technology platforms have fueled the advancement of the gig workforce.
　　　　　– ADP Research Institute, Ahu Yildirmaz, Sarah Klein,
　　　　　　　　　　　　　　　　　　　　　　February 2020.

The way we work is changing, and it has been changing for more years than we may have been counting. The future is always coming faster than we think!

Thanks to advances in technology, we can now take more control over how we work and, consequently, the way we live. We can work flexible hours from a location of choice, earn a side income, or build a career from freelance work. As technology continues to evolve, the options will continue to expand for both work flexibility and the rewards received for time invested, thus allowing for a more robust definition of work.

What started out as subtle waves of change have grown to be seismic shifts in the structure of the world of work. Employers and workers alike have access to new paths for delivering value to the market. If these changes have not reached you personally, it is just a matter of time.

If no one has said this to you yet, let me be the first: Welcome to the gig economy.

It may feel new, but the gig economy has been around for a long time. The word "gig" has been used for many years by musicians, who referred to their part-time, temporary performance work as gigs. But until recently, few people outside the music industry would say they worked a gig. They may have had a part-time job, but those were very much like full-time jobs, except with fewer hours and generally lower wages. Part-time jobs typically required spending a fixed amount of time working at a specific location. People who worked them usually did so solely for the extra income, and there was virtually no entrepreneurial spirit involved.

The financial reasons for working part-time are as strong as they ever were and undoubtedly are one of the motivations for working a gig. But there is much more to gig work than the opportunity to earn part-time income. The ability to work when you desire fulfills a need, such as making it easier to juggle work and childcare. Younger generations consider flexibility essential. The ideal job, or the way we work, is no longer confined to a definition associated with the hours of 9 a.m. to 5 p.m. Millions of people are now attracted to the many choices offered by companies that we describe as being gig providers. These gig-providing companies have changed the way we view work.

As we began our study of the gig economy, we found impressive perspectives and estimates from many sources.

- 57 million Americans involved

- Contributing $1.4 trillion to the US economy

- 40+% of the US workforce is currently involved

- Up to 80% may be interested

- Growing at a rate of 8.1% per year, while the traditional workforce growth is 2.6% per year (pre-COVID-19)

Assuming the growth continues, the gig economy could contribute to a workforce dominated by independent contractors within the next decade, creating a growing interest in flexible income opportunities.

The terms "gig economy" and "sharing economy" are often used interchangeably and have rapidly become a part of mainstream business conversations; however, they are very different in many ways. The sharing economy is not the focus of this book. In the gig economy, the focus is on flexibility in how work is done. In the sharing economy, an asset is often used to activate a gig, the perfect examples being offering a home or even a room as a short-term rental property or using a car to provide a delivery or transportation service.

Gig economy companies such as Airbnb have become competitors to hoteliers. The hotelier must satisfy stringent standards of expectation, even rules, laws, and regulations, not to mention the enormous investments in real estate and construction. Meanwhile, there are now millions of property hosts who represent a new chain of entrepreneurs who use the asset of a home to accommodate those interested in a place to stay and perhaps a home-cooked meal to go with it. The story is similar for Uber, Lyft, TaskRabbit, Thumbtack, Fiverr, Upwork, and so many others. These companies do not make significant investments in assets. Instead, they use technology to connect expertise and assets to consumers or potential clients through independent contractors recognized as gig workers.

As we dug deeper into understanding the gig economy, we began to see that it may represent far more than the opportunity of providing people with flexibility, freedom, and fair rewards for the effort they invest. Adam Smith, the 18th century philosopher often recognized as the father of modern economics and a major proponent of free markets, posited the belief that "*left to their own devices, people will always act in their self-interest, and those interests will inadvertently level out to create the best outcome for all.*" Smith felt that a free marketplace would serve to support the creation of better and higher quality products and services. We see these ideas at work within the gig economy. Many gig economy providers and workers solicit almost immediate feedback from their customers. Consumers rate their service providers via an app that makes a simple request once the transaction is complete: rate the service provider with one to five stars. There is no waiting for the traditional quarterly, semiannual, or annual performance appraisal typical of conventional jobs. The service, product, and the worker are evaluated immediately. In many cases, the gig provider also rates the consumer. This simple process serves to encourage higher quality all around.

Gig work opportunities and the choices available are not limited by specific and designated hours one may have or the need to be physically present at a fixed facility in order to do the work. The gig worker participating in the Etsy global online marketplace (etsy.com) can be located anywhere in the world and market their products around the globe through the Etsy platform. Etsy has more than 1 million small business owners/independent contractors involved and has become one of the most popular global online shopping malls. Etsy ads can now be found on many national and global television channels. Etsy is just one example.

The gig choices available are very numerous. Our research reveals that there are thousands of gig opportunities, perhaps many multiples of such a figure. The impact on labor statistics is staggering and game-changing. More than 40% of the current labor force is involved in some type of gig, and we are rapidly approaching a 50% participation rate within a few years here in the United States. We find estimates that as much as 80% of the current labor force may be receptive to gig work.

What are the primary reasons for the growing interest in gig work? And why is this ever-increasing interest more than just another part-time income opportunity with a new and fancy label? Our quest for answers led to some remarkably interesting books and articles on the subject. One book, *The Sharing Economy*, published by the MIT Press in 2017, impacted our thinking about the relevance of the gig economy. The author, Arun Sundararajan, Harold Price Professor of Entrepreneurship and Professor of Technology, Operations and Statistics at New York University's (NYU) Stern School of Business, has done extensive research on the sharing economy and probably interviewed more sharing economy founders, co-founders, and chief executive officers of new innovative companies than any other author with whom we are familiar. In his book, Sundararajan reminds us that there are trends to be aware of:

...personal assets, brick and mortar institutions, hard currency, salaried, permanent jobs are on their way out and virtual exchange, and flexible on demand work are in. The 'crowd' is replacing the corporation at the center of capitalism.

The Industrial Revolution created significant wealth for a small percentage of the population. This era was known to be asset-heavy. In the new economy that is emerging, companies that we put into a gig economy category are asset-light, representing a significant shift in how products and services are marketed and how consumers are engaged. In Sundararajan's book, we are also reminded of a seldom exposed stat that becomes particularly important in understanding the gig economy phenomenon.

At the turn of the 20th century, almost half of the compensated U.S. workforce was self-employed. By 1960, this number shrank to less than 15% because of the Industrial Revolution. It is also highly likely that the self-employed constituted more than half of the compensated workforce at some point prior to 1900. For the 50 years since 1960, the percentage of self-employed in the U.S. economy has been approximately 10%.

It now becomes evident that our economy has been dominated, for over 100 years, by large corporations and a very traditional form of work – the nine to five. In many ways, Sundararajan's book supports our thoughts relative to defining the gig economy as much more than making part-time work more appealing via the use of technology.

Dr. Paul Oyer, the Mary and Rankine Van Anda Entrepreneurial Professor and Professor of Economics, Senior Associate Dean for Academic Affairs and Senior Fellow, Stanford Institute for Economic Policy Research, also influenced our thinking through his papers and lectures about the gig economy. Oyer is also a Research Associate with the National Bureau of Economic Research and the Editor-in-Chief of the Journal of Labor Economics. In 2016, Upwork retained Professor Oyer to conduct research on the Independent Workforce in America. Upwork is world-renowned for its ability to connect a company's needs with a freelance professional. The company and freelancer do not need to be near each other; in fact, they can be in different countries. Upwork has served over 5 million businesses that desired to connect with a freelancer who could fill a short-term need. The study conducted by Oyer remains available online and provides incredible insight into what we sought to better understand in the publishing of this book. The following is what he shares in the opening paragraph of the research done for Upwork:

> *The composition of the US workforce is changing as demographic shifts impact labor supply and demand, interstate commerce and international trade grow, and technology makes it easier for people to work independently. The independent workforce ("I.W.") has grown to become a sizable share of the American labor pool and is widely expected to grow even more significant in the coming years. This growth has created (and will continue to create) considerable benefits for the US economy, both for the I.W. itself and the buyers of their services.*

We refer to the I.W. as the gig economy.

The study was focused mostly on independent workers who were engaged in freelance work of a professional nature. The study serves to broaden an understanding of how broad the gig economy has become, who is involved, and their reasons for involvement. In reviewing the research conducted by Oyer, we were led to a survey conducted each year since 2014 by Upwork and the Freelancers Union titled Freelancing in America (FIA) https://www.upwork.-com/i/freelancing-in-america/. The most recent report was issued in October of 2019. This report is excellent reading for business leaders who engage independent contractors for any portion of their labor force. Freelancers who use a platform like Upwork to connect with a business that needs their services are well paid in comparison to their counterparts earning at a median rate of $28.00 per hour, which is more per hour than what 70% of workers earn in the overall US economy. For the first time, the survey reported that as many freelancers said they view freelancing as a long-term career choice as they do a temporary way to earn money. In addition, the share of those who freelance full time increased from 17% in 2014 to 28% in 2019.

If, as we believe, the gig economy phenomenon is more than part-time work appeal, we may very well be experiencing a return to entrepreneurship as a preferred way to work. When thinking of becoming an entrepreneur, the cost and associated risk of an entrepreneurial pathway usually required a considerable investment of capital. For small businesses, effective marketing has always been challenging, expensive, or prohibitive. Granted, the direct selling model of distribution of products and services by independent contractors has been around for over 100 years, and so has the franchising model even though its popularity and rapid growth did not occur until the 1980s and 1990s. Getting started as a direct seller is relatively inexpensive, and support is generally supplied via free to minimal investment in initial training. A franchise model requires a more significant investment; however, both models work for the entrepreneurs involved because engagement provides affiliation with a brand and a proven process for business success.

Now comes the gig economy. With, generally, no upfront investment, possibly a reasonable subscription fee, a gig worker can become a microentrepreneur and engage the often very sophisticated support of a gig-providing company. The gig economy label represents new terminology but more of an evolution versus an invention.

We describe this evolution as a phenomenon because the asset of flexibility in how work can be done via gig work is also built upon *trust!* When we as a consumer choose to rent a room or couch in someone's home over the brand identity of a hotel chain, we are trusting considerably basic instincts associated with a belief in the goodness of people and the possibility of enjoying a more personal experience. The same is true when we connect with a transportation service that connects us with a car and driver that will have very little signage. The car might be new or one that is a few years old; hopefully, it is clean, but it may be dirty. Once again, we trust our fundamental beliefs in the brand and the intent of another person to provide a quality product, service, or experience. The same is true of the freelancer who performs a very sophisticated professional service that a company has never used before when it needs short-term assistance instead of engaging a long-term employee.

Something else is happening here. Labor is being provided on demand; therefore, efficiency is gained for all involved. Assets utilized in the gig economy are owned by the crowd versus a select few. Labor is used, perhaps, more equitably and definitely more efficiently. The company does not have to engage in long-term commitments. Gig workers consider the ability to quit work when they want to, even terminate the relationship when they want to, an asset, not a negative. The use of instant performance ratings through technology serves to keep a focus on quality and self-regulation. The consumer wins as quality improves. Pricing also becomes more competitive because more people are involved in delivering products or services. The growth of the gig economy is proof that the entrepreneurial spirit is alive and well around the world, and trust is playing a significant role in making the concept of working with flexibility and freedom more popular than ever! The gig economy is changing the game relative to free enterprise opportunities, especially microenterprise opportunities.

As more and more gig opportunities become available, we may be living through not only a gig economy phenomenon but also a labor revolution. The gig economy will dramatically shift the numbers toward entrepreneurship. With more than 50% of the current workforce forecasted to be engaged in gig work in the next few years, how many will opt to explore their gig and turn it into a full-time endeavor? This is already happening. Living in a COVID-19 environment has triggered many significant business decisions that are far-reaching into organizations, school systems, the way we shop, and, of course, the way we work. Companies are moving beyond the "office-centric" environment as we learn that productivity does not have to diminish in the absence of physical presence. New regulatory oversight and innovation will support the creation of unique work opportunities in support of the most diverse workforce ever. Older workers will not have a fear of being pushed out of the workforce earlier than they would like. The younger generations will find their new and very different definition of work–life balance. More women will find their "dream come true" work opportunities.

Welcome again to the gig economy!

DEFINING GIGS

Most important to understand at this point is how we define a gig. A gig could be considered a part-time job, but it is not. By our definition, a gig offers flexibility and freedom in how, when, and where one does the work for rewards that are basically cash-based. The gig participant is a microentrepreneur, an independent contractor, and his or her own boss. Also, it is essential to understand that the gig economy is a new phenomenon in its infancy. As we continue the journey through this book, discussing various aspects of the gig economy and what might be most important to you as a current or future gig provider or gig participant, we expect a continued evolution. Gig providers, participants, consumers, and local and national regulatory agencies will unveil challenges and opportunities which will be addressed, we believe, to create an even greater gig economy than the one emerging today.

A part-time job differs from full-time employment only in the number of hours worked and the amount of traditional employer-based benefits received. A gig represents the opportunity to work in accordance with one's desires or motivations. Flexibility, freedom, and fair rewards for time invested are key attributes of the gig economy. In the past, part-time work opportunities have been associated with a willingness to work for hourly wages less than the hourly wages earned by those in an equivalent full-time job. The gig economy does not work by these rules. The amount of income earned via gig work includes the value placed on flexibility and freedom enjoyed; therefore, a comparison of gig opportunity earnings with hourly earnings of any type is not a valid comparison. Some hours of gig work will yield more than others in terms of cash rewards; however flexibility also has an intangible value.

For purposes of this book and the information we are sharing, we separate the gig economy into its three primary components:

1. Gig workers

2. Consumers who engage a product or service from a gig worker

3. Gig providers, the companies that connect gig workers with consumers

Gigs are all about simplicity and flexibility for all members of this equation. There are many labels associated with the gig economy, and we share a few, along with a brief explanation. Our focus will be on gigs in which the gig worker is an independent contractor providing a product or service directly to a consumer. You may become interested in understanding more about the other labels we share as all are contributing to a redefinition of not only work but also how our economy functions embracing microentrepreneurship. Perhaps we are moving beyond the centralized society of the industrial revolution to something else. Maybe, we are moving more toward an economy more inclusive versus being exclusive to the smaller percentage who currently control much of the wealth. The keyword in the previous sentence is "inclusive," meaning the availability of entrepreneurial activity to a broader segment of the population along with the attributes of flexibility, freedom, innovation, and creativity in how we approach work and life. As you review the most popular labels, others are emerging.

Sharing economy: Any service allowing an asset previously available only to its owner to be used by other people.

Peer (or peer-to-peer) economy: The direct connection between the people on either side of a transaction, unmediated by a company.

On-demand economy: Services offering cars, food, home cleaning, etc., by signing onto an app.

Platform economy or networked economy: A digital platform connecting customers with providers of goods or services.

Bottom-up economy: The collaboration of small businesses and freelance workers to find and acquire customers or band together for projects with other workers.

Access economy or rental economy: Services that let you pay to access and/or use things like homes, tools, cars, movies, or music for fees versus ownership.

Passion economy: Platforms, both traditional and new, that enable people to earn income in ways that highlight their individuality and/or their interests.

Four Types of Gigs
(Defined by Ultimate Gig Research Team)

- Transportation

- Services

- Selling

- Leasing

From our perspective and for purposes of this book, gigs fall into one of the four categories: transportation, services, selling, or leasing. These four categories are generally used by those who are researching and writing about the gig economy. The number of gig opportunities within each type is too numerous for any one book, but this can be the beginning of an exploration and, indeed, the beginning of an understanding of the various types of gigs. The gig providers within each category are providing what we also refer to as a platform. Uber is a platform within the category of transportation gigs. The term platform arises out of the technology focus all gig-providing companies bring into play. They have created digital platforms in which the connection between the provider of a product and/or service and a client or consumer takes place. TaskRabbit is a platform, and this description applies to every product or service utilizing gig workers to make the actual connection with a consumer or client.

Transportation gigs disrupted the traditional taxi and limousine industry and have transformed how consumers think about personal transportation needs and how products and services are delivered. These gigs have grown to dominate the gig economy since 2013, and consumer and worker interest continues to grow. Transportation gigs include ridesharing, delivery, and moving services. The large players are the following:

- Uber lets you use your vehicle to provide ridesharing services. Uber is a flexible platform that allows you to choose when and where you drive.

- Lyft is similar to Uber. Initially, its primary differentiator to the gig worker was that the drivers kept 100% of their tips. Uber has since changed its tipping policy to match Lyft.

- Via is a new ridesharing service currently available in Chicago, New York, and Washington, DC. The service provides cheaper fares through shared rides only.

- HopSkipDrive is a ridesharing service for kids. The company provides a background check on all drivers, who must have at least five years of general driving experience to qualify for the gig.

- AmazonFlex is a package delivery service gig for Amazon.

- Bellhop provides residential moving services, both local and long distance.

- Roadie is an on-the-way delivery service that connects people who have stuff to send with drivers already heading that way.

- DoorDash is a food delivery app. Its gig workers, called Dashers, deliver food from local restaurants to the consumer.

- Postmates is a delivery service for various items such as dry cleaning, groceries, restaurant take-out, Starbucks, etc. Any mode of transportation, including car, motorcycle, or bicycle, can be used to make the deliveries.

Service gigs focus on offering a variety of services, such as home repair and dog walking. Services are always being added to this sector, as creative entrepreneurs develop new types of contracts between independent suppliers and their customers. The popular players are currently the following:

- HelloTech provides industry experts providing a variety of support services on technical equipment, including computers, gaming equipment, smart home systems, home Internet, and more.

- Care.com provides the opportunity to match people needing childcare, adult and senior care, pet care, and home care with providers.

- Handy is the gig app for home cleaners and handymen.

- Rover matches pet owners with pet sitters, dog walkers, and house sitters.

- TaskRabbit is a same-day service platform that instantly connects customers with skilled "Taskers" to help with odd jobs and errands.

- Behance showcases and connects artists, designers, and photographers with clients worldwide.

- Upwork connects diverse professionals with clients throughout the world.

- Gigster connects the world's best talent with clients that need elastic teams and staffing.

- Toptal connects top freelance software developers, designers, finance experts, product, and project managers in the world with clients.

- Hire-A-Chef connects qualified chefs with those interested in the services.

Selling gigs allow individuals an opportunity to sell products. Some selling gigs enable people who have a product to sell to find buyers through online marketplaces. Other selling gigs provide products to independent sellers who take on the role of marketing. New platforms are being launched frequently. Current favorites are the following:

- Amazon enables you to sell a variety of products, with some specific categories needing Amazon approval.

- Shopify is a provider of the services needed to market and sell products and services created by the gig worker (entrepreneur) or the marketing and selling of products or services branded by others.

- eBay allows you to auction off a variety of items to the highest bidder.

- Bonanza is an online marketplace that allows individuals and businesses to sell their goods. The app aids sellers in building an online brand.

- Etsy has become a leading online marketplace. There is no warehouse, only 2 million gig workers selling, and over 40 million customers purchasing from many regions throughout the world.

- Mercari is an online platform where people can sell virtually anything they feel the marketplace will be receptive to.

- Poshmark is an online sales and social network hybrid for men's, women's, and children's clothing.

- Ruby Lane is a platform for serious antique and vintage sellers.

- Direct selling companies provide people with various products and services to sell, and the companies offer branding, marketing, fulfillment, and training support when applicable.

- Digital services such as Squarespace and Wix enable the build of both websites and ancillary platforms needed to create an e-commerce platform.

Leasing gigs match lessors of assets, such as homes, rooms, automobiles, tools, and even parking spaces, with people willing to rent those assets for a specific amount of time. These gigs can be highly profitable and are gaining traction. These apps are becoming so prevalent that hotel chains have initiated similar offerings. Popular leasing gigs include the following:

- Airbnb is the "Uber" of home rentals. You can rent a room or an entire house. Larger cities with a significant tourist economy have passed laws regarding these types of leases.

- OneFineStay takes Airbnb to the next level by offering only luxury accommodations and preparing them accordingly with clean linens, a greeting service, etc. This service caters to high-end customers.

- Vrbo is a platform for vacation housing that matches travelers with private homes. Expedia owns the platform.

- Parking Panda allows drivers to book a guaranteed parking space in advance of destination arrival – including residential, commercial, and airport locations. It is a popular platform in larger urban areas.

- HyreCar allows individuals to lease their personal vehicles.

- Turo also allows people to rent their personal vehicles and dynamically sets prices based on the market value, location, time of year, and other data.

- Home Away enables extended home rental.

- Vacasa offers extended home rental for vacationers.

Key Drivers of Gig Economy Growth

- Cultural shift

- Technology

- Economic realities

The gig economy has grown for underlying reasons that include a cultural shift in attitudes and expectations, vast advances in the way we use technology, and a clearer understanding of economic realities often covered up by statistics such as employment or unemployment rates that do not measure the quality of life. When we decided to initiate our research on the gig economy, we became most interested in how we got to this new place and why part-time work has become attractive. As we stated earlier, over 57 million gig workers are currently involved in the United States alone, and that number was expected to continue to rise. Behind every new phenomenon are forces that have fueled it, and this is undoubtedly true for the growth and appeal of the gig economy.

Times Have Changed and so Have Cultural Attitudes

The growing number of participants in gig work is driven by the desire to experience more freedom and flexibility in how the work is done. Younger generations consider these attributes to be essential. Half of all freelance gig workers consider their gig(s) their career. Women have long appreciated work opportunities that can be accomplished during hours that are flexible and controlled by the worker, not an employer. Older workers who have been replaced or displaced in traditional jobs or who found retirement different than what they imagined, also seek work that offers flexibility and freedom. Retirement is no longer thought of as a specific moment in time. Quality of life and being able to sustain a quality of life is most important.

Technology Changes the Game!

It does not take a lot of research to understand that technology has played a considerable role in the growth and appeal of the part-time work opportunities we are experiencing and the growth of the gig economy. The mobile phone has been around for a long time; however, our phones certainly got a lot smarter over the past 15 years, a period synonymous with the continuous growth and popularity of the gig economy. Technology has provided us with new tools and amazingly effective ways to communicate, and the impact is evident when we think about our last experience with a transportation gig. Chances are that we simply accessed an app on our mobile phone, contacted our service provider of choice, connected with a driver, and received confirmation that he or she would pick us up, and we were provided with the driver's identity and estimated time of arrival.

Transportation gigs have utilized technology effectively, disrupting traditional transportation businesses like taxi cabs and private limousine services, and they have become attractive to those seeking flexible work. Technology makes engagement and participation so much easier for gig providers, gig workers, and consumers. The trust factor, which contributes to the success of the transaction, will play a huge role once again as we continue to learn more about artificial intelligence and the role that bots will play in our lives. We are not that far away from requesting a needed transportation service, and an autonomous car shows up, right on time. Research supports the idea of autonomous cars being safer than those driven by humans. The trust factor continues to play a huge role.

Technology has also fueled the growth of the gig economy by eliminating the need for some jobs that are being replaced by artificial intelligence and the use of robots that perform flawlessly and deliver more output in less time. The efficiencies enabled by these gains in technology have eliminated many jobs and forced early retirement in others, catching many workers by surprise. Those who have been replaced or displaced are unlikely to be interested in learning an entirely new skill or work another job, in which they continue to be susceptible to workplace innovation and replacement. Therefore, the attraction of being a microentrepreneur, the opportunity to be in control of how and when you work, with the support of a brand that provides useful marketing and is capable of connecting a worker with a consumer, fulfills a need, and the gig economy is answering the need.

One of my favorite authors, Peter Diamandis, states in his recent book, *The Future is Faster than You Think*, "*our biggest companies and government agencies were designed in another century, for purposes of safety and stability. They were not built to withstand rapid radical change.*" Technology has become disruptive in an incredibly positive manner. We can now do more with less and invest less time experiencing the productivity we desire.

Technology changed the game and helped fuel the growth of the gig economy. With new inventors and visionaries like Peter Diamandis, Elon Musk, Bill Gates, Jeff Bezos, Richard Branson, and a host of others, who are consistently investing their wealth in shaping the future, we expect technology to continue to play a significant role in shaping what the gig economy will become. We think we are scratching the surface of possibilities at this moment in time.

Elon Musk, founder, CEO, and lead designer of SpaceX; co-founder, CEO, and product architect of Tesla, Inc.; co-founder and CEO of Neuralink; and co-founder of PayPal, is already planning to take the first civilian to the moon and back, offer space travel to tourist, and provide travel to any place on earth within one hour! These statements have already been presented in unbelievably detailed presentations in some of the most important conferences held throughout the world. Do not take our word for this; read the book *The Future is Faster Than You Think* by Peter Diamandis and Steven Kotler. You, too, will have your "holy cow" moments. Technology has changed our lives and is having a dramatic effect on the way we work. It has become the foundation and a significant driver of the growth of the gig economy.

Economic Realities Are Key Motivators

We are living in a paradox. In the United States, we had been experiencing overall unprecedented economic growth, low unemployment, and the best of times for many. For others, those individuals attempting to earn a decent wage, take care of themselves and their families, enjoy some of life's wonderful opportunities such as owning a home, paying for college education, taking vacations, and investing in a quality retirement, it is a challenging time.

Before COVID-19, it can be said that while average incomes had been growing overall, the appeal of part-time work opportunities supported by impressive advances in technology, and the attribute of flexibility had been growing as well, fueling the growth of the gig economy. COVID-19 has revealed how vulnerable we can become from a health and well-being perspective and an economic perspective. Decisions around the world have been made attempting to strike a balance between the safety of human life and the need for economies to remain open. COVID-19 has also revealed our dependency on traditional labor and exposed the inefficiencies associated with many concepts learned during the industrial revolution. Those forced to work from home have remained productive and may have an even greater desire to find work that allows them the flexibility to continue to work on a flexible schedule. The perceived need to organize work from fixed facilities with fixed expenses has been changing. New thinking is accelerated. The financial stress of rent, mortgage, and associated expenses in operating a facility will not be a priority for all types of labor providers. More employers are expected to explore and provide more flexible work opportunities creating a more efficient business model for the business and adding more choices to gig work possibilities. The use of independent contractors, we predict, will grow even faster than prior growth rates relative to the gig economy. This is not a new conversation; COVID-19 has simply accelerated what we have been experiencing for years.

The alternative workforce: It's now mainstream. For years, many considered contract, freelance, and gig employment to be "alternative work", options supplementary to full-time jobs. Today, this segment of the workforce has grown and gone mainstream even as talent markets have tightened, leading organizations to look strategically at all types of work arrangements in their plans for growth. Best practices to access and deploy alternative workers are just now being invented. If the economy continues to grow, organizations must be more flexible in adapting to these new work arrangements, and plan to use them in a strategic way.

— 2019 Deloitte Global Human Capital Trends.

The preceding references are an example of the many insights into the evolving and changing landscape of work. Our reality is that we have been experiencing what others foresaw many years ago. COVID-19 is an accelerator. The economic stress of change, shrinking jobs, a movement away from 9-to-5 traditional work hours, new forms of work, and the growing appeal of flexibility in virtually everything we are involved are real.

Another financial reality worth noting is the fact that while wages have increased significantly over the past 40 years, inflation has caused our purchasing power to remain relatively flat. On average, we may be earning more as individuals. Still, we may not be able to buy much more with the dollars we spend. When we dig into some of the data, it is easy to see why many Americans, and their counterparts in mature markets around the world, are looking for ways to earn income beyond their traditional jobs. COVID-19 will, we predict, accelerate this concern that has been brewing and maturing over the past decade. Economic pressures are real.

GIG ECONOMY IMPACT

The gig economy has become a popular topic of conversation. The growth of gig-providing companies and the number of gig workers participating are the reasons for the popularity. The gig economy is transformative, innovative, and creative. Our research and writing about this topic has a US focus; however, the impact of the gig economy is global. What is happening here in the United States is also happening in mature markets all over the world.

Businesses are adopting the use of independent contractors because of the efficiencies associated with the model. When you use independent contractors in a fee or commission for performance agreement, you pay after the work is completed reducing the cost of downtime or low productivity hours associated with traditional employer/employee relationships.

Workers are attracted because they can work when and how they want to and as much or as little as they desire. This is indeed a phenomenon, and we predict continuous growth creating more possibilities for both gig-providing companies and those seeking gig opportunities as participants. According to some forecasts, more than 50% of the US workforce will be involved in some type of gig work within the next 3–5 years. Within the next 3–5 years, 50% of traditional companies are also expected to increase their usage of contingent workers/alternative workforce, many of whom will be in gig classification.

The gig economy is still relatively new. It does not have a national or international body that is investing in the kinds of data and research that most established industries and business models have in place. The US Department of Labor is now tracking gig opportunities and so is the International Monetary Fund (IMF). In November 2019, Kristalina Georgieva, a Bulgarian economist who serves as Managing Director of the IMF and is a former Chief Executive of the World Bank, acknowledged the growing importance of understanding the gig economy and its impact on government. The IMF refers to the gig economy as the informal economy, which is an even broader term.

In Georgieva's published speech, she speaks to concerns relative to the informal or gig economy and the need for accurate metrics.

The informal economy can provide income or social safety net. ...Informality results in lower tax revenues that hinder the government's ability to spend on social programs and investment. ...The informal economy is also an important source of income for women. In developing economies, 92% of women workers are informally engaged.

Georgieva's comments reveal some of the challenges already emerging for certain gig providers as government revenue from taxes is critical to the welfare of communities. We will address those issues, in part, in this book.

Georgieva's closing comments, in her speech, speak to the importance of gathering more data on the informal economy/gig economy:

> *Let me conclude with my sense of optimism. I hope you will leave here with a better appreciation for the challenges and opportunities in measuring the informal economy and a broader recognition of the benefits of doing so. We at the IMF will continue our collaboration with member countries and international organizations to improve the estimates of the informal economy and in the process help countries realize their full economic potential.*

The popularity of the gig economy conversation is a result of real impact and enough aggregated thoughts, insights, and data that convincingly indicate, to us, the importance of the gig economy and the manner in which the gig economy has simplified and made possible the most unique, flexible, and variety of work choices modern societies have ever experienced. As we share aggregated information, we will also be providing our own insights, forecast, and predictions based upon the assumptions we have made as observers of gig work ourselves and the survey our research team conducted.

As the gig economy continues to grow, we predict that concerns about regulations and the social safety net will be addressed for the benefit of all. Free economies function on structured labor that adheres to various laws and regulations, including tax codes that enable governments to receive a portion of what companies, organizations, and individuals have earned to provide the services and structure needed by society. Providers of various forms of protection, including multiple types of insurance and retirement savings, are especially important for a workforce growing in its entrepreneurial participation. Currently, most work benefits in America are tied to W-2 employment. The gig economy is beginning to shine a spotlight on what may very well be an anti-quated system. We can expect more regulatory discussions at the state and federal levels as to what constitutes 1099 work versus W-2 work. Current discussions center around health care, minimum wages, unionization, and retirement benefits, all of which are outside of the definition of an independent contractor. The continued growth in technology, the use of artificial intelligence and machines that do a lot of the labor-intensive work, may shrink the industrial revolution–type workforce that current insurance products were designed to protect. Currently, gig workers do not have access to the best of insurance products; however, creativity is already in play and gig workers in the future can expect access to some of the benefits that historically have been enjoyed only by employees. This does not infer that gig-providing companies will fund these benefits, only that gig workers will have access to such benefits currently available to those in traditional (W-2) employment status.

INSIGHTS: GIGS ARE WORTH EXPLORING

Gigs are worth exploring, and that is what this book is all about. You are now on a journey. The journey will include more information and many insights, including conversations with gig workers who share their motivation and how their gig has impacted their work/life balance. We hope that you will find the journey helps you answer the many questions you may have as an entrepreneur, employer, educator interested in the subject, or as an individual seeking to find the ultimate gig.

Gigs, of all kinds, give people who are falling short of their financial goals an opportunity to bridge the gap created when expenses exceed regular income or when a new source of income is needed. The forces that have been building over the past 20 years have served to create motivations for exploring what we now refer to as the gig economy.

More freedom and flexibility in how one might work has become a new norm. Younger generations do not understand or accept the same limitations once perceived by previous generations.

And all ages are beginning to realize that the speed of life and enjoyment can be accelerated when there is more control of income possibilities.

Let us welcome the gig economy! There is much more to understand about this new asset, which has the potential to positively impact people from any walk of life. Fig. 1.1 summarizes key facts.

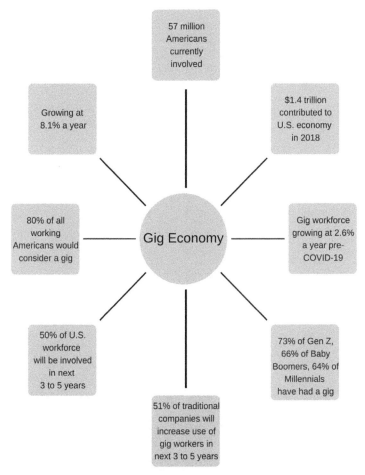

Fig. 1.1. Key Facts of the Gig Economy.

2

AN ACADEMIC PERSPECTIVE

Dr. Greg W. Marshall first shared this important perspective on the gig economy in the Ultimate Gig Special Report, published in 2019. Marshall is the Charles Harwood Professor of Marketing and Strategy in the Crummer Graduate School of Business at Rollins College, Winter Park, Florida. In addition, he is a Visiting Professor of Marketing and Sales at Aston Business School, Birmingham, UK. He serves as editor-in-chief of the European Journal of Marketing, and is former editor of the Journal of Marketing Theory and Practice and the Journal of Personal Selling & Sales Management. He is past president of the American Marketing Association Academic Council, a distinguished fellow and past president of the Academy of Marketing Science, a distinguished fellow and past president of the Society for Marketing Advances, and is a member of the Direct Selling Education Foundation Circle of Honor.

First, let us just initially get out of the way that yes I am a full-time professor (that is, my full-time job is not a "gig"). But before you succumb to a knee-jerk reaction something like "oh great, here comes an opinion from the token egghead," I would like to shore up my validity a little bit in the "real world" outside of academe. First, I transitioned to being a business professor after over 10 years in the retail and consumer packaged goods (CPG) industries. Second, my own dissertation years ago dealt with critical salesperson motivation and performance issues that I had witnessed as a field sales leader in those CPG businesses. And finally – and probably most importantly at the moment – I have stayed very, very close to industry throughout my academic career including the direct selling industry. So I think it is safe to say I am a bit of a hybrid academic – comfortable with scholarly research and writing but also quite happy to bridge over to my own gigs as a consultant and trainer with a variety of organizations.

One of those gigs a few years back was with the folks at the Bureau of Labor Statistics (BLS) within the US Department of Labor, which is the principal federal agency responsible for measuring labor market activity, working conditions, and price changes in the economy. In my engagement with them to assist in their developing a marketing planning capability, I found their leadership team to be amazing and the agency's work to be of impeccable integrity (no, despite "fake news" inferences to the contrary, the BLS is not a propaganda tool of whichever federal administration is in power at any given moment). So I read with keen interest the findings of BLS's first report in 13 years on the state of the contingent workforce, published in June 2018. They essentially found that contingent workers had actually declined since the prior report in 2005! A surprise, to say the least, given all the hype about the rise of the gig economy. The report initially generated some headlines about increased gig work being a blip in the bigger picture of labor trends.[1]

Well, one thing academics are well-trained to do is to question the "why" of things – appreciation of curiosity is built into every facet of our PhD training! In the case of the BLS' counterintuitive findings, understanding what happened goes to the definition of exactly what a gig is in the first place. It turns out that the operative definition of contingent workers used by the BLS study was persons who do not expect their jobs to last or who report that their jobs are temporary. This definition by itself (and thus its associated measures in the study) does not really capture the essence of the current gig culture very well, a culture that is shared by large numbers of millennials and others in today's economy. Complicating measurement just a bit further, a gig

[1]Paquette, D., & Long, H. (2018, June 7). America's gig economy is smaller now than before Uber existed, official data show. *The Washington Post*. Retrieved from https://www.washingtonpost.com/news/wonk/wp/2018/06/07/there-are-fewer-workers-in-the-gig-economy-today-than-before-uber-existed-official-data-show/?noredirect=on&utm_term=.3a97bb82d41b

is also not the same thing as what is often referred to as "alternative employment arrangements" – this work mode is more about roles such as traditional independent contractors (the key difference is that there is a "contract"), on-call workers, temporary help agency workers, and workers provided by contract firms. Ultimately, the results of the 2018 BLS report were controversial.[2]

To their credit, the BLS was not pleased with the level to which its June 2018 publication added clarity to knowledge about the current state of the gig economy, and they subsequently undertook a process of asking additional questions centered on the concept of "electronically mediated employment" – an emerging type of work defined as short jobs or tasks that workers find through websites or mobile apps that both connect them with customers and arrange payments for the tasks (think Uber here). Unfortunately though, once those new data were in, the BLS determined that the additional questions were not perceived and answered as intended by respondents, which left the questions of both the definition of gig work and the desire for clarity of knowledge of the true magnitude of the economic impact of gig-style income-earning activities in gray areas.[3]

WHAT IS A GIG?

An authoritative source on the gig economy is the Gig Economy Data Hub, which is a collaborative project between the Aspen Institute's Future of Work Initiative and Cornell University's prestigious School of Industrial and Labor Relations. I urge you to take time to thoroughly review their website at www.gigeconomydata.org, which aims to provide accessible, comprehensive information for anyone interested in better understanding the scope and nature of independent and gig work. They suggest that, at its essence, a gig from an employment perspective quite simply consists of *income-earning*

[2]Contingent and alternative employment arrangements – May 2017. (2018, June 7). *News Release: Bureau of Labor Statistics*. USDL-18-942. Retrieved from https://www.bls.gov/news.release/pdf/conemp.pdf
[3]Electronically mediated work: New questions in the contingent worker supplement. (2018, September). *Monthly Labor Review, Bureau of Labor Statistics*. Retrieved from https://www.bls.gov/opub/mlr/2018/article/electronically-mediated-work-new-questions-in-the-contingent-worker-supplement.htm

activities outside of traditional, long-term-employee relationships.[4] Although there are innumerable nuances that can emanate from this definition (especially once the labor lawyers and tax accountants weigh in), nonetheless for marketing and strategic purposes I like this definition's simplicity and clarity.

WHICH GIG(S) TO CHOOSE?

For gigs, it seems to be a buyer's market (that is, more gigs than people to fill them)! Hence, gig workers can legitimately think of themselves as a highly valued asset, and as a result more and more firms seeking gig workers are thinking of themselves and their offering as being in competition with a wide array of other offerings for a slice of a potential gig worker's income-earning hours. With this environment, it is a *great* time to be working gigs!

Please note that I am using the word "offering" very deliberately above because an offering denotes a *bundle of benefits realized by a receiver.* Building on the earlier conversation about prospects for gig workers being thought of as customers by firms for one gig opportunity versus another, prospects will be evaluating the *potential benefits* – income and otherwise – of engaging with a given firm versus other gig options. And importantly, these gigs may run a gamut of offerings from direct selling to transportation to any other income-earning opportunity.

Bottom line: From a potential gig worker's perspective, just like any "customer" for any offering, perceived benefits by definition involve their belief that the level of value added to them of a gig is superior to other competitive options. Hence, any type of firm offering gig opportunities need to make sure theirs is perceived as so attractive that gig workers will fully consider it against those other options. *It is the quintessential seller's market for gig workers!!*

The pool of potential gig workers are all about assessing value-adding benefits when they make their choices about with whom to allocate their precious and limited income-earning hours!

[4]Gig Economy Data Hub. (2019). What is a gig worker? Retrieved from https://www.gigeconomydata.org/basics/what-gig-worker. Accessed on May 4, 2019.

And we know from much research on millennials that, beyond just income potential, convenience, technology, and brand/firm culture are three primary value-adding benefits that millennials rank very highly when choosing from among various income-earning options. Put another way, firms that offer gigs in which it is highly convenient for the worker to participate; for which the operative technology is modern, effective, and central to the offering; and with whom the culture appeals to the gig worker will have a significant leg up in attracting gig workers from millennial crowd.

GIG PERSONAS

Let us consider a concept called "personas." Personas are fictional characters created by marketers who represent different key potential user types for an offering. They represent different needs, experiences, behaviors, and goals of different individuals. Marketers use personas to step outside of their own personal viewpoint and biases about who their customers are and recognize that different people have uniquely different needs and expectations.[5] In the case of a gig, different individuals work gigs for different reasons. Let us further illustrate the persona concept by breaking down gig workers into two broad personas:

Persona 1: The Enhancer

This persona represents individuals who have a stable income source from traditional employment, but for whom that employment may not be full time at present and/or may not pay sufficiently to cover their current expense obligations. Alternatively, they may have determined that their traditional employment income is not enough to enhance their financial status over the longer run (such as by reducing debt more quickly or increasing future savings for retirement). Hence, this persona is labeled **THE ENHANCER**.

---

[5]Dam, R., & Siang, T. (2019, March 29). Personas – A simple introduction. Interaction Design Foundation. Retrieved from https://www.interaction-design. org/literature/article/personas-why-and-how-you-should-use-them

The enhancer has strong motivation to do gigs, and this persona should be familiar to direct selling organizations because many of the most successful independent representatives in direct selling currently fit this description. In general, many millennials are of this persona (think massive student loan debt to pay off), but the persona actually is very relevant multigenerational because the need for supplemental income stems from many types of circumstances. At the core though, folks comprising this persona "have a steady job" but are motivated to do gigs to make more money.

Persona 2: The Gig Exclusive

This persona represents individuals for whom a set of simultaneous gigs comprises *their entire set of income-earning activities*, with no traditional income sources in the mix. Hence, this persona is labeled **THE GIG EXCLUSIVE**. Committed gig exclusives are generically thought of as being skewed younger – and probably this persona is in fact more prevalent with millennials than with Gen X and older. But be careful to not totally discount the fact that folks from all generations may be motivated to put together a patchwork quilt of gigs as their sole set of income-earning activities, including individuals who are retired from previous traditional employment.

Some firms that offer gig opportunities are more familiar with one of these personas over the other, and thus their recruiting tends to favor either the enhancer or the gig exclusive. But as firms become more sophisticated in their knowledge about gig workers' needs and preferences, and as the competition for gig workers continues to intensify, we will witness even more responsiveness in the marketplace to all types of gig workers' desire for income-earning activities outside of traditional, long-term-employee relationships.

Firms that are most successful will learn to develop and effectively communicate the benefits of their business opportunity for the two personas. In particular, it is critical to consider that because the gig exclusive has no safety net of traditional employment to fall back on versus the enhancer, decisions by gig exclusives about what opportunities to combine for their bundle of income-earning activities are made much more mindful of the risk differences between the choices.

LOOKING AHEAD

Going forward, gig workers are in a great position to be picky about choosing their opportunities for income-earning activities. It is a seller's market, and prospects must perceive that a firm's work opportunity provides an overall attractive bundle of benefits in order to attract the best prospects for gig work. There is no question that prospects for gigs compare opportunities across industries and types of jobs. A strong value proposition for gig workers, when compared with other choices they have for their precious and limited income-earning hours, will go a long way toward ensuring success in this very competitive environment for talent.

3

MOTIVATIONS FOR WORKING
A GIG

We have four generations in the workforce at the same time, all very different but united by their dissatisfaction with the status quo. Baby Boomers (born between 1946 and 1964) are working later in life than they had planned because they need to support underfunded retirement plans or adult children struggling under the weight of student loans. Most of them have spent long careers in traditional employment in corporate structures that valued paying your dues. But this generation often does not get enough credit for being open to change as it should. Baby Boomers have been questioning authority since their teens and, as adults, have pursued changes that would improve their social and financial positions.

After watching their parents be rewarded for many years of loyal service to their employers with layoffs during the recessions of the early 1980s, the latchkey kids of Generation X (born between 1965 and 1976) entered the workforce with a jaded view of the traditional career path. This generation tends to be pragmatic about employment. Gen Xers typically do not plan to stay in any one job for more than a few years, an outlook that was underscored by the upheaval of the dot com boom and bust and the Great Recession that followed.

Millennials or Gen Y (born 1977–1995) who came behind them have a vastly different attitude about work. They do not fully embrace the traditional work ethic of the 9-to-5 job. They were raised to seek near-constant feedback, especially recognition and reward. Now comes Generation Z (born after 1996). This generation is younger than Google and grew up immersed in technology, only knowing a world in which information and connection to others are available on demand at any time of the day or night. They do not so much chafe at the idea of a 9-to-5 work environment as they do not understand why such a parameter would exist in the first place. They value hard work but expect flexibility.

While these four generations come from different perspectives, they share similar goals. They want the flexibility to juggle their complicated lives, freedom to pursue work on their terms and rewards that meet their financial and psychological needs. And the traditional 9-to-5 employer/employee relationship is no longer cutting it.

Our research spanned all four generations, providing more information as to who gig workers are and why they choose to work a gig. We identified seven primary motivations for gig work. It is helpful for both gig providers and gig workers to understand these driving forces. Gig providers can use this information to shape the focus and effectiveness of their marketing efforts. Gig workers who understand their motivations will be better able to select a gig that will meet their goals.

Major career decisions, such as choosing a college major or a specific profession, are rarely based purely on emotion. People tend to factor in the wisdom, experience, or logic shared by a coach, mentor, family member, or teacher. However, when people decide to pursue part-time, flexible income opportunities, they typically are driven by real-life pressures or emotional aspirations triggered by their circumstances. People turn to gigs because they fulfill a need created by at least one of the following seven primary motivations that we identified:

1. Financial pressures

2. Flexibility

3. Improve quality of life

4. Be your own boss

5. Work from home

6. Scalable income possibility

7. Residual income

FINANCIAL PRESSURES

Fear, worry, and anxiety about money is a common challenge faced by the majority of society. Prosperity and wealth accumulation remains the American Dream; however, the reality of the average American is quite different.

Even as the economy continued to recover and grow following the Great Recession, many Americans remained in precarious financial shape. In a survey of more than 5,400 Americans from the Financial Health Network, a nonprofit financial services consultancy, 70% said they struggled with at least one area of financial stability.

Various trends have been negatively impacting workers and their families for many years (Figs. 3.1–3.4). As the cost of living has continued to rise, nullifying much of the wage increase for most workers, Americans began borrowing at higher levels. Total household debt in the United States is approaching $14 trillion, including $1.5 trillion in student loans. The rising cost of health care is also taking a toll. During 2018, one in five US adults had significant, unexpected medical bills. The median expense for these was between $1,000 and $4,999. US disposable income is matched by a level of debt that has also impacted the personal savings rate, which is now at its lowest rate since 2013 and matching the pace of savings we were experiencing in 2006. The average savings rate is dangerously low and is also contributing to the financial pain felt by many in our society during a period that has experienced some of the lowest unemployment rates (pre-COVID-19) in the last 50 years. During what has been described as the best of times, near full employment by the stats on our overall economy, there is another alarming statistic; approximately 40% of all adults say they would not be able to cover an unexpected expense that required $400.00 cash.

Wage increases in the U.S. rise to the top earners

Usual weekly earnings of employed, full-time wage and salary workers, not seasonally adjusted, in constant 2018 dollars

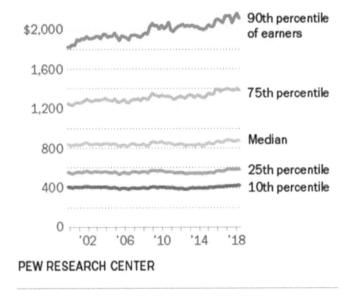

PEW RESEARCH CENTER

Source: U.S. Bureau of Labor Statistics.
Fig. 3.1. Wage Increases in the US Rise to the Top Earners.

Sluggish and uneven wage growth has been cited as a primary factor behind widening income inequality in the United States. A recent Pew Research Center report, based on an analysis of household income data from the Census Bureau, found that in 2016 Americans in the top 10 of the income distribution earned 8.7 times as much as Americans in the bottom 10 ($109,578 vs $12,523). In 1970, when the analysis period began, the top 10 earned 6.9 times as much as the bottom 10 ($63,512 vs $9,212).

Benefit costs have risen faster than wages in recent years

Employment-cost index for all civilian workers in the U.S. in constant dollars, not seasonally adjusted

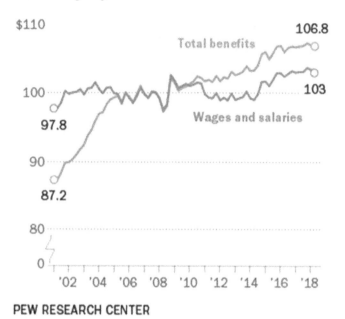

$110   106.8
                    Total benefits

100   103
97.8   Wages and salaries

90

87.2

80

0
    '02 '04 '06 '08 '10 '12 '14 '16 '18

PEW RESEARCH CENTER

Source: U.S. Bureau of Labor Statistics.
Fig. 3.2. Employment-cost Index for US Civilian Workers. *Note:* The employment-cost index is a measure of the change in price of labor defined as compensation per employee hour worked. "Total benefits" includes overtime payments, paid leave, insurance premiums, retirement contributions, and other benefits.

Financial motivations for working a gig are universal across generations, jobs, and professions. Anyone seeking to increase their income earning potential should explore gig work as an option. Most traditional jobs will not provide the worker with salary

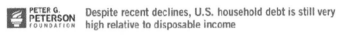

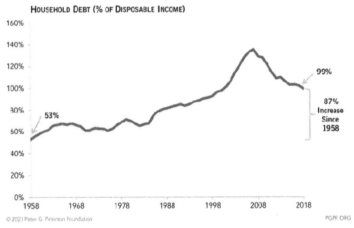

Source: Board of Governors of the Federal Reserve System Financial Accounts of the United States, December 2019; and Bureau of Economic Analysis, National Income and Product Accounts Tables, February 2020.

Fig. 3.3. US Household Debt as a Percent of Disposable Income.

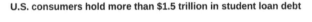

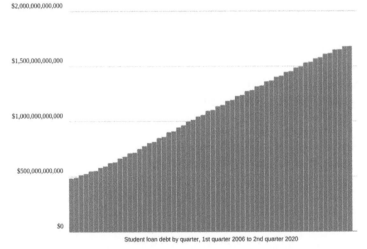

Source: U.S. Federal Reserve.

Fig. 3.4. Total Student Loan Debt Held by the US Consumers.

increases of 10%–20% per year. Yet, by adding a gig on the top of a conventional job, the income derived from the gig could make up for what might not be possible in a salary increase. For a salaried worker earning $60,000 per year, a 20% increase in income would represent an increase of $12,000.00 before taxes. This could make quite a difference in one's life when the incremental income is managed effectively. Gig providers should always be aware of this fundamental motivation that attracts people to the opportunities they create and offer.

Gig workers who can earn $500.00–$1,000.00 per month while maintaining a full-time job will experience the equivalent of a 10%–20% income increase if we use the $60,000.00 per year base example. Incremental earnings of $3,000.00 per year would be the equivalent of a 5% increase in income using $60,000.00 per year as the base example. The average salary increases over the past few years have been less than 5% of annual salary.

The opportunity to convert available hours into potential income, earned in a manner one chooses, can help ease financial stress. When more money is available, if managed effectively, there is more to save, invest, or cover personal or family needs or short-term goals. $500–$1,000 per month can make a difference.

We are not attempting to identify motivations in any order of priority, only describe them in a logical sequence. To jump to the conclusion that part-time income, by itself, is a motivation for working a gig overlooks a fundamental understanding of human behavior and what drives decision-making. When more money is available, when managed effectively, there is more to save and invest toward the personal and family goals.

Our hypothesis is that the gig seeker and worker is not looking to replace a career-type income, at least not in the beginning. Gig seekers are looking for an incremental earning opportunity and the ability to leverage flexibility with an income possibility. They might be a mom or dad who wants to stay at home to care for the kids and earn via a flexible income opportunity or those who simply do not want a job. Those who love their current jobs and career paths can easily experience the financial stress of spending more than they are earning. This dilemma is not confined to any income bracket or any age or type of job or profession. Gig opportunities now provide choices, and the right choice can make a difference. This also serves to further explain why the current labor force is experiencing over 40% of workers engaging in some type of gig. The trend indicates that within a few more years, over 50% of all traditional workers will be involved. The workers represent diverse jobs and professions, and this outlook speaks to the significance of the gig economy.

Research conducted by J.P. Morgan Chase at the end of 2018 looked at the average monthly earnings within various gig categories. Although the report did not list the median income, which we would expect to be much lower than the averages presented, these data are still quite revealing (Fig. 3.5).

As we researched this topic, we found a unique online lending company called Earnest Loans. It looked and felt like a gig company. Earnest is a different type of lender, with a significant focus on student debt, having refinanced over $6 billion in less than six

Source: The Online platform Economy 2018, JP Morgan Chase & Co. Institute.

Fig. 3.5. Average Monthly Earnings of Gig Workers.

years. They also boast that 50% of refinancing applications are processed within one minute using a proprietary assessment tool created by the Earnest team. Because of the younger clientele they have attracted, Earnest (earnest.com) has also accumulated some interesting data on gig workers and gig-providing companies.

When we examined the motivations for working a gig, we found the stories that remind us of the fundamentals that drive human behavior. The desire to work and live in a manner that supports the pursuit of happiness and peace of mind is fundamental to the human spirit and the glue that builds families, communities, and eventually the societies in which we live. Humans always find ways to do it better. This human spirit created the agricultural, industrial, and technology revolutions. We learn to continuously find better ways to do what we do. In this book, we have defined the gig economy, provided insights to help make sense of what is happening in the gig economy, and demonstrated that underneath the gig economy phenomena is always the evolving brilliance of human ingenuity, innovation, and creativity.

When traditional forms of work, in mature societies, make it challenging to earn more than we spend and delay or postpone our pursuit of happiness and peace of mind, innovation and creativity will always kick in to solve the problem. We always create better products and improve the quality of services rendered, and the same is true for how we work. We do not work the same way we did 25 years ago, and 25 years from now, the work will have been redefined again.

FLEXIBILITY

For several decades, alternative work arrangements and flextime have been the subject of conversation in the Human Resource Department of companies. Many organizations offer some type of alternative work arrangements to at least some of their employees, with options such as job sharing, compressed workweeks, flexible schedules, and telecommuting. These policies allow employees to have a more customized or flexible work schedule, relative to what hours are worked and on what days. However, those workers continue to be bound by traditional job rules, including a W-2 worker classification in the United States for tax purposes.

Staffing agencies have long provided businesses with temporary workers to cover for those on leave or to help companies scale their workforces up for busy seasons and down when things get slower. The US Postal Service and many retailers, for example, hire temporary workers to help during busy holiday seasons. Some people have considered these temporary jobs examples of gig work, but this is often a misclassification. Many of these positions are jobs that put a person into a traditional employee status for a temporary period. A person receiving a W-2 in the United States is not working a gig, even if the job is temporary.

Today, the technology-driven gig economy offers a more flexible approach to work. First, most gigs make it easy for an interested worker to get started. Seldom, if ever, is there a request for a résumé. For example, earning part-time income as a taxi or limousine driver requires navigating a complex system of licensing and registration. Becoming a driver for a private transportation company might require a significant upfront financial investment. However, driving for an online transportation platform, in contrast, is simple. The initial sign-up process takes just a few minutes, after which a new driver provides some basic documentation, undergoes a screening process, and, within hours, can start earning money.

Also, most gigs come with a high degree of scheduling flexibility. Unlike the employer/employee relationship where there is minimal flexibility allowed, gig workers set their schedules, taking on work when they wish and only when they wish. While it might not be practical for a working parent to take on a traditional part-time job, he or she may find a gig an option for earning an income while balancing childcare and other responsibilities.

Retirees or those from Generation Z seeking flexibility and the ability to earn a supplemental income are finding gigs to be part of the solutions they seek; so are educators, who work gigs in between their professional responsibilities and students looking for the additional $200.00–$300.00 or more per month. For all these groups, many consider gigs, and the choices available, to be a dream come true. You name the profession or the type of skilled worker who may be seeking an incremental income opportunity or a way to earn an income based on available personal hours, and you will probably find a gig opportunity that fulfills the needs.

When I graduated college in 2015, I knew I wanted to do gig work; I just didn't know that's what it was called. My dad helped guide me through the type of work I wanted, so we listed out what I wanted in a job and started looking for ways to do that.

Today, I love working from home and having flexibility to make appointments throughout my week or go to lunch with friends, and not be tied to a schedule. As long as I can knock out my work for the week, it doesn't matter what time I do it. I'm not a big morning person, so I would rather start later and work later. I also want to be a mom, so my hope is that I can continue to work and be a mom at the same time.

– Brooke H., freelancer

According to PYMNTS, flexibility is a primary motivation that drives workers to replace traditional employment for full-time gig work.

A quarter of surveyed gig workers named this as their top motivation for joining the gig economy. This becomes even more important for younger workers, as 22% of full-time gig workers, aged 18–24, and 30% of those in the 25–34 age bracket cited flexibility as the main reason they participated in the gig economy.

About 18% are in the 45–54 age bracket (pymnts.com). Most interesting is what PYMNTS also reports:

> *In Q2 2018, PYMNTS found 47% of gig workers had a regular, nine-to-five job, a drop from 55% in Q1 2018. This shift indicates that a growing share of workers see gig work as a viable career path over traditional work.*

In a 2018 study, researchers at Gallup Inc. found that independent contractors and people working through online gig platforms reported higher levels of work/life balance, motivational pay, meaningful feedback, and creative freedom than those in traditional work environments.

Another way in which people desire flexibility is when it comes to exploring entrepreneurship. The phrase "home-based business" has generally been used to describe anyone working out of their home, from an in-home office, or merely providing expertise or skills that were within a label of self-employment and not dependent upon a formal office or fixed facility. The gig economy is adding more possibilities to the ability to work and build a business from home, minimizing the risks associated with the expenses of starting a new business venture.

The gig economy and its many choices that allow for flexibility and freedom in how people work is a part of labor revolution. Who would have thought of the next-door neighbor being in the transportation business by simply driving her own car? The handyman is now a professional Tasker, and the friend we met on Facebook who told us about the wonderful new products she is enjoying is building a gig business.

IMPROVE QUALITY OF LIFE

The idea of the "American Dream" is rooted in the premise that if we work hard, life will yield prosperity and enjoyment in our pursuit of happiness and peace of mind. The pursuit of happiness and peace of mind is an aspirational attitude, and different people define it differently. The list may include cars, homes, other nice personal assets, more support for kids and their interest, becoming debt-free, having more time to enjoy hobbies and leisure activities, more money for savings and investments, postsecondary education expenses, and more.

We also know that achieving this dream is challenging for many people. Many students graduate from college, facing overwhelming debt. And many adults have such little savings that they cannot pay cash to cover minor emergencies.

The data illustrate this story. The first chart depicts the savings rate of Americans over the past 40+ years. It is interesting to note that our savings rate was close to 15% in 1975. The rate declined through the years 1975 through 2005, before beginning to climb again (Fig. 3.6). Has the gig economy contributed to the increased personal savings rate in recent years?

The second chart represents how 44% of Americans would deal with a modest $400 emergency expense (Fig. 3.7).

This is the current state of average American life and an excellent reason for seeking a way to accelerate and change a personal/family situation.

Fidelity, the financial services company, recommends a level of savings, at the age of 67, to be approximately $600,000.00. Therefore, we note the desire to be in control and accelerate the pace or state of one's life as a primary motivation for working a gig. Incremental income could change the dynamics of whatever the income vs expense relationship might be. The amount saved per month could improve the quality of one's life, as shown in the next chart over a short 5-year period. What a difference five years can make! (Fig. 3.8)

I'm an entrepreneur at heart. Currently, I own and manage my own salons. In my early career as a product educator with a hair color company, I learned the value of the science behind the product. I was introduced to direct selling in 2006.

I am still involved 14 years later. Today I have the advantage of growing my business in conjunction with my salons, with social media and the excellent support of

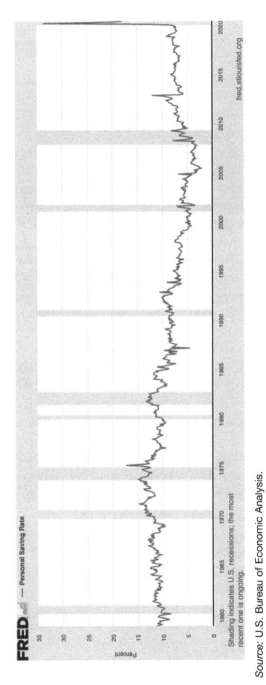

Source: U.S. Bureau of Economic Analysis.

Fig. 3.6. US Personal Savings Rate Over Time.

44% of U.S. adults in 2016 said they would not pay for a $400 emergency expense with cash or its equivalent. Here's what they would do instead.

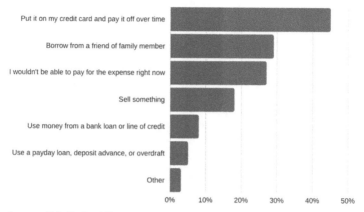

Source: U.S. Federal Reserve.

Fig. 3.7. How US Adults Would Pay for a $400 Emergency Expense.

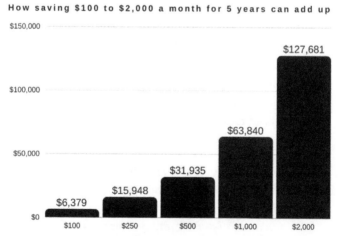

Fig. 3.8. The Compounding Effects of Increased Monthly Savings.
Note: The above calculations are based upon a 2.5% interest rate compounded monthly.

my company's digital marketing and leadership building resources. I believe that gig economy opportunities offer low-risk and high-reward opportunities for the part-time entrepreneur. This allows anyone to realize their dreams at whatever level they choose to engage. Whether that is an additional $500 a month to cover immediate financial needs or they want to grow into an unlimited business opportunity.

– Connie L., direct selling

I come from a family of truck drivers; we love to drive. That and a health issue that challenges me as a full- or part-time employee is probably what 'drove' me to a transportation gig. My company's immediate income is essential; the bonus is meeting and speaking with all kinds of people AND making my car payment! At the same time, I started my transportation business, a friend introduced me to another gig. In a lightbulb moment, I realized the sales and residual income component could be a game plan for retirement.

– Dawn B., transportation gig and direct selling

My brother is an architect, and when he asked me how much of my home I actually use as living space, a whole new project took shape. I remodeled to create a rent-able casita!

Four years later, my casita is a highly desirable short-term rental property. My parent company's support systems are designed to inspire trust for the consumer, combined with a full suite of training and systems for me to attract renters/customers. I am rated a 5-star property based on testimonials of guests that have stayed and enjoyed their experiences. I love to provide excellent customer satisfaction and build a repeat clientele!

– Michele M., home rental

THE ABILITY TO BE YOUR OWN BOSS

As we travel along life's pathway, most of us inherently desire to be in control of our journey. We are willing to work hard to reach our goals, and the more confident we are that our hard work will pay off, the more focused and motivated we become. The process of go to school, study hard, get as much education as possible, find work, and possibly build a family is in the human DNA. Our desire to be in control is not always the "control" or safety valve that prevents some of life's challenges. We are willing to incur financial pressures, often when we know we are walking near the edge of disrupting that positive balance between earning more than we are likely to spend. The belief that we will prevail is what drives us to work harder and seek new ways to earn from our experience, talents, skills, or willingness to learn something new. It is at this point that we may embrace the idea of something that might be meaningful to our desire to be the architect of our own destiny. This fundamental motivation becomes of great importance when one seeks to find a gig that is easy to engage that could also fulfill a need and accelerate the attainment of a goal to be the boss.

For many people, opportunities in the gig economy represent not just a way to earn money but also build a future they control. These individuals relish the idea of being able to direct their own work and to build a business where they call the shots. Gigs make possible the opportunity to be the boss or at least to some extent.

> When I was working corporate, most of my work consisted of things that I didn't really enjoy all that much. Going freelance just allowed me to do more of the work that I actually enjoy — the creative stuff. And since I have a number of clients, I get to work on a lot of different projects instead of just one company, so things stay fresh and interesting.
>
> Will I ever take a corporate 9-to-5 job again? Very possibly. The difference is, I'd likely be taking that job because I really wanted to do that work, not just because I needed a paycheck. It puts a different spin on

*the idea of planning your future when you aren't quite
so beholden to the traditional job market. You have a
bit more choice in the matter.*

– Ben H., freelancer

Being your own boss in the gig economy does not require
choosing a single gig and going "all-in" on the endeavor. Many
individuals create a personal business by combining multiple gigs
that, together, represent a way to build the lifestyle they desire.

*Currently Spencer and I are using Airbnb and also
TaskRabbit. Spencer is full-time working with TaskRabbit, and the Airbnb portion is more of a part-time position. We like how flexible it is and how many different
types of people we get to meet. Our eventual goal is to
build up enough clients and properties to where we can
choose when and where we would like to work.*

*Because it is so flexible and so random, it can branch to
anything new. Spencer did construction for a doctor's
office; then, through conversation, they asked if I could
do a sewing project for them, so now I'm making face
masks for them during this coronavirus pandemic. We
plan to use Airbnb for probably the rest of our lives
— unless there's a better website that comes out in the
future. We do plan to do rental properties from here on
out. With TaskRabbit, we are currently just using it as a
tool to meet new clients and meet lots of new people.*

*Our goal is to be extremely flexible while bringing in
enough money to not only take care of ourselves but
also to be generous with other people and go on trips
with families and all that good stuff.*

– Keagan H., home rental and service gig

WORK FROM HOME

The phrase "home-based business" has generally been used in a vague
manner to describe anyone working out of their home, from an in-

home office, or simply providing expertise or skills that were within a label of self-employment and not dependent upon a formal office or fixed facility. The gig economy is adding more possibilities to the ability to work from home, and this can be motivation for those who envision themselves as entrepreneurial and desirous of eliminating the risk associated with the expenses of starting a business not knowing exactly how successful the business will become. Building a business from home with the digital support and global presence of a company that supports microentrepreneurs is now a reality.

For anyone interested in working from home, it has never been easier, and there are virtually no limits to the possibilities. If you have an idea, or merely the desire to work from home, companies such as Shopify, Etsy, eBay, and others enable the ability to start, market, manage, and grow a business for the commitment of a minimal monthly subscription fee. Women, in particular, may find this to be their most important motivation in conjunction with flexibility.

I've got a small hand embroidery business. I do wall decor for kind of anything: office, anywhere in your home, baby nursery stuff, wedding hoops. There is some jewelry, enamel pins, some banners, but it seems that hand-stitched embroidery is the main thing. I've always been a maker ever since I was a kid. I finally started realizing, especially in the past few years, I need to be selling things instead of just making it, so that's how I got active on Etsy and doing shows and stuff.

In the evenings, I am stitching, working on orders, working on my website. I'm on Instagram promoting, going to events and going to network. My actual, physical job is a barista, so that is where I am getting an actual paycheck. Right now, my Etsy business isn't doing enough where I could quit my other job, but it is supplementing my monthly income and helping me pay rent and take care of bills, so that's pretty awesome.

– Kara H., selling gig

Growing up, I had entrepreneurial role models in my grandfather, who owned his own grocery story, and my dad, who opened his own pet store. I experienced first-hand the demands and fulfillment of owning your own business. In the early days of eBay, around 1999, I looked over my husband's shoulder as he posted and sold video games through eBay. It didn't take much time, and the income was pretty good. I knew I could do that! It was a way to generate income from home on my schedule.

What started small eventually became an important side hustle, and at one point, the income from eBay helped us through a time when my husband was between jobs. For various reasons, I wound down my eBay business. Now I work part-time as an established substitute teacher in my community. While we do not typically think of teaching as gig or freelance work, it's been an ideal part-time option for me. But, the COVID-19 pandemic highlighted how even a teaching position isn't as secure as you might expect. With schools closed, I wasn't teaching. My husband's expertise in marketing is currently in use through freelance consulting work. With 'freelance' teaching out of the question, I've returned to eBay, which I was thinking of doing even before COVID-19.

The best way to succeed on eBay or similar platforms like Etsy is to provide unique, desirable, priced-right products. Twenty years ago, I was selling my kids' outgrown clothes. Then I transitioned to graphic clip art CDs and scrapbooking supplies and even dollhouse furniture – all of which have strong demand from buyers. My product offering now is, wait for it, vinyl stickers! My research shows they are in demand as kids AND adults love them to add lively personalization to everything from bikes and cars to laptops and insulated water bottles. I also see high demand for lanyards. And,

*I can get my stock and shipping supplies at an afford-
able price, allowing for a good return on each sale. The
ultimate decision driving factor for selling the stickers:
they ship in an envelope with a stamp or two. eBay's
technology and analytics support product decisions and
provide data so I can focus on products that sell and
avoid dud options. I work as orders demand; I'm here
for our two girls in high school; the mailbox is my
logistics partner, and the family's financial pressure
valve is relieved!*

– Kim R., selling gig

SCALABLE INCOME

In some gigs, the worker is purely trading time for money. Once the
gig is complete, the income stops. For example, transportation gig
drivers get paid when they drive the car and stop earning when they
turn their app off and stop accepting rides.

Some gigs, however, offer opportunities to grow a business over
time. In these gigs, the effort someone puts in during the early days
of the work can continue to pay off. Such gig workers may invest
time in growing their customer base so they can enjoy the benefits
of repeat sales and expanded word-of-mouth advertising. A direct
seller, for example, has an opportunity to scale a business and earn
income via the purchases of customers who continue to buy the
product or service. Freelancers who start out as gig workers,
working at their gig a few hours a week, may find themselves
building a client base that grows into higher income.

With so much digital marketing support available, it is possible
to start small and grow into a more robust or even large business.
The gig worker building a business using a platform such as a direct
selling company, Etsy, Shopify, YouTube, Kajabi, and others, look
forward to being able to grow a business and market their products
or services, even globally, to a growing audience.

*I am a printmaker, painter, and designer. I sell my orig-
inal linocut art prints and archival-quality productions*

*of my drawings and paintings as well as greeting cards
and vinyl stickers.*

*I've been doing this seriously since about 2011. Before
that, I had studied drawing and painting in college, and
I was pursuing more of being a gallery artist with oil
paintings. Obviously, paintings represented in a gallery
are not necessarily accessible to the public. So, I decided
that I wanted to make an effort to create work that was
more accessible that would be easier to get into any-
body's home, which was still high-quality. Now that I
do print-making, each of the prints is original, so I love
that what I'm making is original, but it's also affordable
and accessible.*

*I love my job. I can't imagine doing anything else. I love
that I have the opportunity to be creative and to share
my work with the world and to be home also. That is a
huge plus for us because childcare is expensive, so this
has been a great way for us to supplement our income.
It has consistently grown over the years as I've been
able to dedicate more time. I really hope it continues to
grow and become something where my husband could
potentially quit his job. We have really big dreams for
this business.*

– Anna T., selling gig

RESIDUAL INCOME

Creating a residual income is not a common trait associated with
the gig economy, but the possibility does exist. We are defining a
residual income opportunity as one that attracts customers who
purchase, frequently purchase, and refer others to the source of the
products or services with which they have become familiar. Work
from home opportunities that are based on selling something to a
potential customer base that continues to purchase through an
online e-commerce platform is a new form of store that potential

customers appreciate. There is no longer any debate as to whether customers will purchase through e-commerce platforms or not. What is most appealing, innovative, and game-changing are the tools available that can support microentrepreneurs. A gig can become an enterprise. Using tools such as those provided by such gig-supporting companies as Shopify, Etsy, Fiver, Gigster, Toptal, direct selling companies, and others, a microentrepreneur can now open an e-commerce store and compete with big brands locally and globally. When shoppers come back to platforms actually owned and managed by a microentrepreneur, the potential to grow a larger business becomes a possibility and a reality for some.

SUMMARY

The gig economy is not the result of a boom in the appeal and interest in part-time work. The gig economy is leading a revolution in how we work.

Gigs of all types offer people an opportunity to bridge the gap when expenses exceed regular income. This enables people to pursue happiness and peace of mind, in whatever form that takes. Regardless of the differences in our individual goals and dreams, our success in managing our lives is often the difference between what we earn and what we spend. When that ratio becomes negative, it negatively impacts the way we live, eat, and enjoy our work and life. When we earn more than we spend, we can eliminate financial pressures and enjoy more of what life – and even work – has to offer.

Gigs also provide flexibility in how or when work can be accomplished. Many offer freedoms associated with operating an independent business like being your own boss. Flexibility and freedom in how work can be done have become a new norm. Younger generations do not understand or accept the same limitations once perceived by previous generations, and all ages are beginning to realize that they can reach their goals faster when they have more control over their income possibilities.

4

GIGS REDEFINE
ENTREPRENEURSHIP

From the increasing use of contingent freelance workers to the growing role of robotics and smart machines, the corporate workforce is changing – radically and rapidly. These changes are no longer simply a distraction; they are now actively disrupting labor markets and the economy.

Today, more than one in three U.S. workers are freelancers – a figure expected to grow to 40 percent by end of 2020. This year's survey confirms that the contingent workforce has gone global. Fully 51 percent of executives in our global survey plan to increase or significantly increase the use of contingent workers in the next three to five years, while only 16 percent expect a decrease. Companies such as Airbnb and Uber embody this trend, but they are not the only organizations profiting from the "gig economy."

– Deloitte University Press, Global Human Capital Trends,
published 2016

Earlier, we discussed the primary drivers of gig economy growth, trends in labor, stagnation in the purchasing power of real wages, and the effect of technology on traditional jobs. It is quite possible that the labor force will downsize before new jobs are created that demand a completely new and different skill set that current workers may not be willing to learn. This will continue to fuel the interest in opportunities that allow people to leverage what they already know rather than having to learn something new and potentially uncomfortable.

External factors have caused virtually every segment in the working population to explore gig economy opportunities, and we see this as the precursor to a massive shift in how labor will be performed. We envision the gig economy as a significant part of a change in who owns the labor pool. Signs indicate that the labor force is growing toward ownership by millions of people from all walks of life rather than the select few of the more industrial economy. In the new economy, more people work in accordance with their own time frames rather than within the rigid hours of the industrial economy format. COVID-19 has increased people's understanding of how flexible work can be as productive or more productive than traditional work models. Moving forward, we will not be retrofitting the work methodologies of the past. The future is different. It is happening now.

As we shared in previous chapters, motivations to join the gig economy can be related to the desire to create some sort of entrepreneurial experience. Even those who are not aiming to build their own business are looking to have more control over their income, taking on a new work endeavor in order to bring in an extra $500 to $1,500 per month. Gigs allow people to become entrepreneurial while eliminating many of the risks associated with starting a business venture.

In the past, we thought of an entrepreneur as a bold, confident businessperson – part of the engine of commerce, involved in the distribution of goods and services, or the owner of buildings and land. This definition, and the accompanying financial investment that was required, distinctly separated entrepreneurs from the laborers who did the work. It also meant that the entrepreneur enjoyed a significant portion of the profit from the enterprise while the laborer would work for fixed wages.

This perception of the entrepreneur may be a bit dated, but its roots reach back to the origins of America and virtually every mature market in the world that embraces free enterprise. By the end of the nineteenth century, entrepreneurs had become an elite group in America. Henry Ford, Andrew Carnegie, Pierre S. du Pont, and John D. Rockefeller are synonymous with the origins of free enterprise and entrepreneurship in America. Today, the names are more likely to be Sam Walton, Bill Gates, Steve Jobs, Jeff Bezos, Mark Zuckerberg, Elon Musk, and others who have made remarkable contributions to the entrepreneurial model and society overall. Even though some of these businesses were started with a minimal amount of capital, they required extraordinary vision, talent, and marketing savvy. Their stories are inspirational.

Over the past 100 years, the entrepreneurial model has evolved. Two specific innovations – direct selling and franchising – both made it easier to start a business. Direct selling, which we discuss in more detail in Chapter 6, was among the first business models to allow individuals to affiliate with an established brand and build their own business in accordance with schedules they design themselves. Starting a direct selling business has always been relatively inexpensive, typically less than $100.00. When it was first introduced, franchising offered a unique way to be in business as an entrepreneur with the support of a proven brand and its established marketing and sales processes. The franchise support came with fees that often exceeded a few thousand dollars, even a few hundred thousand dollars to get started. Most franchises also required people to establish a fixed facility, which further increased investment costs. These two models give people with an entrepreneurial spirit the ability to leverage someone else's brand and provide access to proven processes for starting, managing, and building the business.

Today, the gig economy offers a host of new choices when it comes to entrepreneurial opportunity. No matter who you are or how you dream of improving your life, there are options that likely could work for you. Within each of these gig choices is a path for exploring microentrepreneurship, making gigs much more than another avenue for working part-time.

Gig economy opportunities, in many ways, have taken pages from the playbooks of both direct selling and franchising but added their own twist. Today's new gig-providing companies require minimal investment from participants and often provide substantial business support. In addition, they share three key attributes that reduce the complexity traditionally associated with becoming an entrepreneur: simplicity, customer focus, and brilliant use of technology. Gig-providing companies use these attributes effectively, often marketing them so subtly that it is easy to take them for granted.

SIMPLICITY

Part of the appeal of gigs is their simplicity. But do not misconstrue our meaning here: Their simplicity does not minimize the importance of the work or the sophistication of the tools and marketing concepts they use. Some are pure genius. Rather, part of the beauty of gig work is that gig-providing companies offer an opportunity to quickly start work and receive payment when the work is completed, not days or weeks later. This performance-based concept works well for the company providing the gig opportunity and the gig worker.

Part-time work opportunities have been around for decades. The gig economy has made part-time work more appealing by making it so simple to take on. The most popular gig opportunities have few, if any, barriers to entry. They have low or no fees to get started, require minimal training, and offer plenty of support and guidance along the way. This makes giving a gig a try an easy, low-risk proposition and is a big part of why they have such wide appeal. Contrast that with business or work opportunities that require big upfront investments, lots of training, or even a lengthy interview process, and it is easy to see why the gig economy has created a powerful competitive advantage within the market for work (Fig. 4.1).

The simplicity is working. As easy as it is to start working a gig, it is easy for people to stop or switch to a new gig if they did not enjoy the experience. Job satisfaction among gig economy workers is high. In an August 2018 survey, Morning Consult found that 80% reported being either very satisfied or somewhat satisfied with their current gig. In hindsight, we do not believe such strong job

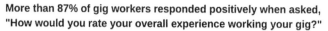

More than 87% of gig workers responded positively when asked, "How would you rate your overall experience working your gig?"

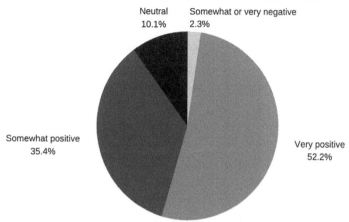

Fig. 4.1. Satisfaction of Gig Workers.

satisfaction scores would have been found in a simple survey of traditional part-time work.

There is something else going on that adds to the gig economy's appeal. Many gigs are providing people with a simple way to turn an underutilized asset into an opportunity to make some extra money. Take cars, for example. Cars are one of our most significant purchases. For many people, their car payment is second only to their mortgage payment or rent when it comes to monthly expenses – and that is before you take into consideration the cost of insurance and maintenance. Yet, our cars sit unused much of the time. In Arun Sundararajan's book, *The Sharing Economy*, he references a study that measured the usage of cars owned by Californians. Not to anyone's surprise, the average usage was 10% of the car's life. The gig economy offers opportunities for people to get value out of the remaining 90% by offering it as a short-term rental or using it to provide transportation or perform errands. Turning underutilized assets into income opportunities is applicable to other gigs as well. An underutilized talent or skill is, in many ways, no different than allowing a car to sit unused in our garage. Gigs offer simple solutions to turn both into an income earning opportunity – work that a person can start and stop as they choose.

*I cannot speak to other gigs, but I would recommend
Lyft if you were thinking about that type of gig. Lyft
has mastered ease and flexibility. However, you need to
know how to work the "system" regarding where the
"good rides" (the longer rides) are in order to make the
$17 to $20 per hour that they promote. I made about
$10 an hour. I was really surprised by the ease of the
process. You receive the information you need, as you
need it.*

                                        – Bobbie W., transportation gig

Bobbie's observations about earning potential raise an important
topic worth discussing as part of the analysis of the simplicity of
gigs. Clearly, there is money to be earned by participating in the gig
economy, and there are definite trends toward self-employment via
gig work. People from all walks of life are giving it a try. Credible
surveys indicate that up to 80% of the existing working population
expresses receptivity to part-time work or some form of a gig. This
is a considerable number. The survey represents part-time interest,
not new full-time career paths to entrepreneurship. Aspiring
entrepreneurs who are looking to earn the equivalent of a full-time
income from a gig are a much smaller segment of the marketplace
than those who are looking for an additional $500.00 to $1,500.00
per month.

While the earning potential is there, we believe it wise to be
careful about evaluating a gig income opportunity in traditional
terms. Gigs are not designed to accommodate an hourly wage
comparison, although most will compare favorably. Instead, gig
selection is more focused on the flexibility and freedom associated
with how work is accomplished. We also advise against comparing
the opportunity to market professional skills as a freelancer, which
generates gig earnings, to the salaries earned by professionals who
work traditional jobs. The more accurate comparative analysis
would be to evaluate the return on investment of time and effort.
How do you do this? A gig seeker would be wise to take the time to
clarify his or her personal goals and specific objectives for taking on
a gig. Planning remains essential to everything we do in our lives,
and, as exciting as the gig economy may be, the gig economy has

not discovered or uncovered an elixir that replaces thoughtful decision-making. The need for immediate income, incremental or otherwise, may make one type of gig more appealing than another.

CUSTOMER FOCUS

The world's most successful companies are excellent examples of the importance of customer service, and they demonstrate this in many ways. Gig-providing companies understand the importance of customers, and many have designed their business models to focus on connecting customers with providers of products and services. Transportation gigs, for example, generally provide a gig worker with easy access to customers. Upwork, the world's largest online workplace, is a gig provider in the service gig category that makes it easier for people who need a professional service to connect with someone who can provide the service. Through its platform, Etsy provides an online shopping mall for microentrepreneurs to sell their products. The global exposure provides exposure to a marketplace of potential buyers that is much larger than most new microentrepreneurs could create on their own with a limited marketing budget.

When a gig allows the worker to share in the customer relationship, as Upwork, Etsy, direct selling companies, and many others do, it creates more potential for the gig worker. People working such gigs can potentially increase their income by focusing on consistently acquiring and providing great service to new customers and then turning those customers in repeat buyers. In gigs with this structure, workers can start to see their returns on the time they invest in the gig increase over time as customers return again and again.

In December 2019, the Deloitte research team of John Hagel, Jeff Schwartz, and Maggie Wool published an article titled *Redefining Work for New Value* in Deloitte Insights and MIT Sloan Management Review (mitsmr.com/ZOFAAa8). In the paper, the Deloitte team emphasizes that the future of work will need to create new efficiencies and better value for the customer. We see the gig economy continuing to increase the value that consumers receive. Entrepreneurs and microentrepreneurs know that their compensation is based on results, and gig workers quickly learn the entrepreneurial rules. With more microentrepreneurs learning how best to attract and serve consumers, we will continue to see even more choices for customers and gig workers alike.

BRILLIANT USE OF TECHNOLOGY

Technology has fueled the popularity and growth of the gig economy and is integral to many gigs. Even better, being tech-savvy is not required. The technology used in most gigs today is very intuitive. Getting started is often as simple as downloading an app, and the onboarding process to begin working can usually be completed within a few hours. Once completed, the income earning opportunity begins.

Technology also fuels a number of innovations that make it easier for people to build their own gigs. Companies such as Shopify, Squarespace, Etsy, Kajabi, Teachable, and many others have simplified the process of starting your own online business. Another technology-fueled innovation is the concept of affiliate marketing. Affiliate marketers are gig workers who promote another brand, typically using digital tools and working on schedules they create for themselves. Such big-box brands as Walmart and Amazon use affiliate marketers, providing guidelines and tools to help promote their products. The affiliates earn a commission on the purchases made by the customers they influence. For example, someone who has a personal blog might decide to become an affiliate marketer by placing a banner on their website, promoting products sold on Amazon. Technology allows Amazon to track the sales that come from that banner and to pay a commission back to the affiliate. Some affiliate marketing opportunities, but not all, also reward affiliates for the future purchases of the customers they create for a brand. Affiliate marketing gigs come in all shapes and sizes. Those who work these types of gigs often work on their promotions in the middle of the night, or between homeschooling a child, or during regularly scheduled hours for working their gig. Serious affiliate marketers, especially those who learn and apply sophisticated marketing expertise to the brands they promote, can earn significant incomes.

We will dive more deeply into the role technology has played in the formation and growth of the gig economy in Chapter 5.

ADDITIONAL FINDINGS AND ATTRIBUTES

As we conducted our research, we identified many other positive attributes of the gig economy. While simplicity, customer focus, and brilliant use of technology are the core three attributes, there are other attributes that are noteworthy and game-changing.

Traditionally, entrepreneurs tended to build their business through a hierarchical structure that creates opportunities based on traditional values and levels within a business structure. Corporations have many layers within the structure, and so do small businesses. The franchise model relies on the structure of owners, managers, and workers. Even direct selling models, which have long offered independent contractors the opportunity to work and develop businesses in accordance with personal flexibility and freedoms desired, created many levels of achievement to distinguish outstanding levels of performance.

We do not see this within the gig economy. When people first decide to work a gig, there is no need to wonder who the manager or boss might be, whether their résumé will match the job description created by the human resources department, or if there are job openings at the moment. Within the gig economy, we do not find hierarchy. Titles and structures are replaced by a simple and easy-to-understand focus on performance. Some gig-providing companies have the ability to rate the performance of their gig workers, which encourages improvement and the quality of service provided by workers. Gig workers are rewarded for the work they do, not the titles they achieve because there are no titles. The gig seeker needs to display one thing: an interest in doing the work. Most importantly, the gig worker reports to himself or herself. No hierarchy!

THE POWER OF INNOVATION, CREATIVITY, AND TRUST

Behind all forces that change the game of life and work are ingenious minds that find a way to deliver innovation and creativity in quantum leaps, whereas we sometimes go from "what was" to "what is" overnight – or it feels that way. The first flight into space was in 1961. Those flights were controlled by the governments of either the Soviet Union, the first to fly into space, or the United States, the first to land astronauts on the moon. NASA ceased its space shuttle program in 2011. Private enterprise entered the picture (first approved to build spacecraft in 2004) and has been responsible for transporting supplies to the space station ever since NASA closed its space shuttle program.

As we wrote this book, SpaceX (founded by PayPal and Tesla Motors founder Elon Musk) just took its first astronauts to the International Space Station. It seemed like suddenly something amazing happened, and it did. A sleek new rocket, Falcon-9, flew a Dragon Crew capsule and two astronauts to the International Space Station. The events that led up to what happened on May 31, 2020, had been developing throughout the past decade. Private enterprise first exposed their versions of spacecraft around 2004. When Dragon Crew returns the astronauts home within a few weeks or months, they are expected to land on a dime, an expression for the precision now accomplished in returning rockets and spacecraft. Within the next decade, space travel will be commercialized, taking passengers into space and to many destinations on the planet. Companies we should continue to watch are SpaceX and Virgin Galactic.

We use the quick snapshot of space travel as an example of how innovation and creativity can trigger a startling difference in many aspects of life and work. It is always happening, even when we are not aware. Gig-providing companies continue to change the game relative to how work can be accomplished, and their stories are as innovative as the story about the evolution of space travel. Accelerated innovation and creativity is happening, and we are participating.

When we examined Airbnb, we found a visionary CEO in Brian Chesky, a designer trained at the Rhode Island School of Design. The acronym Airbnb comes from the words Air Beds and Breakfast. Chesky and his roommates were thinking of creative ways to pay the rent. The idea of making a few airbeds available to people possibly interested in a short-term stay and a light breakfast came to fruition when they realized hotels had sold out all accommodations the weekend of a very popular design conference being held in their city. The year was 2007. Today, that idea has resulted in Airbnb having hosts in more than 190 countries and listings in over 80,000 cities around the world. Since its inception, Airbnb has hosted over 500 million guests.

We also found John Zimmer, co-founder and president of Lyft, to be another fascinating story. Lyft, a popular transportation gig-providing company, was launched in 2012, but the idea of the founders probably started earlier, around the same time Brian Chesky was inventing what became Airbnb. Today, Lyft operates in the United States and parts of Canada, serving approximately 1 million customers per day through their drivers (gig workers).

Zimmer also had an interest in hospitality. Excellence in hospitality success is based upon delivering a good experience that attracts high acceptance. Zimmer took note of the high underutilization of cars by owners who were making large investments. Arun Sundararajan, author of *The Sharing Economy*, quotes Zimmer as saying:

> *Vehicle utilization is about 4%, occupancy in those cars is about 20%. So you basically have a 1% utilization rate on something that accounts for about 13% of global GDP. I saw that as a big opportunity.*

The original idea Zimmer and his co-founder Logan Greene started with was more of a ride-share model than a gig-providing model. Not long after launch, they switched to the more gig-providing model that they use today. Once again, the innovative and creative idea of how to turn a familiar and underutilized asset into positive value versus depreciation changed the game when it comes to transportation.

Sundararajan, an economist, goes on to provide a very bold thought that he offered in his book. The thought is profound:

> *There's immense excess capacity in cars around the world. Americans alone spend about a trillion dollars each year buying new and used cars. Around the world, governments spend billions of dollars building elaborate public transit systems, often imposing crippling costs of*

both money and inconvenience on their city economies.
Could apps like Lyft promise a different approach to
building urban transportation infrastructure, foresha-
dowing a new kind of crowd-based, public-private part-
nership, one that uses digital technology to tap into
decentralized excess capacity rather than creating new
monolithic centralized systems.

The idea expressed by Sundararajan is demonstrated in the
success of France-based BlaBlaCar, which has become popular
in Europe. An app is used to connect a driver going to another
city who has empty seats with passengers who want to buy an
empty seat. BlaBlaCar transports more people every day from
city to city throughout Europe than the entire United States
Amtrak System.

We view the gig economy as a connector that changes and disrupts traditional thinking relative to work. In some cases, those
with underutilized assets are provided an opportunity to use those
assets for revenue generation without disturbing more traditional
work, family responsibilities, or routines. The gig worker is an
independent contractor. New forms of gig work provide services
never thought of 25 years ago; other forms of gig work such as
direct selling have been around for over 100 years. Who would ever
have thought that ordinary people, from all walks of life, would be
turning underutilized assets (homes, apartments, cars, talent, and
professional skills) into significant income earning opportunities,
whereas the worker is actually provided flexibility and control of
when work can be done?

The direct selling channel of distribution has been built upon
foundational concepts of utilizing independent contractors to
consummate the final transaction with the consumer. Most direct
sellers have always been involved in earning part-time income on
their own terms. The gig economy has taken a page from the direct
selling playbook, adding innovation and creativity in how consumers and providers of goods and services can be connected. As
we discussed in Chapters 1 and 2, a great percentage of the
population happens to be most interested in utilizing time more
effectively to achieve goals. However, as great as the values of
innovation and creativity are to any endeavor, there is another

component worth noting that has fueled and enabled the growth of the gig economy as entrepreneurship is being redefined. It is labeled: Trust!

Those of us who have participated on the Ultimate Gig Core Team remember the days when the Internet was not trusted. Having been directly involved with the direct selling model, it is easy to remember conversations, whereas the Internet was viewed as a threat to traditional business models, even corrupt in the minds of some who were very short-sighted in how the use of the Internet might eventually reach and serve consumers more effectively. Our level of trust in online sources and services has reached a level of dependency. Today, we cannot imagine being without the Internet. We bank online, we do not see a teller, and the money goes wherever we want it to go. We use transportation services when we have no idea what the car or driver will look like until we place our request. Professionals connect to clients who need their services that may be in another city or even another country. Traditional brick and mortar retailers are attempting to reinvent themselves through online platforms. Direct selling companies are no longer dependent upon their direct sellers needing a physical presence to introduce products and services. The Internet is no longer a demon; it has changed the world.

Just as the SpaceX launch that took astronauts to the International Space Station was not an overnight phenomenon, the emergence of trust has not been an overnight phenomenon in fueling the growth and acceptance of products and services from those we have not been acquainted. Once again, we found a nugget of information in a quote in *The Sharing Economy*.

> *There is a new kind of relationship of trust for people to build on: trust in online profiles. This is not an incremental change to society – It's not a bit more, or a bit better of what went before – it is a disruptive change. Nothing will ever be the same. The building block of society, interpersonal trust, has been transformed from a scarce into an abundant resource. Our potential to collaborate and create value (is) also transformed.*
>
> – Frederic Mazella, QuiShare magazine interview,
> January 14, 2013

Notable in the quote is the date January 14, 2013. The seeds upon which the gig economy is growing were planted, nurtured, and observed almost 10 years ago. The gig economy is redefining entrepreneurship, growing the importance of microentrepreneurship, and making it possible for the masses to be more in control of one of life's most important components – our work. Entrepreneurship is redefined.

FUELING THE FIRE AND FANNING THE FLAMES

If the gig economy is part of a new grassfire of economic shifts in how a growing number of people will work, it is evident that there must be some companies that are fueling the fires and fanning the flames, and there are many.

With approximately 60 million Americans already involved in gig work, it was not surprising to us to find the very innovative and intriguing stories of brands such as Uber, Lyft, Airbnb, Upwork, TaskRabbit, Get-A-Round, and others to be playing a massive role in the growth of the gig economy. However, companies such as Shopify and Wealthy Affiliate, which are not gig providers but supporters of those who desire to create and work their own gig, also are playing a significant role in the growth of the gig economy and fueling the fires of microentrepreneurship.

When we read the Shopify mission statement, we knew we had found microentrepreneurial fuel.

We help people achieve independence by making it easier to start, run, and grow a business. We believe the future of commerce has more voices, not fewer, so we're reducing the barriers to business ownership to make commerce better for everyone.

Shopify was founded in 2004, in Ottawa, Canada, by entrepreneurs Tobias Lutke, Daniel Weinland, and Scott Lake, who set out with the goal of selling snowboards. When they realized they had developed an incredibly unique software platform, they switched to supporting microentrepreneurial businesses. As the saying goes, the rest is now history. Shopify has become one of the most successful and admired companies in Canada and throughout the world, valued at $119 billion (Canadian). Shopify supports more than 1 million merchants (many of them gig workers) in over 175 different countries around the globe who sold more than $60 billion in merchandise value in 2019. Shopify provides a complete e-commerce platform that helps the newest of gig seeker as well as established companies like PepsiCo and Staples with online, multichannel sales platforms. The Shopify support platform can be engaged by a new microentrepreneur for as little as $10.00 per month. The company employs more than 500 people.

"The vast majority of people are employed by small businesses, and they struggle the most during a crisis," said Tobi Lütke, Shopify's CEO said in a statement released along with the companies first-quarter 2020 earnings. "The spread of COVID-19 is going to be a tough time for all entrepreneurs. We are working as fast as we can to support our merchants by re-tooling our products to help them adapt to this new reality. Our goal is that, because Shopify exists, more entrepreneurs and small businesses will get through this."

We also were impressed with the involvement of the big-box retailer Walmart and online retail giant Amazon in stoking the growth of the gig economy. The No. 1 and No. 2 retailers in the world both use affiliates (gig workers) to bolster their online marketing. Other brands are also involved in contributing to the entrepreneurial spirit fueling the growth of the gig economy. Walmart is newer to the game, and the fact that they have chosen to be in this game is noteworthy. Affiliates for both companies focus primarily on online promotions of the brands. The commissions range between 4% and 10%, and there are limitations as to what can be earned on the different categories of products. Both brands represent approximately 10 million products that are sold under the respective brand names.

CHAPTER SUMMARY AND INSIGHTS

The gig economy formula is working. The choices for gigs have never been as abundant as the choices that are currently available. These opportunities will continue to increase as innovation, creativity, and technology continue to change the way we have done things in the past. The gig economy is recognized as a formidable force that is reshaping the way work can be accomplished.

In the next chapter, we explore further the role technology has played in the evolution and growth of the gig economy. However, it is the combination of simplicity, customer focus, and new digital tools that are redefining entrepreneurship, redefining the way we work, and providing more people from all walks of life the opportunity to engage in microenterprise. The gig economy phenomenon is redefining entrepreneurship.

5

HOW TECHNOLOGY IS SHAPING GIGS

The gig economy is founded upon the excellent and innovative use of technology. In fact, technology is part of what makes gig work so appealing to people across all generations.

Technology certainly impacts decisions made by potential gig workers. People assume gigs will include features powered by technology that they never imagined 20 years ago. An app is a primary example. We now expect to have an app to access information that we use and share. Transportation gig workers live and work by an app, as do Airbnb hosts, Grub Hub gig workers, Taskers, those who use platforms like Upwork, and those supported by platforms such as Shopify and Etsy. Every gig-providing company leverages an app. In this chapter, we take you behind the scenes to provide a glimpse at the incredible changes technology brings into our lives. We approached the development of this chapter in segments, each devoted to understanding a specific role technology plays in support of the gig economy. Each segment of this chapter is the result of specific contributions from leaders who own and lead businesses that utilize a great amount of technology. Robert Cavitt, CEO of Jenkon, contributed the first two sections. Yogi Shankar, CEO and founder of Prescriptive Insights, contributed the third and fourth sections. Vince Han, CEO and founder of Mobile Coach, contributed the section on artificial intelligence (AI) and chatbots. Paul Beldham, founder and CEO, and Karen Dworaczyk, Chief Revenue Officer, of PayQuicker, provided insights relative to the banking systems and processes that make it possible to pay gig workers quicker. We know you will find this chapter informative and insightful.

A GENERAL OVERVIEW OF THE CRITICAL IMPORTANCE OF TECHNOLOGY

Technology is the engine driving the twenty-first century gig economy. Gig business models are predicated on the use of technology to make it easy for an entrepreneur to provide a product or service. Gig entrepreneurs will be able to choose from, and conduct, a vast array of business and career opportunities from the mobile device of their choosing. Mobile devices will not only be smartphones but also become "wearables," IoT technologies (the Internet of Things) where tiny computers reside on almost everything that we purchase or use, and even nanocomputers that can be embedded in our physical beings.

Dr. Haya Ajjan, Faculty Fellow for Innovation and Director of the Center for Analytics at Elon University, emphasizes the significance of how technology has been utilized by companies, such as Airbnb, VRBO, Uber, and Lyft, to create what is in effect, the largest hotels, and taxi services in the world. The largest theater in the world is Netflix, but it has no cinemas. Many people regard the Uber and Lyft corporations as software companies, not ride-share companies. Why? Because Uber and Lyft develop and evolve a software platform upon which riders make requests and payments, and driver entrepreneurs obtain ride information and get quickly paid.

Similarly, GrubHub, DoorDash, and JustEats create online software solutions for customers to request delivery of meals and delivery entrepreneurs to obtain location information. VRBO, HomeAway, and Airbnb create web-based software that allows property owners to list and market properties for temporary rental and customers to query and select from many destination options. All these software platforms pay the gig microentrepreneur within minutes, hours, or a few days of their service. Upwork may be the most extensive professional search firm. It has now served over 5 million businesses in identifying available freelance talent in the world, and it has all been accomplished with the effective utilization of technology.

Consumers and microentrepreneurs will continue growing in their expectations, and confidence, with the use of gig technologies. Gig companies are focused on not only the end customer experience (CX) but also the *microentrepreneur experience*. Consequently, many business solutions are being created to simplify their journeys in the distribution of company products and services.

Gig-providing companies use technology effectively to accomplish the following:

1. Identify and connect retail customers with a gig worker who makes it easy for the consumer to access products and services.

2. Relieve gig workers/microentrepreneurs of routine customer service responsibilities.

3. Quick compensation for the work or service provided.

Most amazing is that the gig-providing company's online software or app manages many tasks and steps in the typical marketing and sales process of acquiring customers. Some gigs provide workers with customers, and the gig worker is simply the connection between brand and consumer. In these situations, the gig worker does not need to have marketing or sales skills; they simply provide the work. The technology used connects with sophisticated currency systems that move money quickly so that the gig worker is quickly paid a commission or generated a form of credit. Consumers remain engaged through encouragement to use the product or service again and provide referrals. Compensation is often in the form of loyalty rewards or discounts on future purchases. All of this is a result of very sophisticated technology. What we see is usually a simple, easy-to-access app on a smartphone.

Some of the world's largest consumer goods companies are now offering gig-type opportunities to expand the reach of their brands. Unilever, a company with one of the world's highest market capitalizations, provides gig opportunities in Southeast Asia. Members of Unilever Network can refer to or promote the company's consumer products in skincare, cosmetics, personal hygiene, and health. This is obviously a test, and positive results could mean expansion throughout the world. Technology is the key driver.

The Body Shop, formerly owned by L'Oreal, the French-based cosmetics company, is utilizing technology in a very innovative manner. The company is now owned by Natura, the Brazil-based direct selling cosmetics company that also recently acquired Avon Products, Inc. The Body Shop built its brand in a very traditional way: selling their products in malls and retail outlets worldwide. Today, they offer a new type of gig opportunity in the United Kingdom, Australia, and the United States. Having once experimented with direct sales, the new model is quite different. The Body Shop at Home uses online technology tools, rather than stores, to sell their skincare and health products through independent representatives earning commissions. Perhaps, The Body Shop at Home's tagline best encompasses the future of gig entrepreneurs: "Use It, Love It, Get Paid to Share It."

In all of these cases, software technologies are automating business processes that historically required someone's time and effort. For example, Apple's Siri and Amazon's Alexa use advanced speech recognition to understand what we are saying. You may have already noticed that Siri and Alexa get better at understanding us as we communicate more with them. This improvement, or "learning," occurs because of the ever-increasing examples that they accumulate when conversing with us. As you continue interacting with them, Siri and Alexa will improve their ability to understand your requests.

You may have also noticed that Siri and Alexa will begin providing better recommendations or answers to your queries for information. These usability improvements are happening because the software is looking at the results or data of your past interactions. The software then uses that information to have Siri or Alexa provide better results with future communications of a similar nature.

If you have ordered products on Amazon's website, you have been exposed to some of the most advanced forms of AI and machine learning (ML) in business. Their software is tracking not only what you have ordered but also what products you have viewed, how long you saw them, where you were at that time, what you queried about them, the sequence of your queries, and much more. They use this information to make real-time and future recommendations for more products. Hence, they keep your attention on their website, while continually upselling you in their online marketplace. The impact of Amazon's success with AI and ML, while also continually improving CX, has become known as the "Amazon effect." The Amazon effect has impacted virtually every business in the world, seeking to sell products or services on the Internet. The game has changed as a result of the enormous advancements in technology usage.

Consequently, improving CX is now an obsession for all successful businesses in the gig economy. This obsession takes the form of new technology solutions for both consumer and gig workers. It means that gig companies are continually working to make it easier for customers to buy the products and services that gig workers provide. Equally important is making it easy for you to run your own gig business from devices and touchpoints that are already part of your everyday life.

Apple's Siri, Amazon's Alexa, Google's Assistant, and Microsoft's Cortana are all virtual assistants (VAs), predicated on AI and ML. The primary way of interacting with VAs is through our voice. Because of AI and ML, speech recognition and natural language processing are improving at incredibly fast rates – so fast that our youngest generation, who are learning to use their first mobile devices, is primarily talking to their phone – speaking, instead of using their fingers to tap, enter text, or diverting their eyes' attention.

The result is that virtually every device of the future requiring interaction with a human being will come embedded with some form of a VA. Unlike Siri and Alexa, who seek to answer any question, many VAs will be very much targeted in their functionality based on the device to which they are applied. However, like Siri and Alexa, their goal will be to help you more quickly complete tasks through verbal communication and even digital identification, such as a face or retinal scanning.

We will always be talking to displays or being digitally verified by everyday objects that have a tiny computer attached. Talking, or being scanned, rather than using door keys or pushing buttons, will become the most common way to turn on microwaves, faucets, and stoves. Even our use of laptops and workstations will rarely involve keyboards. In fact, keyboards and touchpads will be stored away in drawers for the rare occasions that we use them.

THE INTERNET OF THINGS

Computing technology will continue to shrink in size and cost at such a scale that, eventually, a digital processor will be part of almost every physical product or device that gets created. The reasons for doing so will be many but always be driven by our desire for information related to the specific device hosting the processor. This microcomputer may be required for the device to function correctly, or the microcomputer may include a small microphone for accepting our verbal instructions using speech recognition software.

In some cases, the microcomputer is capturing information used by embedded ML software to operate the device more efficiently. ML may start accurately anticipating how and when you want to use the device. The processor may also be Wi-Fi or Bluetooth-enabled so that it can connect to the Internet for accessing relevant sources of information or for sending valuable information and notifications to your smartphone. The processor may include a small camera for sharing information with a product support person, medical technician, personal coach, or family member.

We already see these technologies today in many areas of life. Security systems, personal health monitors, highway toll collection, package delivery systems, and smart-home appliances are just a few examples of what is to come. Things with embedded digital processors and sensors are connecting to the Internet without human intervention. As scary as this might seem, these connected devices will enable us to share or receive information to make our lives easier or better. This IoT may be a technological phenomenon that is impacting society at the scale of the first microprocessor, smartphone, and emergence of the Internet. In a sense, everything will be connected. The value of this ubiquitous "network of everything" is information. Humanity's inherent desire and use of information created the Internet and, now, the IoT. Yes, information security needs to be addressed. By all measures, information security and proper regulation have historically been a major laggard in the evolution of information processing. Having said so, data security requirements will also start evolving more quickly to become a more integral part of this ever-changing landscape.

Riding on the backbone of 5G networks, IoT will be creating data at a level exponentially beyond anything in history. We will need new ways to manage, understand, and use this asset of information that we have created.

LEVERAGE TECHNOLOGY TO ENABLE ANALYTICS AND OPTIMIZE DECISION-MAKING

Optimizing growth and profit in today's complex and highly competitive environment is an extremely challenging task. Companies struggle to find the right answers to business problems because they are frequently asking the wrong questions. Intuition based on business experience is still the driving factor in decision-making, leading to wrong solutions being developed for the wrong problems. The better process involves understanding what happened, what is happening, why it is happening, what will happen next, and, ultimately, how do we solve it. Success in a competitive world will depend on a company's ability to amass, assimilate, and act on torrents of data (both structured and unstructured). Management needs insights built on a process that is agile, adaptable, and fast.

The use of advanced analytics describe one of the more critical attributes of gig-providing companies. They are using analytics very effectively, gig workers are benefitting, and so are consumers (Fig. 5.1).

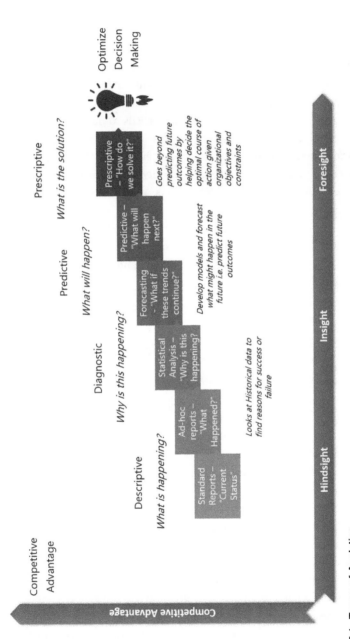

Fig. 5.1. Types of Analytics.

Types of Analytics

Descriptive analytics focuses on summarizing existing data to give insights about the past. But these insights only highlight whether something is right or wrong, without finding reasons for success and failure.

Diagnostic analytics focuses on past performance and tries to answer the reasons for the performance – What happened? Why did it happen? These insights seek to isolate the drivers of success and failure.

Predictive analytics incorporates date from descriptive and diagnostic analytics to predict future outcomes. Trend lines and models are developed and calibrated to show future trends.

Prescriptive analytics goes beyond predicting future outcomes by recommending a possible set of current and future actions to optimize business performance. These actions are monitored continuously and adjusted to ensure an optimal return on investment.

The Value of Analytics

The benefits of having an enterprise-wide analytics process in the current global environment are just too many for companies to ignore their implementation. They include the following:

- Increased profitability/cost reductions

- Ability to manage business risk proactively

- Faster and high-quality decision-making

- Faster innovation of new products and services

Even though the term "business analytics" has become ubiquitous, companies still experience huge barriers in deploying fact-based decision-making. Some of the most common obstacles to implementing enterprise analytics are as follows:

- Lack of understanding of how to use analytics to improve the business

- Lack of intellectual bandwidth due to competing priorities

- Ability to get data

- Absence of executive sponsorship

Unfortunately, even among the companies that claim to have an analytics process, most tend to focus on descriptive and diagnostics analytics, which severely restricts their capacity to rapidly react to changing dynamics in the market, while best-in-class companies tend to use all of the aforementioned types of analytics in their day-to-day business operations. A survey published in the *MIT Sloan Management Review* in 2017 across 3,000 executives shows that even though 85% of them believe in predictive analytics, only 5% of the companies were using these techniques regularly.

Companies need to remove the barriers to implementing analytics. Still, they also need to formulate a data analytics strategy that is continuously evolving and improving. Multiple studies have shown that companies with the most developed analytics capabilities commanded a larger market share and were also twice as likely to be in their sector's top 25% for profitability. The end goal for all companies is to have an active, adaptable, and actionable insights infrastructure that allows for speedy integrated analysis and recommends clear guidelines for action.

THE CRITICAL IMPORTANCE OF DATA

To ensure that the analysis performed is accurate, it is imperative to have rich and clean data. Richness refers to ensuring that all pertinent internal and external attributes of the business are being captured with meaningful history, while cleanliness refers to ensuring that data have been captured, scrubbed, and harmonized and do not contain errors.

With the advent of the Internet and increased use of digital and social media platforms, the variety and complexity of data have exponentially increased and have resulted in the creation of two broad sets of data: structured and unstructured. Structured data refer to internal data (transactional sales, financial, and operational data) and external data (market, third party, and syndicated data.) These types of data allow companies to generate insights on areas like demand forecasting, price optimization, marketing mix, market structures, market baskets, etc. Unstructured data in the context of business analytics refer to text and multimedia content that contains consumer conversations and consumer feedback about brands and products. These conversations and feedback occur via social media, review sites, blogs, forums, call center transcripts, email, etc. These types of data are playing a critical role in helping companies understand the positive and negative drivers of customer sentiments behind category, brand, and product conversations.

This collection of structured and unstructured data is called big data, which has three defining properties:

Volume – The variety of sources containing data pertinent to a company has increased substantially, leading to an exponential increase in the amount of data that provide high-value information.

Velocity – With the rapid adoption of digital and social media platforms by consumers, the speed at which data are being generated and refreshed has also increased exponentially.

Variety – Data come in all types of formats: numeric, text, audio, video, graphics, etc.

Only companies that excel in leveraging big data can genuinely flourish in the current ultracompetitive environment. Big data helps companies in the continuous transformation of the business process to accommodate the rapidly changing market environment.

A few great examples of companies successfully leveraging big data include the following:

- Amazon has gone from a simple business model of selling books online to a global entity with significant businesses in e-tailing, cloud computing, and entertainment, among others. They ingest consumer purchasing and consumer Internet surfing data to create a detailed profile of each customer that then allows them to upsell and cross-sell a wide range of products and services.

- Netflix uses a highly sophisticated recommendation engine that personalizes suggestions to viewers based on their tastes and preferences.

- Target leverages advanced data analytics to improve demand forecasting, reduce inventory levels, and generate operating efficiencies.

- Procter & Gamble (P&G) uses analytics across the enterprise to better understand consumer needs and drive product innovation. They are famous for creating "Decision Cockpits" that incorporate data from around the globe and allow decisionmakers to respond to changes in business trends rapidly.

- American Express uses predictive models to generate forecasts for churn and product loyalty.

Increased Use of Machine Learning, Deep Learning, and Artificial Intelligence in Analytics

Business analytics is experiencing a momentous increase in the number of use cases and business applications that use analytics due to the advent of ML and deep learning. Research in the 1950s and 1960s laid the groundwork for some of the core principles behind ML, deep learning, and AI. But over the past 10 years, the explosion of big data, along with the emergence of new computing technologies, has brought forward these concepts and technologies from scientific labs to mainstream corporate business operations. These technologies are radically changing the way companies analyze vast amounts of data and generate insights and enabling them to transform operations and proactively manage customer expectations and changing trends in the business.

AI involves computers to perform or simulate actions that traditionally would require human intelligence. ML is a branch of AI and is the study and use of algorithms that allow analytical models to learn and improve from experience automatically. Deep learning is a subset of ML that uses artificial neural networks to recognize patterns in data and continuously improve and adapt to changes in the data. Companies are currently using ML and deep learning algorithms across the spectrum in a myriad of applications: Apple's Siri, Amazon's Alexa, Uber's efforts to mine customer complaints to detect patterns by locations, Coca Cola's work managing its global product innovation of 500+ brands, Disney personalizing the theme park experience for each visitor, and more.

These new technologies enable companies to leverage vast amounts of real-time and historical data and be digitally connected to their consumers. They also generate both macro- and microconsumer-centric metrics that have implications on a company's sales, marketing, and supply chain processes.

Institutionalize Data-driven Decision-making

To leverage analytics and generate meaningful business value, an analytical infrastructure (including people, processes, and technology) that allows for speedy integrated analysis and recommends clear guidelines for action is needed.

People are the most critical component of the analytics infra-structure, and well-defined roles have been created for achieving maximum value. Some of the key roles in analytics initiatives include the following:

- *Chief analytics/chief data officer or other C-level executive sponsor* – This is needed to ensure that everyone in the company sees data as an asset. This position will be the thought leader/ change agent in the company and will lend credence to data-driven decision-making.

- *Domain experts* – Analytics solutions cannot be developed without the proper identification of business rules. These domain/ business process experts are internal resources and are critical to helping assess the effectiveness of the analytical solutions.

- *Data scientists/data analysts* – In most companies, these are a combination of internal and external resources that have the expertise to extract, integrate, model, analyze, and present data.

- *IT analysts* – A combination of internal and external resources with the expertise to develop and maintain databases and applications and ensure the execution and accuracy of all data processing activities.

Analytics technologies are rapidly evolving. Solutions should be selected and viewed through the criteria of features, scalability, flexibility, security, costs (price–performance), and innovation. The CIO, along with the chief analytics/chief data officer, should always have a short-, medium-, and long-term analytical road map that identifies the information and insights they need, who will use the information, and how they will use the information. This exercise will then enable the selection of the right technologies and tools for data storage, data extraction, data mining, querying, data analytics, and data visualization.

The analytics process brings together people and technologies. To achieve the highest efficiencies, the analytical process must be implemented enterprise-wide and will determine the guidelines and rules on how information is transformed into insights and actions. This would also include creating a repository of lessons learned so that they can be reapplied across categories, products, and brands. P&G is an excellent example of creating an immersive data environment that transforms decision-making by harnessing real-time business information from around the globe. According to P&G, their process allows complex data to be presented visually in business processes allowing leaders to view the data more efficiently, process the information faster, and drive faster actions.

To create an immersive analytical environment, the following components to infrastructure are essential:

- *Data lake* – A central repository that allows a company to ingest noncurated data from a wide variety of internal and external data sources and cost-effectively store them. This ensures that if any valuable data are needed down the road that is not lost or corrupted.

- *Analytical data warehouse* – One of the most critical elements of the analytical infrastructure is a central repository/database of integrated data that is created by the extracts of multiple data sources (including those from the data lake). The data warehouse contains data that are cleaned, normalized, transformed, and continuously updated. This enables the generation of meaningful views of the business for easy analysis and reporting. One of the most substantial barriers to analytics in most companies is the lack of a robust data warehouse.

- *Analysis and insights* – Identify drivers of customer acquisition, retention, and productivity. Understand customers' life cycle (awareness, consideration, purchase, retention, advocacy, and growth) and link the operational process (sales, marketing, and supply chain) to the customer journey.

- *Predictive and prescriptive models* – Develop analytical models that generate early warning indicators, future trends, and recommendations for critical operational areas.

- *Strategy development* – Use analytical model outputs and other insights to develop champion and challenger strategies. In addition, for each strategy being executed, leverage a robust test and control methodology to measure each strategy's effectiveness against a control group.

- *Strategy monitoring and validation* – Analyze the results of strategies executed and measure return on investment and variances versus expectations. Continuously monitor, document, calibrate, and optimize procedures.

- *Integrated reporting* – Deliver insights and actions via integrated intelligent dashboards leveraging advanced visualizations. Ensure that these dashboards are used across the enterprise.

If correctly implemented, the above components can significantly transform and enhance the operational effectiveness of an organization. Our analysis of different domains (such as consumer goods and services, financial services, entertainment, etc.) reveals that business models are constantly getting disrupted by rapid changes in technology. These rapid changes in technologies are influencing and changing customer preferences and behavior, forcing many companies to be in a reactionary mode. Examples of these disruptions are numerous and present in our everyday lives. Apple iPhones have not only reduced the need to buy cameras and camcorders, but the launch of Apple Pay has enabled the rise of contactless and secured purchase of goods. The availability of Uber and Lyft has not only dramatically reduced demand for rental cars and taxi services but also increased the potential pool of eligible workers. Amazon is rapidly expanding into product categories such as online groceries, and Prime Pantry is now having an impact on traditional grocers. These are all a result of innovative uses of technology.

The launch of these new businesses was primarily driven by companies leveraging analytics and insights to identify new market opportunities, predict future consumer preferences, and analyze potential responses by competitors. Best-in-class analytics enables companies to proactively manage these continually changing market forces and make corresponding adjustments to their product portfolio, operational strategies, and business processes. These proactive set of actions can only be undertaken if they are underpinned with analytics-driven fact-based decision-making. Every step of the way, business leaders need to answer the following questions about their business: What is happening? Why is this happening? What should be our action?

THE ROLE OF AI AND CHATBOTS IN HELPING GIG ECONOMY PARTICIPANTS

For millions of people, the gig economy represents the promise of flexible work hours coupled with the opportunity to earn income, whether it be for part-time extra income or the more significant entrepreneurial pursuit of full-time income. However, this promise is often met with the reality of aspirations, goals, and plans unfulfilled. Why? A significant reason is that new gig economy entrants often have considerable skill and knowledge gaps. These gaps by nature are blind spots; they are hard to recognize because "you don't know what you don't know."

Success, therefore, can be contingent upon how quickly a new independent worker can recognize and bridge these gaps to see success before either their money or motivation runs out. This is where AI and chatbots can and will make a significant contribution.

A chatbot is a form of AI in that it is a computer that simulates conversation. Chatbots can be important catalysts that accelerate the gig economy entrant's productivity by helping someone quickly learn the skills and the knowledge required to do the job. In our research, we often found gaps in the guidance provided to new gig workers. Direct selling companies were the exception in this area as they typically include a lot of guidance that is generally a part of an onboarding process. Companies looking to close this gap can benefit from chatbots and other AI designed to share information and offer guidance to gig workers who are getting started in their gig work. The goal is to make the information easily accessible, easy to understand, and easy to learn.

The list of essential skills and knowledge that will support an independent worker's success can be daunting. They can include the following:

- Organizational and time management skills
- Self-discipline

- Sales skills, relationship building skills

- Budgeting, accounting, and money management

- Customer service

- Emotional intelligence and communication skills

- Writing skills

- Understanding relevant business laws and regulations

- Marketing knowledge

- Customer acquisition and social selling skills

- Technology savviness

It's likely that anyone willing to jump into the gig economy intuitively feels like they have enough of these skills to get started. Still, the magnitude of what they *need* to learn versus what they *already* know cannot really be known until they begin.

AI can help mitigate gaps by doing a lot of the work for the worker, thus reducing the skills they need to master. For example, an Uber driver can get away with not having any customer acquisition or marketing skills because Uber has an automated algorithm that chooses customers near them and brokers the service on their behalf. Not only that, the Uber app also utilizes AI in the mapping function to calculate the fastest and most efficient routes to take, thereby eliminating the driver having to be proficient in knowing how to get around the town they are in.

Another prominent example of AI helping a gig economy worker is with online advertising algorithms. In the past, marketing to the masses was an exclusive exercise reserved for big brands with huge marketing budgets. Today, any entrepreneur can advertise their products and services to online audiences on Google, Facebook, Amazon, and with banner ads on websites that potential customers visit via ad remarketing techniques. They can set their budgets (which can be modest) and enter in variables that describe their target audiences such as geography and demographic information and rely on AI to strategically place their ads in front of audience members that fit the search criteria.

AI can also automate social media postings, predict revenue, correct grammatical errors in written communication, and automatically alert entrepreneurs of potential risks and problems before they occur. Gig economy workers that choose service platforms that already leverage these types of uses for AI have a significant advantage over workers who choose platforms that require workers to be much more skilled and knowledgeable than they might be.

While algorithms help gig economy workers automate many essential job functions, ultimate success still relies on that worker to perform the service at a level of satisfaction for the customer receiving that service. This is where critical skills like communication skills, problem-solving skills, and demonstrating in-depth knowledge of their goods and services will determine whether the worker will succeed or not.

Such skills and in-depth knowledge are not something that is learned overnight. In fact, these types of valuable skills are valuable because they tend to be scarce. Those that take the time to master them find themselves in the enviable position of great success. These skills and amassing of in-depth knowledge can only be mastered by practice, study, repetition, and internalizing feedback to improve over time.

Most gig economy workers do not have the luxury to go to school for years to learn these skills; they are already employed or are looking to the gig economy to deliver immediate financial needs. Therefore, they are left to try to gain these skills while they jump into the market.

This is where chatbots can be incredibly valuable resources. Chatbots can be programmed to coach gig economy workers on these relevant skills and be available 24 hours a day to answer questions on demand when workers need the most help. Chatbots deliver an invaluable frictionless experience because users can chat with them just as if they are chatting with a friend. They are instantaneous and can scale to handle millions of conversations at once. Chatbots can also be programmed to learn a user's learning style and employ *adaptive learning techniques*, which means it can adjust its coaching and lesson plans to the user's learning style and tendencies.

Chatbots can also engage with users wherever they are already messaging with their friends and family, whether it be via SMS,

WhatsApp, Facebook Messenger, and so forth. While the gig economy is now seemingly in full force, it is still relatively in its infancy. There are still new industries, new markets, and new audiences that will emerge that will continue to accelerate the value of the gig economy. These new opportunities will continue to be powered significantly by AI and chatbots, so any major player, whether it be companies looking to attract gig economy workers or the workers themselves, would be wise to choose platforms that leverage these technologies to help workers bridge the skills and knowledge gaps keeping them from their goal to earn a living on their terms.

GIGS PAY QUICKER

Gig-providing companies are using technology to reward gig workers monetarily by paying quicker. The traditional one-month or two-week time frame to receive the monetary rewards associated with work accomplished has been revolutionized by the gig economy. How about being paid within hours after performing the work? It is now possible, thanks to technology and its impact on banking and money transfer.

The gig economy provides work on demand. This has created a workforce that expects to be paid immediately for their sales and services. Many join the gig economy as their primary or supplementary source of income. In addition, almost three out of four workers live paycheck to paycheck and want the financial security of knowing they can immediately access their hard-earned money for their daily living expenses and emergencies.

Paul Beldham, founder and CEO of PayQuicker, recognized drawbacks with both traditional payment methods and newer wallet payout solutions. Beldham knew workers prefer being paid more frequently and drew from studies that indicated paying often aligns work with reward and directly correlates to reported happiness and work satisfaction. He began to rethink the way workers could be paid using new technology. Traditional methods were too slow, inconvenient, and expensive to administer. New payout wallets also had drawbacks. Wallets were not providing payees access and ownership of their funds at the time of payment notification, nor providing payees instant use of their funds. Wallets were holding the payments in commingled accounts. Beldham realized that payees get frustrated when they receive a payment notice and try to spend using the wallet's prepaid card, and the transaction is declined due to insufficient funds, in addition to getting charged decline fees. Payees often did not realize they needed to login and request the funds be transferred to the card. On top of this frustration, if they lost the card – the money was gone. Beldham knew clients and payees were not happy with these solutions.

Beldham and the PayQuicker team set out to develop a secure instant payout platform that delivers payouts to a payee-owned bank account and associated debit card, like a checking account. As soon as a payment notification is received, the funds are immediately available in the account and can be spent in a variety of ways, including online with a virtual card, at retail with a plastic debit card, or by loading the card to a mobile wallet like Apple, Google, or Samsung Pay. Instant payment means instant spending, and it is now possible. The solution makes payees happy.

Gig-providing companies are taking notice. Being able to pay workers quicker makes the work more appealing and, perhaps, increases productivity, performance, and work satisfaction. If workers are motivated to do more because they know they will be paid promptly, the business will also benefit.

During our research, we were fortunate to be personally introduced to Beldham. He is a pioneer in payments, and we were delighted to find him and his team at PayQuicker to be interested in the Ultimate Gig project. We asked several questions relative to the importance of how gig workers are compensated and received many insights that we now share with our audience. The following thoughts and insights are attributed to Beldham and Dworaczyk. They provided us with descriptions of the key elements they have incorporated into their own platform. We considered the descriptions they shared as being a checklist for any gig-providing company as merchant processors are a very important part of what the gig-providing company provides. Those seeking a gig will also find the following to be a checklist of what should be expected. Both of

our audiences should benefit from what Beldham and Dworaczyk
shared.

1. *Gone are the days of waiting to be paid. Our clients
can pay as frequently as they desire with no cost per
transaction. We have clients paying their reps within
three hours of the sale.*

2. *A significant benefit is the payee commission
account, which qualifies as a bank account for any
gig worker who gets paid as an independent contractor.*

3. *The client-owned funding account and payee-owned
bank accounts are on the same banking platform meaning transfers between funding and payee accounts process instantly. The payment process is streamlined and
seamless.*

4. *Onboarding must be easy. Payees receive their payment notification by email with a link to register online
for their account. They provide minimal information:
their name, address, and date of birth, to register. They
instantly obtain their virtual card for immediate online
spending and can order their plastic card, which is
delivered within a week or two.*

5. *A low-cost, fully customizable, client-branded experience that becomes our client's competitive advantage.
We also provide an advanced global payment gateway
that integrates directly with our client's portal, powering
it with the PayQuicker solution features and benefits.*

6. *Return on investment in a payment system is essential. The apparent return on investment comes from the
reduction in costs associated with the traditional processing of checks and Automated Clearing House
(ACH) transactions, handling sensitive banking information, KYC (know your customer) banking requirements, escheatment, call center support to handle*

payment issues, and the collection and distribution of tax-related documentation.

7. Spend back is another feature we offer. It allows gig workers to use their commission account to spend back with their gig-providing company when appropriate. The gig-providing company avoids merchant processing costs on order fulfillment. This is a significant cost savings for our clients, shipping tangible goods to their gig workers.

8. We eliminate the need for shadow accounting. A shocking 70% of businesses still manage commissions through internal processes. Frequent payouts, immediately after the sale or services are rendered, help eliminate expensive, productivity-sapping, shadow accounting reconciliation.

9. The instant payment, instant spend trend, while still early in its lifecycle, is increasing rapidly. For evidence of its mainstream appeal, look at the number of applications now available for daily pay in the traditional employment arena for salaried and hourly employees. The interest incurred by workers using pay-day loan services costs consumers more than $9 billion annually. Getting paid quicker, which is a benefit in the gig economy, is becoming a revolutionary new benefit for all business models.

10. The psychological boost of paying bills on time, or being able to cover emergency costs, pays dividends on and off the job. Surveys show that workers who have instant access to their pay feel more positive about their company, more supported by their management, and are more likely to stay with the company longer.

11. Smartphone-enabled fintech solutions are now mainstream, and the latest studies from global leaders like FIS Worldpay show significant changes in behavior using these systems to increase our convenience to spend. Virtual cards and mobile pay solutions incorporated into smartphones (Apple Pay, Google Pay, Samsung Pay) will surpass traditional spend methods in 2023 in the US and are already the majority of transactions in Asia.

12. Clients can start making payouts in 2 to 4 weeks by deploying a PayQuicker card. Branded card programs take 4 to 8 weeks, accounting for network approval of card artwork. Overall, client onboarding includes bank due diligence, card artwork approval, client training, and launch. Payments can be made by batch file uploads or through easy API integration.

13. Multilingual support is essential. Client Relationship Managers train and assist clients. Payee Support is available to account holders via phone, email, live chat. Our development team supports clients through API integration.

14. When you have two generations – Millennials and Gen Z – growing up with instant everything and everything on demand, the transformation to instant pay is guaranteed to continue.

15. Over the next five to ten years, competitive companies will implement an instant or daily pay cycle. Companies will continue to convert their legacy systems to take advantage of the efficiencies and growth resulting from the instant pay, instant spend model.

16. Companies with strategic plans to expand globally will need scalable payout solutions that enable their global expansion. Partnerships with global banks, processors, and global card networks and fulfillment, to provide a seamless, scalable global payment platform that allows businesses to make instant secure mass payouts in local currencies around the globe.

17. The gig economy and its payout systems are expanding across all industry verticals.

Paying quicker is a very important component of what has made the gig economy so appealing. We wanted specific descriptions of how payment systems work. Beldham and Dworaczyk were the experts we were looking for, and they provided us with specifics.

As you now know, technology has changed the game. This is the beginning of the story, not the end. Much more innovation is expected within the next two years, and gig workers can expect to benefit.

6

DIRECT SELLING – THE FIRST GIG?

While the gig economy is a relatively new phenomenon, the concept of flexible, independent work has been around for centuries. Throughout history, people have picked up small service jobs or sold products to others to supplement their income. Yesterday's Airbnb looked like renting a spare room to a boarder. Etsy looked like selling baked goods or handicrafts at the local market. TaskRabbit looked like performing odd jobs for neighbors for a slight stipend.

One of the most enduring gig opportunities is direct selling. Direct selling is a channel of distribution, much like e-commerce or brick-and-mortar stores. Instead of relying on traditional advertising, marketing, and sales strategies, direct selling companies use a sales force of independent contractors, often referred to as distributors, associates, or consultants, to sell their products or services to customers. These independent contractors represent the brand.

I decided to devote a full chapter to direct selling because I consider direct selling to be a form of gig work, and possibly, the first form of gig work. I have been involved in the channel of distribution directly and indirectly for more than 50 aggregated years and would be remiss if I did not share enough about direct selling and why its attributes might fit within what any gig seeker is looking to identify. The historical perspective is important because the model has a history of more than a few years. For those familiar with direct selling, this chapter may reinforce your pride in the choice you made. For new gig seekers, you will learn a lot about direct selling as a potential choice of gigs or a compliment to a gig already chosen or a current job.

Direct selling's roots reach back to the dawn of civilization. In 2000 BC, a Babylonian law known today as the Code of Hammurabi protected the welfare and integrity of peddlers who traveled from place to place selling various goods. Record of this type of trade exists through ancient Greece and Rome, the Middle Ages, early modern Europe, and colonial America. In the mid-nineteenth century, "Yankee Peddlers" traveled the countryside, bringing products to consumers who might not have a well-stocked general store nearby.

As America moved West, so too did the peddler. These hardworking nineteenth-century vendors ultimately created trade routes and distribution networks surpassed only by industrial mass production and freight transportation.

In the later part of the century, more and more retailers began to use mail-order catalogs, putting new pressure on peddlers and local general stores. The first catalog was produced in 1872 by Montgomery Ward. Ward closed its stores and shut down its catalogs in 2001. Catalogs were considered an innovation at one time. Today, every retailer uses some type of catalog to promote their brand, products, and services. Innovation does not last forever. As the mail-order catalog grew in popularity, a few consumer product companies found success by building on the person-to-person sales experience from the peddler days. The first notable example came in 1855 when Rev. James Robinson Graves founded the Southwestern Publishing Co. The company, known today simply as Southwestern Advantage, has trained generations of college students to sell books door-to-door and enabled many of them to not only pay tuition but also earn a few thousand dollars over summer months. Thirty years later, David McConnell, seeing the natural ease with which women sold products, revolutionized the American workforce by intentionally recruiting women as sales representatives for his new California Perfume Co., known today as Avon. The direct selling business model was becoming more popular even though the words "direct selling" were probably not used to describe the business model until many years later.

In 1939, Carl Rehnborg began the California Vitamin Corp., later known as Nutrilite products, which brought more innovation to direct selling. Through two of its independent distributors, William Casselberry and Lee Mytinger, the company introduced a multilevel compensation plan that allowed sales representatives to earn a commission based on their own sales efforts and the efforts of those they sponsored and trained to sell the products.

Unlike a mail-order catalog experience, direct sellers provided a personalized shopping experience, providing consultation and one-on-one service. They worked independently of the company whose products they represented, setting their hours, and cultivating their customer base. In the mid-1930s, Norman W. Squires began outselling his peers when he stopped selling Stanley Home Products door-to-door and started gathering small groups for a combination of social events and product demonstrations in someone's home. Direct sellers for Tupperware and many other brands followed suit, creating a new category of direct sales company: the party plan.

This high level of flexibility and autonomy made direct selling one of the first significant opportunities for many women to experience entrepreneurship. Through direct selling, moms could fulfill the role of primary caregiver to small children while earning additional income by sharing information about products they loved with friends and neighbors. The companies provided the products and necessary information, and the sellers provided the customer base and distribution.

During the 1950s, the direct selling channel of distribution continued to grow and gain national recognition. In 1954, Tupperware, which had been in business for eight years, saw its sales leader, Brownie Wise, make history as the first woman to appear on the cover of *Business Week* magazine. In the later half of the twentieth century, some of the biggest names in direct selling emerged: Amway, Mary Kay, Herbalife, Nu Skin, Primerica, USANA, Telecom Plus, Vorwerk, Oriflame, Yanbal, Ambit, Jeunesse, PM International, Belcorp, Pola, Coway, Medifast/Optavia, Arbonne, Team National, to name just a few.

DIRECT SELLING TODAY

Today, direct selling companies offer a wide selection of products and services, including beauty, fashion, personal health, home décor, energy, finance, insurance, subscription services, pet products, and much more. Not all companies use the term "direct seller" to describe the members of their sales force. It is common for companies to refer to their sellers as independent business owners, distributors, social sellers, consultants, affiliates, or brand ambassadors. The titles and descriptions are numerous, with new terms cropping up all the time.

Unique compensation plans are also an attribute of direct selling business models. Sellers earn commissions on their first sales to customers and can qualify to earn on all future purchases by those customers who remain attached to the direct seller. While gig opportunities in the transportation and service sectors tend to focus on transactions in which the company makes the connection between gig participant and consumer, the direct seller finds the customers of the brand and technology allows the direct seller to market to potential customers, encourage a purchase, and receive credit for the sale. Parties, group selling activities, and personal interaction remain key tactics for direct sellers; however, what has changed is the nature of the transaction, which is now technology-based and more online versus offline.

The direct seller is often someone who was a satisfied customer who became a passionate advocate. A new direct seller starts his or her business slowly, as customer acquisition and retention require time and effort. The first business activities may depend upon scheduling an event, having personal interactions with family and friends, planning a virtual meeting or conference call, or using other social tools. What is exciting is the opportunity to earn a commission on the sales made to 10 or 12 customers or more within a reasonable time frame. Once the first customers are acquired, retention and repeat purchases become a primary objective alongside the ongoing acquisition of more customers. The possible result is, within a few months, there is a base of customers who will continue to shop frequently and consistently because of their love and enjoyment of the products or services they have purchased. The costs associated with customer acquisition may be higher than those associated with customer retention dependent upon the type of direct selling opportunity engaged. The attribute described here is the chance to aggregate customers and maintain the ability to receive a reward for the purchases those customers continue to make. There is no limit to the number of customers a direct seller can acquire and encourage to become a frequent shopper. The direct selling company provides a direct seller with the digital tools and services needed to build a business without the original direct selling business model's geographic restrictions, whereas a physical presence with a prospective customer was considered essential.

Some direct sellers take the process a step further and build a team of other direct sellers with whom they shared the opportunity to become a direct seller. By doing so, these direct sellers enable an expansion of customer acquisition through the efforts of others. This effort results in a larger scale business than what the direct seller could build by building a business strictly on their personal selling and customer acquisition efforts. Like the rewards a sales manager receives in a traditional corporate structure, where the manager can earn a percentage of the sales made by all salespersons they supervise, direct sellers can usually earn on the sales performance of those they recruit and sponsor, directly and often indirectly. Commissions are not paid on the act of sponsoring someone else but on the sales made to customers by the direct sellers personally or indirectly sponsored.

OUR DIRECT SELLING S.W.O.T. ANALYSIS

Approximately nine years ago, while serving as Publisher/Editor in Chief of *Direct Selling News*, a trade publication for direct selling company executives, we published an analysis of the direct selling business model. Businesses often assess their current state when planning using the simplicity of examining strengths, weaknesses, opportunities, and threats (S.W.O.T.). When reflecting on what was written nine years ago, we found similarities to what we will share today. The original analysis published by *Direct Selling*

News defined the S.W.O.T. as follows: strengths, what matters most, opportunities, and the future. We took a similar approach for this exercise.

Strengths

The primary advantage of the direct selling way of doing business over the past 100 years is a focus on unique products and personalized service delivered through a personalized presentation, most often through personal or group interaction. Direct selling companies have always offered an opportunity to engage in the free enterprise system with minimal financial investment, minimal risk, free training, and the opportunity to earn in proportion to the invested time and effort. Today, direct selling companies are another form of a platform under the gig economy umbrella. Perhaps, direct selling was the first form of gig work.

A key strength offered by direct selling companies is the basic skill training and a focus on the individual's personal growth and development. This is a strength of the business model and a point of differentiation between direct selling and many other gigs. Many transportation, service, and selling gigs are very intuitive, and the gig-providing company does not offer a lot of guidance or training. A transportation gig provider, for example, does not have to provide driver training. Most direct selling companies opt to offer guidance and training because most of the participants come into direct selling with no previous sales experience. Many direct selling companies also provide their participants with ample personal development opportunities. This type of training and guidance is generally focused on goal setting, planning, the importance of self-esteem, belief, and confidence, and even leadership development for those who intend to build a business by attracting others who will also learn to be direct sellers. Direct sellers can build a sustainable business that is capable of growing in value based on their personal efforts and those of others they may recruit directly and indirectly. This opportunity to build a business that becomes an asset remains a definite competitive advantage of direct selling compared to many other gigs.

What Matters Most

The personal relationship between the customer and direct seller and between direct sellers and their team of other direct sellers is a strong attribute. Over many years of experience in working within and with direct selling models, some teams that we have encountered recognize the concept of "team" to be stronger in direct selling models than one would ever expect. You do not expect people with no prior business experience to be a very successful leader, teacher, and coach of a team of direct sellers; however, it happens, and the stories are incredible.

The recognition, rewards, and compensation direct sellers earn are unique attributes of the model. In our observations, we find the newest to the most accomplished direct seller will experience a company that recognizes their presence upon joining and their performance and achievement throughout the building of the direct selling business. Recognition pins and ribbons are considered badges of honor. Special prizes, even travel to some of the most exotic destinations in the world, are known to be incentives that serve to motive and inspire consistent performance throughout the ranks of direct sellers. We find no other business model to be comparable to our experience and involvement with direct selling companies.

Compensation plans that reward the behaviors that drive growth in customer acquisition, retention, and the recruitment of others who become direct sellers are found to be unique and diverse in design within direct selling companies. The many compensation plans we have reviewed are unique, and many are also complex. When easily understood, the direct seller can look forward to more than pay for work accomplished relative to a specific task. We have been witnesses to many examples of direct sellers who have turned what was initially a part-time effort into what has become high income, recognition, and rewards.

Opportunities

Our approach to this portion of the analysis is based on interviews and observations with those inside and outside of direct selling, many of whom are dear friends and established subject matter experts. A few of our interviews are included later in this chapter. We sorted our collection of perspectives into internal factors and external factors to enable a focus on the significant opportunities that exist for direct selling opportunities, from our perspective.

Internal Factors

Direct selling companies that were focused primarily on the personal interaction between direct sellers and customers, and other direct sellers, are reevaluating and implementing new strategies more focused on the use of technology-based tools and e-commerce platforms. The handwriting has been on the wall for several years, and direct selling companies will become, we believe, more of a platform with distinct attributes. COVID-19 has become the accelerator of this type of thinking. Gig providers are also expected to learn from the direct selling model as they continue to innovate and improve their value proposition; therefore, the competition for a direct selling company is the new economy of platforms that link consumers directly with the products, services, and type of gig they seek.

There has also been a shift toward the utilization of other labels, initiated by direct selling companies, to distinguish themselves and their approach to how their products and services are offered in the marketplace. Some direct selling companies define themselves as network marketing companies, party plan companies, social selling companies, or some form of social entrepreneurship. Those attracted to the networking term embrace the opportunity to purchase products and services at discounted prices and gain financially from sharing the product or service with others. This activity is not the same kind of sales activity as in traditional direct selling; however, it is becoming more and more popular. It also contributes to a "blurring" of the definition of direct selling, a trend that we expect will continue as direct selling companies introduce innovative ways to acquire and retain customers. We do not expect these labels to be as meaningful in the future as they may have been in the past.

Direct selling companies are now competing with every other online retailer, many of whom have been developing their e-commerce and customer service models for many years. The customer service representative is no longer "Mary or John," who we got to know well. Direct selling companies, with their focus on people, have an opportunity to design better technology-based customer service with innovative and personal touches. "Now" is the new expectation as to "when" we desire to have the product or service. There are also new benchmarks of customer service excellence provided by big brands, Amazon, Walmart, Wayfair, Zappos, and others. Direct selling companies, recognizing the new competitive marketplace that competes for customer satisfaction, are paying attention and are expected to emerge with customer service that rivals and equals the best customer service in the marketplace. The work is currently being done and already complete in some direct selling companies. The contemporary and competitive direct selling company realizes that the future market share for direct sellers is bright. The offer of unique products and services in conjunction with excellent customer service and unique microenterprise income opportunities can compete well with other platforms and become a preferred choice.

Digital marketing strategies, created by the direct selling company and replicated through direct sellers, are expected to be a powerful method of marketing and selling products and services. An army of independent contractors (direct sellers) can provide new competitive advantages for direct selling companies at a time when digital marketing is an essential ingredient in the sales and marketing mix. The definition of personalized service is changing, but its importance remains a potential competitive advantage for all direct selling companies. The direct seller, equipped with excellence in digital marketing tools, will find ways to personalize the tools, thus delivering a more personalized connection with a potential customer or another potential gig seeker. With excellent digital tools and no limit to the number of customers that can be contacted and engaged, nor any limit to the number of prospective gig seekers that a direct seller might become acquainted, personally or digitally, the future looks very bright for this model. We believe this moment in time to be an excellent opportunity for direct selling companies and those they support.

The common value proposition of a direct selling opportunity is the uniqueness of the business model. No different than the franchise industry, which found a way to collaboratively promote the primary attributes of the model through the International Franchise Association, direct selling companies are expected to benefit from collaboration. Collaboration accelerates learning. Collaboration, inclusive of not only the companies involved but also suppliers, should unlock incredible potential for all. The World Federation of Direct Selling Associations, of which the US Direct Selling Association is a member, provides member companies and suppliers to direct selling companies with opportunities to share insights and thoughts relative to the current and future state of the model. The increased speed of change appears to warrant a higher frequency of exchange between all who have a vested purpose in a shared value proposition.

External Factors

Direct selling models have been challenged to become more e-commerce and platform focused for many years while maintaining the primary attributes of the model. The model is rooted in personal interaction. Direct selling companies that have been paying attention to the changing dynamics of how consumers purchase are well-positioned to grow and succeed in a marketplace that is finding the convenience of online shopping, reliable and quick delivery, being a time-saving and preferred experience. Add to these favorable trends the appeal of gig economy income opportunities and the flexibility to work more as one desires, and we predict this combination of factors will serve the direct selling model well.

The Internet was first viewed by the direct selling community with skepticism because it threatened the more personal approach to selling products and services. Today, the Internet is a valuable asset not to be ignored by any channel of distribution. First known as a community of websites, the Internet is so much more. Websites are more sophisticated than ever and only represent part of the Internet's capabilities. A quick assessment of direct selling company websites indicates that direct sellers overall have much to gain as they continue to update, upgrade, and embrace more consumer-friendly presentations of their products and services. Mobile applications are essential. All corporations and organizations realize the importance of their digital presence. Information on a company, organization, products, or services must be readily available. The consumer expects this, and so do all who are seeking income opportunities. The Internet has created a self-empowered consumer. Smartphones are "game-changers."

Social media platforms make it possible for companies to utilize a new way of communicating with both its consumers and those who represent their products and services. Direct selling companies are expected to venture into virtual environments where much of what they have traditionally focused on – personal interaction and the use of small and large events – might be possible in a different format. Virtual platforms such as Second Life (secondlife.com) are not to be overlooked. In 2003, Linden Labs, headquartered in San Francisco, founded Second Life, which has now become an economy itself. Second Life is enjoyed by millions of people, organizations, corporations, and even branches of the military, and billions of dollars are transacted among users in its economy.

The shift in power from men to women can be a new advantage. Unlike 20 years ago, today, there are more women in the workforce than men, and there are more women who are breadwinners in the family than previously. The direct selling model is composed of approximately 75% women, and they are time-starved because of being responsible for the family, household, and often career. A more technology-focused business model for direct sellers will be perceived as positive for the women who represent most direct sellers. Ironically, the first direct sellers were men exclusively.

Demographic shifts are certainly increasing the pool of potential recruits for those who identify with ethnic segments authentically. All segments in the marketplace are becoming more complex. Most direct selling companies embrace all generations. COVID-19 has impacted the citizens of virtually every country in the world. Seniors have lost much of what was thought to be a secure retirement triggering a renewed interest in the available opportunities. Middle-age unemployed are looking at never being employed again in the traditional manner. The youngest in the population are looking at an economy with fewer jobs and a continuing shrinkage of jobs in the immediate future. We foresee the new jobs or at least many of the new jobs to be gigs and microentrepreneurship.

The Future

The future is now. We are living the future expressed in the thoughts, insights, visions, and wisdom of a few short years ago. The new future is always coming faster than we think. The future for the direct selling form of a gig opportunity, from our perspective, is promising. The business model is not easily compared to any other. Over 100 years of growth and evolution may be the beginning of a new beginning. Providing individuals with an opportunity to market and sell products and services directly to the consumer is, with the support of a parent company, perhaps, more desirable today than at any other time in history. Could the external factors impacting the pace of life and the financial security of so many people be the very forces that will redefine the importance of the direct selling business model?

Direct selling has historically invited all segments within the population to a business opportunity that remains unique in terms of its diverse makeup and its predominance of women. As we mentioned at the start of this assessment, the core value proposition is the business model. The potential to earn money, along with ease of entry, a unique system of compensation, and recognition appear to be the strong attributes of the direct selling model. These features will become even more appealing as direct sellers take on more of a digital face than the need for a physical face. Perhaps, the business model of direct selling is simply on the doorstep of its most significant moment in time. We think so!

HIGHLIGHTS OF CONVERSATIONS WITH DIRECT SELLERS

Many who try a direct selling gig do so because of the positive experience with a company's product. That was the case for Jeri T.

Twenty years ago, Jeri went to a home products trade show intending to do some research to open her own business. There, she met the founder of a direct selling cosmetics company demonstrating a lipstick that did not come off. Jeri tried it and was hooked.

At the time, I knew nothing about direct sales. I just knew I wanted to have my own business with products I love. Through trial and error and great corporate support and personal development, I have learned to overcome and thrive. Every day I wake up with the goal to work the fundamentals of my business: selling, customer service, sponsoring, and building leaders.

Perseverance with a "keep on, keeping on" attitude and consistency with grit is crucial for long-term sustainability in this business model. I believe and teach work/life balance, as success and balance go hand-in-hand. I am blessed knowing, with my business, I'm creating a legacy for my family!

– Jeri T., direct selling

Vicki is another example of how a direct selling business can change someone's life. The significance of including these testimonials is simply related to the fact that the business model has been around for over 100 years, and it continues to impact participants in a very positive manner.

I majored in biology in college, with the goal of becoming a doctor. During a working period with a couple of doctors, I came to the realization that the medical field was not for me. However, I also needed income to put my son through a Christian private school. More importantly, though, I needed something to be passionate about.

At first, the answer was NOT direct selling, or so I thought! Then a friend in direct sales asked me to hold an event for her company around my kitchen table. I

*watched the faces of my friends and family light up
from the joy of using the product and begin the process
of placing an order. I thought, "Hey, these are my
family and friends. I could do this, too!"*

*That was 16 years ago. From a little part-time business,
which got me out of the house two to three days a
week, it has grown into a full-time, passionate devotion
to making a difference in the lives of so many women,
helping them find purpose and discover their God-given
gifts while continuing to develop my own independent
business.*

— Vicki P., direct selling

For some participants, direct selling is just one of multiple gigs.
Hannah H., 28, says she has never worked a traditional job. After
graduating from college, she waited tables for six months while
building her own wedding photography business. While she was
running her photography business full-time, she began a direct
selling gig on the side, as a representative of an essential oils
company.

*I also babysit once a week, and I help a friend with
managing one of her social media pages. I did not have
any experience in sales unless you consider wedding
photography sales. I think the experience of running a
business on my own, establishing a sort of like a brand
and working social media is why I have found success
in direct sales.*

*I have never had a typical job. I have always worked
for myself. When I graduated from college, I waited
tables for six months before I was able to make enough
money doing wedding photography. After I started my
direct selling business, I was shooting weddings for
another year and a few months before I was able to
transition out of that and do this full time.*

I wanted to work to live, not live to work. I have good friends who have found a lot of success in direct sales. I can see the trends and sales over the past two years of my business, and I know I am growing at a really good rate. In the next five or ten years, I fully believe that this is going to be such a blessing to our family and to many other people because I am able to build, but I'm not the one paying them. They get paid by the company. If I do a really good job training them and establishing relationships with them, then the work that they do benefits me, and I am very inspired by that. I am inspired by the way women work together and the way we are able to lift each other up and help each other instead of competing and tearing each other down.

For the rest of my life, I plan to be doing this. At a certain point, my business will basically run itself, and the income will be residual and incredibly dependable. Right now, I am still building, so I am putting in a lot of effort.

Our personal goal is to be debt-free. We are only two months away from that, which is such a blessing and after that to be able to have a work-life balance while we are raising young kids, potentially fostering/ adopting kids and have an income that is residual that will fund our life and allows us to be incredibly generous with others and to help others who have just fallen on hard times who need resources. That is what motivates me the most.

– Hannah H., direct seller

Toni V. and Jay T. work their direct selling business together, and we have experienced the stories of many husband–wife teams or partners who do the same. The conversation we experienced with Toni and Jay was very inspirational.

My early experiences with two direct selling companies were driven by the desire to stay home with my then, young family and the need for income. As many women know, the juggling we do to achieve work/life balance can be brutal!

2014 was a year of change for me, my family, and business. I found a company with core values aligned with mine, a unique product in the direct selling channel, that afforded the opportunity to "repurpose" my husband into our business, that believes in the power of a "vehicle" to earn $300 to $400 or simply enjoy its incredible products. It is a business we can build person-to-person, face-to-face, or via virtual communication platforms.

Flash forward to 2020, and our business is thriving. Our family is involved, as are friends and customers around the world. We have it all!
                                        – Toni V. and Jay T., direct sellers

Fiercely entrepreneurial, Maribel left her home in the Dominican Republic to chase the opportunity of a better life in the states with her with her husband. After working in manufacturing and taking on side gigs selling apparel and accessories, the couple started two used car dealerships. Business was good but it took too much time and energy away from their growing family.

"We went into business for ourselves to have more freedom for family time, not to complicate our lives. But it wasn't working out that way. I knew we had to make a change." She discovered the direct selling opportunity and, after falling in love with the products, found she was great at selling but slow at building a business. Knowing the seasonal nature of the car business, Maribel committed to working her business a little more each day over the winter months. "I gave myself one year to see what I could really do. Too many people want instant gratification and don't give themselves time to learn from their mistakes. I'm always chasing

new goals with a great joy for life. Even after 24 years, I still get excited about my business every day. I love being my own boss."

Maribel has never looked back. "Even now I talk about the business the same way I did then. It's a low-risk opportunity to own your own business, make a little extra money, spend more time with family and enjoy a better life."

– Maribel G., direct seller

"When I started my direct selling business, I was appearing in musical theater and television. I'd graduated college and was working in a career I loved, but not feeling secure in the money I was making." While lucky enough to be working her passion, Lilia needed something more.

She and her then-future husband went to a meeting with a group of friends. After hearing stories about how the business was helping them earn extra income and enjoy more flexibility and a better life, Lilia saw more than an opportunity. "The idea of helping others while helping myself appealed to me. I saw the potential and wanted to pursue it as I do all things—with passion."

For a few years, she worked her business around her busy performance schedule. After she got married and had her first child, Lilia decided to focus on her business full-time. "I loved being able to work my business and travel with my daughter. It was exhilarating. You typically don't have that flexibility in a traditional job."

After four years, Lilia's business had grown to the point where she could return to taking on various roles as a performer. All the while, she turned her focus to mentoring her team. "I had a slow start, so that motivated me to help others develop their business and leadership

*skills, too. I made it my mission to teach, encourage and
lead people to discover their true potential. It's become
my purpose."*

– Lila S., direct seller

A third-generation business owner with his direct selling company, Anthony was determined to pursue his own goals before
joining the family business. He was a gifted guitarist and songwriter
who struggled in high school and longed to perform. After being
accepted into the prestigious Berklee College of Music in Boston, he
got the opportunity to go out on tour.

*I thought I could save my college tuition money and
start pursuing my passion right away. I deferred Berklee and did over 800 concerts in three years. During
that time, I reconnected with my childhood best friend
who had just learned about the direct selling company
he joined. We'd always wanted to do something
together and it felt like the right time to learn more
about the business from my parents. It was a big decision for someone who loves music as much as I do but I
knew I wasn't going to make enough money as a
traveling musician to live the life I wanted. My friend
had set his sights on building financial flexibility
through a successful business, committing to going all
in for at least five years.*

*I wanted to create my own success from the ground up,
not ride on my parents' coattails. I saw myself as a
musician, the son who was kicked out of school three
times. I was afraid that people wouldn't look to me as a
leader. My grandmother's words inspired me. She told
me, 'Whatever you're weakest in, when you overcome
it, you become the greatest teacher in it.' I overcame my
fear and became a mentor to others. I'm living proof
that this type of business is a vehicle for pursuing what
you want in life.*

– Anthony M., direct seller

Since his teens, Jorge wanted to own his own business. Like many entrepreneurs, his path was riddled with failures and successes. In Cuba, he opened his first martial arts studio, but the tough economy forced him to shut his doors. He then earned a computer science degree, hoping to put his analytical mind to use. He soon found working for someone else frustrating and felt the familiar pull of his entrepreneurial drive.

I moved to Miami, opened another martial arts studio and again was forced to close due to a sluggish economy. I had to put my dream on hold. I took a job in construction and began working 80 hours a week, seven days a week, at a job I didn't even like. Overtime was mandatory. I had no time for my family and friends. I wasn't enjoying my life.

I remembered that, while opening my second studio, a cousin told me about the company with which he chose to build a direct selling business. I was not ready, but I did encourage my wife. She started bringing in extra money. I saw the business working and couldn't turn away. It really spoke to my entrepreneurial spirit, especially because we could build a business together. I also liked the low start-up cost. With my studios, I needed tens of thousands of dollars just to open the doors and had to be there morning to night. With my direct selling business, I was in business for only the cost of a starter kit. My wife and I now run a successful business together.

We went from working different jobs, frustrated and unhappy, to working toward common goals. It's incredible to see our business continue to enhance our lives and the lives of others.
                                                    – Jorge M., direct seller

I decided to start a direct selling business once I understood the importance of health and once I saw how

*dedicated the company is in making high-quality prod-
ucts and not taking any shortcuts! Once I fell in love
with the products – and the results – it was easy to see
the possibilities of sharing it with others and promoting
something I really believe in, which is helping people
take an active role in taking care of their health!*

*I have loved being a part of the company and commu-
nity, and I really enjoy the friendships I've made with
people across the country. It's given me opportunities
to travel, to expand my impact on people globally, and
to push myself to improve in all sorts of skill sets! I also
love that I can do it on my own terms in my own time.*

*I own a lawncare business, and I would not be able to
dedicate the hours to that company seasonally if I had a
regular 9–5 job. With this, I can continue to grow both
AND be very present for my new daughter! Having the
freedom to CHOOSE where I spend my time is
invaluable.*

                                              – Alexis C., direct seller

*We decided to become a part of our direct selling
company for the opportunity to build an online business. Throughout our journey, we have helped people
in our team develop and prosper introducing customers
and others. We have been doing this full time for over a
decade. We love empowering our team members to
become independent leaders of their own teams. It's
so rewarding to see them reap the benefits of success
with their business, creating wonderful communities
and experiencing improved health and lifestyle.*

                                    – Jared & Crystal C., direct sellers

*I was looking to make some part-time income to help
pay off my debt. A good friend of mine introduced me
to my direct selling company. I had never heard of the
company, but the more I learned about the company,*

*the more I was impressed by the products, growth, and
integrity. I love the science that goes into the products
we sell. The scientists involved are passionate about
developing world-class products. I love how they
participate training calls to help people understand
the science that goes into all of the products.*

– John G., direct seller

A CHECKLIST FOR SELECTING A DIRECT SELLING COMPANY

Direct selling companies have always understood that most of their
sellers have little or no experience in building a business or selling
products or services. Hence, they typically provide good coaching
and guidance. One of the significant benefits of working with a
direct selling company is improving professional and personal
development skills.

With hundreds of direct selling companies to choose from, it can
be challenging to determine which might be the most ideal. First
and foremost, prospective direct sellers should look to find a
company whose products or services in which they have an interest.
Often, direct sellers start as customers of the company before
entertaining the idea of selling as a gig. Enthusiasm for the products
or service and alignment with personal values are fundamental to
feeling proud of the brand being represented. There appear to be
seven attributes that a potential direct seller should consider when
exploring direct selling opportunities. Our checklist is based upon
our learning from the study of the gig economy and our familiarity
with the direct selling model (Fig. 6.1).

This checklist enables any gig seeker to better evaluate a direct
selling opportunity. When we developed the checklist, it became
apparent that such a checklist, when completed, would result in
meeting good criteria for any gig.

Direct Selling Checklist

☐ Clarity

The value proposition should be easily understood, and the focus should be on customer acquisition and retention, the opportunity to share in the rewards associated with the customer acquisition and retention effort and the opportunity to share with others and benefit from those sponsored directly and indirectly who build direct selling businesses based upon the premise stated.

☐ Easy Engagement

Joining a direct selling company should be simple and easy. To get started, new participants usually submit basic registration information and incur a nominal fee to affiliate with the company they've chosen. In exchange for that fee, sellers may receive access to online reporting, training, news, and a replicated website to market the products or services. Reasonable and minimal startup fees are to be expected when selecting a direct selling company.

☐ Digital Tools and Guidance

Excellent support and guidance in the form of a suggested success process, which can be easily embraced, understood, and executed. Digital tools are considered essential in the form of product flyers, product education sheets, catalog, newsletters, mobile apps, video promotions, and the opportunity to personalize.

☐ Fair and Timely Compensation

Direct sellers can often earn 25% or more on the sales they make to customers, which makes it relatively simple to predict their potential income. The diverse product categories offered by direct selling companies offer an opportunity to determine what products are most exciting to the potential direct seller. There are usually other incentives, commissions, and bonuses for having sponsored other direct sellers who also build a direct selling business.

☐ Incentives, Recognition and Events

Direct sellers can offer very enticing incentive programs not found in the typical workplace nor in typical gigs. Direct selling companies are also known for their special events. Events are regular group gatherings, online meetings, opportunity meetings, education seminars, leadership conferences, and annual conferences. Direct selling companies possibly invest more time and money into their events than any other form of business. This is a component of the business worth checking into.

☐ Strong Ethics/Code of Conduct

Considered essential. Most direct selling companies make their code of conduct very visible. Such a document should be expected and reviewed.

☐ Predictable Income for Time Invested

There are no guarantees relative to income potential. However, the direct seller should be able to estimate their first phase of income potential based on what they believe they can accomplish by sharing the product or service with a warm market potential of friends, co-workers, and family. The new direct seller should be experienced with the product or service they will sell and be able to represent the product or service with authentic experience.

Fig. 6.1. Checklist for Direct Selling Components.

UNDERSTANDING DIRECT SELLING

I have a favorite way of describing direct selling gigs as opportunities that attract people from all walks of life regardless of background, experience, or inexperience. Over many years, I have personally witnessed the previous statement in action through the many diverse people I have been fortunate to meet and become friends. Some were young, and some were older. Most were women, and yes, some brought with them a great degree of experience and educational achievements. Some got involved with absolutely no business skills that could be described on a résumé. They brought with them the skills learned through the lives they had been living. Basic skills related to the nurturing and care for a child easily translate into customer relationship building skills, even leadership development skills that are learned and taught. The direct selling model has always embraced diversity in all of its many forms, including those with or without previous experience.

The mistake that far too many writers have made, and continue to make, when they observe and attempt to write about the direct selling model is to define success as if success is only about earning a significant amount of money. The direct seller is certainly a microentrepreneur, and the core definition of an entrepreneur is always inclusive of a willingness to take on greater-than-normal financial risks. This is true for those who seek any form of entrepreneurship. The pursuit of success, however we define it, is part of the fabric of America and all free economies in the world.

The pursuit of opportunities to earn money under flexible guidelines has always been a fundamental attribute of the direct selling model. In Chapter 3, we shared the various motivations that encourage and inspire the exploration and engagement of a gig. The opportunity to earn more is certainly a motivator, but the reasons for exploring opportunities to earn more should be clearly understood. Motivations are not about one sole motivation, and the dream is more often the opportunity to earn a few hundred dollars with the hope that the experience might grow into greater earnings. A few hundred dollars of incremental earnings could tilt the budget from negative to positive when earnings begin to exceed expenses. This can be life changing and a primary motivation for seeking a flexible income earning opportunity.

AN AMAZING STORY OF A DIRECT
SELLING ENTREPRENEUR

This is a story about a direct seller who, after 32 years of involvement, continues to speak about her career and her company as if she just got started. We do not provide full names of those who are actively engaged or the identification of the company, so we will call her GMB.

GMB started her direct selling experience like any other. Inspired by parents who were always encouraging, GMB was confident in her abilities, seemingly naturally courageous, and quite accomplished from the educational point of view. GMB has a bachelor's degree from Howard University, has a master's degree in business administration from Harvard Business School, and has been honored with an honorary doctorate degree from the University of Maryland Eastern Shore.

When we gained the opportunity to interview GMB, we knew immediately what our first question would be: How did a Harvard Business School graduate become interested in a direct selling opportunity? We have edited our interview with GMB to allow her to tell her story uninterrupted, with editing only for clarity.

> *My journey into a direct selling organization started when a girlfriend of mine invited me to her house for a skincare class. And it happened at a time when, in the back of my head, I wanted more, but there was no way I could fit something else into my life or, at least, that is what I thought. I was absolutely up to my eyeballs. I had an hour commute. I had a one-year-old, a two-year-old. I was on the boards of some of the companies in the Boston area. I was running a Girl Scout troop for my pastor, through the church, but I really wanted more. And because I knew I was going to be going through a divorce, I was thinking while the skincare class was going on, how am I going to make more? How could I possibly fit something else into my life? And then, when I saw how the class was conducted, I was not thinking about any form of entrepreneurship. My journey is one that I now teach all the time; take a person as far as they can see, and they'll see further.*

At that time, my parents were living in another city, and they really did not know the extent of my domestic problems and challenges. I had a sister that lived nearby, and she knew I had challenges, but no one really knew the extent. So, my parents did not understand why I would go into direct selling or why I would add anything to my plate at all. However, my mother had worked with another direct sales company and had done very well. My mom was a teacher with a nursing background. She had four girls, and she worked her direct selling gig for the extra money. So, she knew the model, but she just didn't think I should or could add anything else to my plate.

I was on a fabulous executive track making fabulous money and had fabulous benefits. So, she was very afraid of me going into a direct selling business. Number one, she didn't know anything about entrepreneurship and number two, how to make it work.

I am motivated by recognition. When I got started, my first goal was to earn a jacket and then the use of a car, and I did both in my first five months. When I got started, I had no fear of success, I wanted to be successful, and the recognition was a measurement. I kept my job for two and a half years when I first got started in direct selling. When I decided to walk away, I was a half-million-dollar retail producer, and my earnings were significant. Today I have been able to teach a lot of other women how to work the business. I never tell them that you have to leave their current position. You leave the other job if you ever want to when you have become successful.

I knew that I was going to make direct selling my new career when I broke my first company record. I qualified for a special level at a record-breaking pace. My performance helped my sponsor win a trip, and I liked that. I was motivated to help someone else by performing better myself. Afterward, I received a lot of recognition for my performance, and my income had increased. That achievement inspired me, and it gave me the confidence to believe that I could make a career out of direct selling. I also knew that if it did not work out, I could always go back to a job. I always knew that I could get another job anytime and anywhere, but more importantly, I had gained confidence that I could build an entrepreneurial business with my direct selling company.

I tell people: I left a job that I loved; I just happen to love what I currently do a little bit more. My last job was assistant director of admissions at Harvard Business School, and I fell in love with my admissions work. I was recruiting students into Harvard Business School, and my passion for the job was very high. It was a unique job. I was traveling to Africa and Europe to explain to different schools that they should have a relationship with Harvard and their students should be in our programs. And I was also mentoring young kids about what they would do if they came into Harvard. My sister had gone to Harvard before me, and my husband at the time was a student at Harvard. So, I had a lot of legs at Harvard University.

I owe a lot to others. I let people know that I am blessed with a high degree of energy; otherwise, they may not understand me. My mother and father had a high degree of energy. They never believed in slowing down. So, I am blessed with a high degree of energy. Intelligently, I got help. I believe I had more help than most women get in either their professional career or their entrepreneurial career. I had great babysitting help, and then I was able to find live-in support that rocked my world. And she was with me for 11 years. You must have a support team.

Part of my success in attracting and teaching others how to succeed in their businesses is my ability to be transparent. People can always see inside my world to see what is going on, how I manage my life. People have many questions when they are deciding who they might work with. Questions like: What's going on? Where do you live? What do you really do? How do you operate a home and business at the end care for the family at the same time? Do you have a live-in? Therefore, I attempt to model for others how they can do it.

I also believe that confidence is important. I know that integrity and understanding of our faith are the major priorities, but confidence is next. It is very important. One of my core competencies is the way I speak about the importance of financial security in our lives, especially for women. I honestly believe that you need income to change your choices. And I don't mean that it's more important than, or less important than, anything else. I just know that for me, it is critical, and I'm going to be in your face about it. And if you can earn more money, whatever the amount may be, you will have different types of choices for yourself, for your children, for your family and your community. I'm really passionate about this, and I've talked about it my entire career.

I believe women do well in this industry because there's a direct relationship to the things she cares about the most, which are her children, herself, her household and the first amount of money earned generally goes directly to the children, their school, their vacation, other family members, and I am not talking about the mortgage. I'm talking about the extra money that they earn. And they can do it whenever they can, at 11 o'clock at night, at two o'clock in the morning, getting up at four o'clock to get things done. Women are accustomed to working like this because they have so much to do.

One of our biggest challenges is being able to describe what direct selling is all about. When someone talks about becoming a nurse or a teacher, a lawyer, it is understood immediately. Others don't easily understand what I do so I have to teach, I have to care, I have to look into their eyes when I can.

I believe women love connecting with other women, and that's what we do. We are also transparent in the way we build relationships with our customers and our team members. Women want to be transparent, and they don't get to be transparent in their other professions. They must hide; they have to hide their laughter, their energy, and they have to hide their compassion. We do not hide any of these things, and it is unique to the way we build our businesses. We are there for everyone we are in a relationship with. We show up at celebrations, we get to know their birthdays, and we often know when someone is sick.

In my company, it is a culture of celebration. We love recognition, and women know how to give it. They're just good at it. Because I'm in a company that is made for women and have mostly women, recognition and praise are important, and I am constantly involved. Authenticity is also important. In other careers you have to change who we are no matter how smart we are, no matter what our background is, we think we have to dress a certain way. We feel we need to act a certain way, say it perfectly every time, do it perfectly every time, sometimes we feel guilty unnecessarily. I always let my team members know; you're good, you're okay. A lot of my success is attributed to my learning that I am okay; I am good, that it okay for me to be authentic.

The joy that people get in direct selling is that they are allowed to be themselves in so many ways, the way they dress, the way they travel, the way they laugh out loud with girlfriends, the way they get to cry with girlfriends. When we travel on trips together, we travel differently.

When I was still in my corporate job, I traveled a lot, but not the way we do it in my company when we qualify for a travel incentive. When I travel with my girlfriends who are also building their direct selling businesses, we just can't wait to get off the plane to spend time together.

Another aspect of my direct selling career that I love is the opportunity to be rewarded based upon performance and my effectiveness in how we use people skills. I have learned to enjoy this world that is always focused on bringing the best out of people. When you get to live and work in a world like this, where you understand, you only have to work with people, build relationships with people, you don't beat yourself up when everything is not perfect. It is a different world, and I teach this all the time. Because I am in business for myself, I also get to choose what I really like to do, even the customers and team members I spend most of my time. It's a great way to work. It's really been a great journey.

What I love most about my journey is who I've become in the process to achieve what I've achieved. I've become more transparent, an unapologetic powerhouse that likes to run the race, and I am competitive. Direct selling gives me the opportunity to compete for recognition and prizes with other great women who make me better. I know that my iron sharpens your iron. So I don't have any problem telling my girlfriends that if they are outperforming me at any given moment that I'm coming after you, and in this world that I am living and working, it's okay.

The second thing I love about my direct selling experience is related to the women that I've gotten to hang around with. My friends who have made me better, who told me it was okay to travel, who told me my kids would be okay if I'm not there, that the family would be okay if I were not cooking dinner every night, who told me it was okay if I made a big income, who told me it was okay if I had a beautiful home. These relationships with other women have been so important to me, and it is another part of being with a direct selling company that I love. I hang around women who are happy, and this has also been important for my kids to see. Of course, the recognition, especially the events our company has been known for, allows my family and friends to see what I have accomplished. I do not know of another business model that puts so much into recognition of the people who do the work. And that's very important to me because it's important for my children to see this kind of world.

The recognition our company provides also inspires many of us to greatness. Recognition for outstanding performance along with what I've earned, and my ability to live out loud, has been a great joy! Other people often tell me that I work so hard at what I do. I admit I do work hard, and I am not going to apologize. That's just who I am. Direct sellers work as they desire to work in accordance with their goals. I have always chosen to work hard.

What I have been able to achieve and accomplish may have impacted my four children who have found their own pathways to success. Each of them is fabulous people and doing great. I am also doing great and now looking forward to my retirement. It will be a celebration of a relaunch, the beginning of the next phase of my life after 30+ years as a direct selling entrepreneur. I've made up my mind that I'm going to be happy when I leave my current role. I like to say this: "I've eaten freely at the banquet for many years."

There's nothing left for me to eat at this banquet, so it's time for me to move on and someone else's time to step into the spotlight I have enjoyed for so many years. I will continue to be involved in some form of teaching, educating, and inspiring others to believe in themselves, and I intend to do it on an even bigger scale than what I do today.

I know that the women I have met and become friends with over the years will always be in my life. I've been there when they've had babies and been there when their kids graduated from college. So 32 years is a long time to be involved in the lives of many others. I also don't think I'll ever stop training women about confidence. I think I am a confidence-building expert. I did not realize how important this one component of life is until my direct selling experience. I have now gotten to know women who are smart, but they do not have enough confidence. Sometimes they can be confident in one area but not confident in another area that is also important.

This pandemic has also shifted many things. Women and men have more time to think more. I walk around my property where I have resided for the past 20 years, and I now see things I never saw before because I am thinking more and differently. I've actually amazed myself when recognizing the beauty of a tree that was always there but overlooked by me. I am thinking more about the opportunities I have been blessed with, the choices I made, the hard work, overcoming challenges, and what I have been able to achieve. It has been an amazing journey, and I could not have scripted my journey any better.

Most importantly, I am grateful.

INSIGHTS GAINED

When accumulating the insights gained from the work on this chapter, we reached out to our friend Alan Luce, principal, Strategic

Choice Partners, for his perspective. Luce has been involved directly and indirectly with many direct selling companies. He has served as a chief legal officer, chief executive officer, consultant, and advisor. His perspective is unique, and his thoughts influenced the insights we share.

1. *Direct selling companies understand the power of independent contractors.* All direct companies build around attracting independent contractors to sell their products or provide their services. The decision to choose a direct selling opportunity is based upon a belief that the opportunity can support income goals and time constraints. There is also a belief that the products or services can be sold easily and with little or no learning curve. Direct sellers remain active when they believe that the possibility to earn an income for time invested can become a reality. The process can happen very quickly when the new direct seller is enthusiastic about the products or services and equipped with excellent marketing support. Some direct sellers are known to accomplish multiple sales within a few days of getting started.

2. *What the early direct selling companies learned:* Over the decades, direct selling companies learned some basic principles that were essential to follow to achieve enduring success with a workforce of independent contractors.

   • Establishing a healthy level of trust between the company and the army of independent contractors is critical to long-term success. Independent contractors must believe that the company will always act in the best interest of the direct sellers.

   • Direct sellers should be viewed and treated as valued assets of the company.

   • Recognition and celebration of the direct seller's successful performances is a critical feature of creating trust and belief in the company.

   Recognition of the importance of the independent contractor changes the process by which the company makes decisions in very fundamental ways. A company dependent on independent contractors will benefit from asking the question: How will this decision impact our independent contractors? Doing so can significantly impact the effectiveness of attraction, retention, and performance. This simple method of examining all business decisions with the independent contractor in mind has been a key learning for direct selling companies.

3. *Lessons direct selling companies are learning from the new generation of gig companies:* The new generation of gig companies that have sprung up over the past decade has established new standards of what gig seekers are looking for in the ideal gig opportunity. The new generation of gig companies has raised the service standards that all potential gig workers have come to expect. Using new technologies is now essential for direct selling companies. The following is a short list of new expectations that direct selling companies are embracing or already providing:

- Quicker pay

- Quick and easy access to company information and guidance on a 24/7/365 basis

- All business processes, from enrollment, onboarding, digital marketing tools, to daily status reports and sales or service opportunities, managed easily on the smartphone

- Social media platforms to support communication, sharing of ideas and promotion of the direct selling company's products, services, and part-time income opportunities

4. *Outlook:* The shift from traditional employment to the growing use of flexible, part-time gig workers to drive sales and provide services will continue. These new phenomena will serve direct selling companies well as they are, and always have been, gig-providing companies. In the coming years, society will see new best practices to attract, reward, retain, and support gig workers. New safety nets will emerge.

5. The incentives direct selling companies have long used to inspire performance have always included travel to exciting destinations throughout the world. Stephanie McVeigh, founder and CEO of Strategic Incentive Solutions Inc., a full-service incentive

marketing and meetings and events firm, shared an outlook on
how travel incentives have been impacted as a result of COVID-
19, and there are positives:

> *We are now seeing stability as well as client willingness
> to be creative and flexible in the design of their incentive
> programs. Reward and recognition programs continue
> to play a pivotal role in ensuring clients and employees
> are focused, inspired, motivated, and valued during
> challenging times. In fact, it is more important now
> than ever to drive loyalty and engagement with distrib-
> utors and preferred customers.*
>
> *Companies are creating solutions for their rewards pro-
> grams that adapt to make sure they are relevant with a
> focus on the behaviors that will have a positive impact
> on the organization's growth, keeping budgets, health,
> and their employees' and customers' well-being in the
> forefront. Rewards are currently trending towards a
> higher number of gift cards, points-based programs,
> merchandise, and individual travel rewards as a result
> of travel restrictions and concerns. Group travel incen-
> tive programs are predicted to surge once a vaccine or
> cure is found for COVID-19 as a result of people
> having cabin fever and a strong desire to travel again.
> Individual, short-distance travel continues to increase.
> People are staying closer to home and choosing desti-
> nations they can drive to. When designing incentive
> programs, it is critical to ensure the scope of work
> aligns with the relevancy to your participants and
> align objectives to drive a faster recovery for your orga-
> nization. The desire to do resort buy-outs and source
> luxury getaways that offer outdoor experiences in wide-
> open spaces is the new hot trend.*

7

WOMEN AND THE FUTURE
OF GIGS

The story behind the phenomenal growth of gig economy partici-pation, we believe, will increasingly become a story about women. A few years ago, the gig economy attracted roughly two men for every one woman. There were good reasons for the statistics, but we predict they will continue to change. Transportation gigs were among the first of the new gig companies to gain the attention of the marketplace. These new gigs disrupted a predominantly male industry; women represented fewer than 5% of all taxi drivers in most US cities. As a result of the technological innovations introduced by companies such as Uber and Lyft, women now represent around 20%–30% of the drivers in the new gig economy.

As longtime observers of the direct selling model, we predict that the gig economy will soon reach gender parity and ultimately come to have a higher participation rate of women than men. Direct selling is a form of gig work with a history of over 100 years. Approximately 75% of its participants domestically and globally are women. When David McConnell, the founder of Avon, decided to build his company with women as the sales force, his decision was intentional. He saw in women attributes that he felt would benefit his direct-to-consumer model of business. His business decision was radical at the time. Avon provided women with the flexibility and freedom to work as they desired before women could vote in this country. Avon, and virtually every direct selling company that has come after it, helped empower women changing the landscape of flexible work available to women.

The gig economy will become more and more about women because women are shifting their attitudes about work. Much has been written about women who have abandoned the climb up the corporate ladder or the pursuit of any form of work that is not flexible. In preparing to write this chapter, we were directed to Sheryl Sandberg's book *Lean In*, where she states that approximately 40% of highly qualified women are no longer interested in traditional jobs. In *Lean In*, Sandberg uses her research and personal experiences to help women develop strategies to achieve their goals. More of these goals will be supported by the gig economy and the flexible choices it offers.

Women are also well-suited for the growing choices of gigs. Women tend to multitask effectively and manage time efficiently, especially when a family is a part of the responsibility. Most women have natural communication and relationship-building skills that can be leveraged, especially when they have the flexibility and the ability to do the work while maintaining other priorities. These skills and assets become very valuable when exploring gig opportunities.

Gig-providing companies can learn from the direct selling model, which enabled women to maximize their skills and willingness to work outside of the traditional workplace. As gig-providing companies market their opportunities more specifically toward women, we expect to see the rate of participation increase as well as the quality of personalized service.

Here are the reasons why we hypothesize the way we do:

1. *Women appreciate flexibility and freedom in how work can be done.* The gig economy offers many attributes and many choices. Gigs may not be the ideal solution in all cases, but women will recognize and appreciate the options. Gig work provides a path to juggling rewarding work, with childcare, eldercare, and household responsibilities that fall disproportionately to women. Gigs making effective use of technology have made it possible for flexible work to be efficient, in some cases providing earning opportunities without leaving home.

Part of the flexibility of gigs is that these can be short-term work arrangements. People can take on gig work when it fits their schedule, and they are free to stop and start that schedule as they choose, without jeopardizing a relationship with an employer. The gig economy has completely redefined part-time work and created microentrepreneurial opportunities favorable to women who desire to work on their own schedules.

The May 24, 2019, Asia Pacific edition of *Entrepreneur* magazine carried a very interesting article written by Sanjay Lakhotia, cofounder of Noble House Consulting Pte., who has more than 20 years of experience in working across all areas of human resources, including HR transformation, leadership development, HR technology deployment, and performance culture. In the article, titled *Gig Economy: A Boon for Women*, Lakhotia speaks specifically to the importance women place on flexibility and freedom in how work can be done. He also said, "The work from anywhere culture is at the core of the gig economy and comes as a solution for women looking to gain flexibility and work from home opportunities. This will surely boost women's participation in the workforce and eventually, the global economy."

2. *Gigs offer an alternative to trying to break the glass ceiling.* When working a gig, there is no boss and typically no organizational politics. Gig workers usually are not competing with others to get the same job or the same promotion. In the gig world, the gig participant is her own boss, certainly a refreshing option that eliminates many of the challenges women have been fighting in the workplace for many years. Flexibility and freedom in how work can be done also remove age as a barrier to obtaining work and the challenges associated with reentry to the work world for those who have stepped away. In her latest book, *Comeback Careers*, Mika Brzezinski, cohost of the popular "Morning Joe" show here in America, talks about work after 40, 50, and beyond. Mika and Ginny, Mika's sister and coauthor of the book, note that: "Gig work can be an on-ramp back into the world of work, or even a bridge to solid ground after job loss." The final chapter in their book is titled *Gigs, Side Hustles, And Making It on Your Own.*

As we finalized this chapter, the COVID-19 pandemic was taking a more substantial toll on women in the workforce than men. Women comprise the majority of many frontline essential positions, including those in health care, education, and retail. Many found themselves struggling to juggle those in-person jobs at the same time they had fewer options for childcare. Women who were able to work from home also were facing challenges, as studies showed that they continued to shoulder the majority of childcare and homeschooling responsibilities even if their partners were also working from home. Being forced to work from home has accelerated the preference to work from home, making gigs even more appealing to women.

3. *Gender equality may be another hidden benefit of working a gig.* Many gig participants market their services with company support or digital formats that do not reveal the gender of the worker. Therefore, customers make their choices based on what they see (the product or service), not who is providing the product or service. This is another asset that the gig economy offers, perhaps without even realizing it.

   In fact, gig economy opportunities may be eliminating gender inequality. The following is a great study: The 2018 APAC Workforce Insights Study, Gig Economy: How Free Agents are redefining work, the closing of the inequality of pay gap relative to gender. In traditional jobs, the difference in pay between men and women is about 12% (favorable to men); however, the gig economy appears to be less, maybe as low as 5%.

4. *Quick payment for services rendered.* Quicker pay is an attribute of most gigs and is considered to be a short-term motivation that women may have for seeking a gig. Gig-providing companies were among the first to offer a more immediate compensation opportunity paying the gig worker almost immediately for services performed. This attribute associated with the attribute of flexibility and the many forms of gig work choices is appealing.

5. *Short-term work opportunities are appealing.* Many women are not seeking long-term employment but would enjoy meaningful,

short-term work. Part-time jobs satisfied this need and desire at one time; however, the gig economy has completely redefined part-time work and created microentrepreneurial opportunities favorable to women who desire to work on their own schedules. There are both more types of part-time work and more opportunities available in the gig economy than ever before.

Maria Locker is among those working closely with women entrepreneurs, both in the gig economy and outside it. Locker is the founder and CEO of RevolutionHER, a media company that connects members with events, knowledge, and a community of like-minded women. We had the opportunity to interview her about how RevolutionHER supports female entrepreneurs. She lives and works in Milton, Ontario, a young and fast-growing community about 25 minutes outside of Toronto.

"A lot of women in my community are young moms who the majority of the time left their jobs and decided not to go back to corporate," Locker said. *"They wanted something else."*

That is Locker's story as well.

"I'm the second daughter of immigrant parents from Italy, and I have three other siblings. When I was two, my parents opened an Italian bakery and grocery store in our hometown, which is still running now. My entire family still works there except for me," she said.

Initially, Locker pursued her childhood dream of becoming a teacher. However, when she had her two children 18 months apart, that dream changed.

"I realized there was no passion for me to go back to teaching 30 kids and leaving my two," she said. *"It just didn't make sense. I discussed it with my husband, and we both agreed. So, I left my teaching career, and for the first year, I just enjoyed being a mom. To make a little bit of money on the side, I went back and helped my parents. I opened up their Facebook page and did some freelance marketing for them."*

"I was working on the side, and I'd go to the park with my kids and meet other women. I felt like I was always the one striking up the conversation to ask what they did. And honestly, nine times out of 10, the woman I was talking to was an entrepreneur."

It blew my mind. Number one, that they weren't openly talking about it. It was like the women were keeping a secret, and thinking to themselves, "I'm a mom; you're not supposed to talk to me about work right now." And number two, that there were so many women that I was meeting at the parks who also were entrepreneurs. I thought, "You know what? We need to all just get together."

That was how RevolutionHER – first called Mompreneurs – was born. Locker organized her first coffee group with about 10 women and said to them:

"I keep meeting other women that look like they're struggling to talk about being an entrepreneur. Can you guys tell me what you are looking for? What could be done to help you feel better about owning your business and shouting from the rooftops that you have this incredible business."

RevolutionHER is a diverse organization. Its youngest member joined when she was 19 years old. Its oldest member is 96 years. RevolutionHER has more than 23,000 members and subscribers in businesses, including patented consumer products, accounting, finance, dieticians, house cleaning, construction, direct sales, and more. *"If you name a business, I'm telling you, we have them in our group,"* Locker said. *"They're from all walks of life. It's pretty incredible, actually."* The organization publishes a magazine and creates a community for women from all walks of life, entrepreneurs and nonentrepreneurs alike, where they can share ideas and offer each other support online or through in-person events.

While not all RevolutionHER members participate in the gig economy, Locker says she sees a growing number of people enjoying the gig economy's opportunities, particularly as a part-time pursuit. *"I find many women will focus on a side business, even if they already have a full-time job or they are an entrepreneur already,"* she said.

In my work with a truly diverse group of women who were direct sellers engaged with the Avon brand, I also observed that micro-entrepreneurship provides women with a platform to learn more about themselves. The growth of the gig economy will allow more women to find and realize their entrepreneurial and leadership skills far quicker than possibly imagined. Those of us who have worked with the direct selling channel of distribution have had the privilege of being able to get to know and work with women who were moms focused on mentorship and nurturing of children and who were also the general manager of households and, as mentioned previously, often working in full-time jobs. It was amazing to observe and a great opportunity for me to personally learn from their example.

You are now beginning to understand why we hypothesize that women are the future of gig work. It is because of the natural attributes and skills women bring to microentrepreneurial opportunities. Gig opportunities fuel a labor revolution, but we also see women as a significant force in increasing the quality and value of more personalized marketing, sales skills, relationship building, and leadership development. In our observations of how social media platforms are used, women typically share products they feel good about, while companies and men may use more of a harder sell positioning when women are not involved in the marketing strategy. In my 15 years with Avon, I never felt that the Avon Representatives were selling. The sales were the result of their very personal and passionate advocacy of the brand of products we were so proud of. As we learned, Avon was as much about empowering women as it was about any specific product. The same is true for the many other companies that use direct selling as their channel of distribution. Gig opportunities can change lives, especially for women, and the possibilities have never been greater.

In the course of our research, we interviewed Lori Bush, the former president and CEO of Rodan + Fields and now cofounder and CEO of Solvasa Integrative Beauty. Bush is someone we put into the category of being a strong woman. She has climbed the corporate ladder, served as a senior executive in a few very significant companies, and continues to bring an entrepreneurial spirit and a deep passion and commitment to a purpose rooted in empowering women.

"In Rodan Field's early days, the brand was sold in department stores, behind glass counters where all of the premium cosmetics and skincare products were kept. But the company's message just wasn't coming through," Bush said. They decided to change their distribution method, turning to a path that would leverage the power of word of mouth instead: direct selling. *"We put our message in the hands of*

women who are really experiencing our products, sharing our passion," she explained. *"It's taking advantage of a modern way in which information gets shared and distributed. It's almost like crowdsourcing your sales, your marketing, your sales organization management. In that way, it's a meritocracy that allows people to earn an income in ways that might not have otherwise been accessible to them."*

When we spoke, Bush was in the early days of launching Solvasa Integrative Beauty. She identified several intersecting trends that are driving the brand's growth, some of which relate to the product and the brand, but two, in particular, relate to global trends that touch the gig economy as well.

"One of the trends," she said, *"is work from home. WFH is now an acronym. Work from home used to be a home-based business, or it was something related to the internet. But now work from home means a whole different thing. A lot of people do not want to go back into an office environment for various reasons, so that's one of the things that we need is a new definition of working from home and what that means to people, especially women. Social entrepreneurship is also very important, meaning doing well by doing good and having a triple bottom line that relates not just to profits, but also to people and to planet or to people and purpose. People want to join something where they feel a sense of purpose. Whether it's a gig or a sharing economy opportunity, it's more of a purposeful business model in terms of being part of something."*

Having worked her way up the corporate ladder herself, Bush knows better than most the challenges of being a mom on the corporate track and the benefits entrepreneurship can bring. *"My nanny was much better known at the schools than I was,"* she shared. *"I would show up, and it was, 'Oh, you're Zack's nanny's boss.'"*

"For women, it too often ends up being a choice: career or family. It's not as often a choice for men. It's very difficult to be present in your child's life and working your way up that corporate ladder in a male-competitive world. However, the answer to that is often for women having their own businesses."

Bush found her own pathway and climbed the corporate ladder, achieving the ranks of officer, president, and chief executive officer – no easy task for man or woman. She is an example of an achiever who used her influence and continues to use her influence skills, experience, and knowledge, to create a pathway for many other women who desire to create their own pathways, explore and test their own leadership qualities, and pursue side hustles or gigs, and the opportunity to grow a business into long-term successful and growing enterprises.

On the subject of leadership, especially the leadership styles embodied by many women, I share that over the years, I have read many books, attended many seminars and events, and participated in many exercises focused on leadership development. All these experiences served me well. However, it was the experience I gained while serving as an officer on the sales side of the sales and marketing equation that made a lasting impact on my leadership style. It was during this period of my life that I grew to understand how natural it was for many women to demonstrate effective skills in networking, building relationships, extending kindness in how information was shared with others, and how to motivate and inspire others to do what they never thought of doing. It was indeed an amazing experience during a period of my life that I will never forget. I will always hold in my memories an attitude of gratitude for what I learned from so many women. The many women I was fortunate to work with demonstrated a style of leadership that I often found difficult to describe even though I worked hard to adopt the style.

A few years ago, I had the opportunity to work with Janet Meeks, a woman who has achieved extraordinary success in corporate environments in the finance and healthcare industries. With a solid foundation provided by her parents, an excellent education, and the determination to achieve and help others reach what she describes as "peak performance," Meeks helped me explain what I had observed when working with women. Her book, *Gracious Leadership: Lead Like You Never Led Before*, is one of the best books on leadership that I have ever read. It helped me understand how to describe the attributes of leadership that, I believe, women are endowed with more naturally than men. This is also why we hypothesize that the future of gigs is about women, certainly a more significant percentage of women than we see today.

We were anxious to find out what principles Meeks might share with the women reading this book who are looking at micro-entrepreneurship/gigs rather than climbing the corporate ladder. After 40 years of climbing the corporate ladder and arriving at some of the highest levels imaginable, she announced her retirement in 2015. Upon retirement, many of her colleagues wanted to know more about what had driven her and enabled her to successfully navigate environments known to be partial to men. Fortunately for all of us, Meeks took and kept notes about her experiences, notes that became the essence of what she teaches in *Gracious Leadership*.

"I decided that I had not only the opportunity but also the responsibility to put down my thoughts, my convictions, about what great and respectful leadership looks like," Meeks said. *"And so that's what led me to want to write the book, to create a game plan of sorts that is easy to understand, simple to implement so that the leaders of today and tomorrow can focus on how to be respectful in taking their teams to peak performance. I wanted people to know that you can be tough and kind concurrently. You can be compassionate and require accountability at the same time. It was an opportunity to teach the leaders of today and tomorrow that if you are a gracious, fully respectful leader, it's about the intersection of ultimate respect and optimal outcomes."*

In *Gracious Leadership*, Meeks shares how she defines a gracious leader and lists the attributes as follows:

- Respectful
- Values relationships
- Listens with purpose and responds with care
- Sees problems as opportunities
- Asks the right questions
- Matches passion with purpose
- Develops their people
- Requires accountability
- Courageous

- Seeks feedback

- Provides feedback

- Compassionate

- Grateful

"There is so much potential to unleash the human spirit through showing respect," Meeks said. *"And that does not mean being soft. It's about applying the key ingredients of Gracious Leadership."*

When leaders embody these qualities, they create an environment that supports the development and success of those on their teams. This kind of support is just as critical for gig-providing companies to exhibit to their independent contractors as it is for leaders within traditional corporate structures. Yet, in our research, we have found that the average gig worker rarely receives much guidance or support from a gracious leader. The focus is primarily on the work. This illuminates a tremendous opportunity for gig companies that wish to set themselves apart in the marketplace.

Gig workers also can benefit from the lessons of *Gracious Leadership.* Most gig opportunities require interacting directly with a consumer, and the style of the gig worker often correlates with the outcome of the relationship. A gracious leadership style, as Meeks defines it, creates positive customer experiences that can fuel success in the gig economy.

"I think it's possible for both men and women to fully embrace the key ingredients of Gracious Leadership," Meeks said, *"but I think it's more natural for women to do so. As you read that list of 13 key ingredients, they certainly feel very nurturing – giving feedback, showing respect, valuing relationships. It just feels like a more natural fit with us as women. And when you have all 13 key ingredients, that truly is where the secret sauce comes to life."*

INSIGHTS

Women's workforce participation rates in the United States have shifted over time. Despite our modern perceptions, in the eighteenth and nineteenth centuries, women were significant contributors to their household income. They were key contributors to running family farms and producing other goods and services that kept their families afloat. It was not until the manufacturing economy took hold that women began to step away from directly participating in paid work in large numbers, as families split their efforts – men heading off to factories and women focusing on children and household management. Women notably stepped back into the workforce during World War II, filling those factory positions as men moved into military service but then reversing course following the war. We saw another surge in women's workforce participation from the 1960s through the 1980s, before beginning to slow again in the 1990s. During this period, the percentage of women earning college degrees also increased dramatically, helping to shift the types of work in which women engage. According to the US Bureau of Labor Statistics, in 2018, women accounted for 52% of all workers employed in management, professional, and related occupations, a participation rate that outpaced their 47% share of total employment.

As the gig economy continues to grow, we expect to see yet another shift in how women participate in paid work. New types of gigs become available every day, creating new opportunities that appeal to different types of people. We have already seen the gig economy expand far beyond transportation-related services to include categories that currently have higher participation rates among women. As innovation continues, the gig economy will touch virtually every field, opening up even more appealing opportunities. Watch particularly for new gig opportunities related to nursing and teaching – two job categories dominated by women in traditional employment settings – to attract more women to the world of gig work.

Cultural shifts toward equal division of household and childcare responsibilities are happening but slowly. As a result, we anticipate that mothers will continue to shoulder a greater portion of society's needs in these categories – particularly in childcare – than fathers for quite some time. Because of this, the flexibility offered within the gig economy is likely to continue to attract more and more women. The workforce statistics already reveal how much juggling childcare continues to play a role in women's participation in paid work. In

March 2018, 62% of women with children younger than 3 years were in the workforce, according to the US Bureau of Labor Statistics, compared to 76.5% of women with school-age children 6–17 years old. Women also are twice as likely to work part-time than men, 24% compared to 12%. The ability to earn supplemental income on an exceptionally flexible schedule, as the gig economy offers, will have considerable appeal to mothers of young children.

While we have focused our analysis on the US market, we expect to see similar trends play out across the globe. Women's workforce participation varies greatly by country and culture, but the gig economy's attributes of highly flexible work with fair compensation for the effort invested are nearly universal in appeal.

We also expect that organizations such as RevolutionHER will play an important role in supporting the expanding role of women in the gig economy. Locker and others like her are building networks of entrepreneurially minded women interested in developing part- or full-time business opportunities on their own terms. These communities provide social and practical support for their members, giving people a place to turn for firsthand advice. They also shine a spotlight on individuals who are achieving success. Those success stories are inspiring and can create a snowball effect. People are more likely to give something new a try when they see examples of people like themselves having a positive experience. People do not join the gig economy in a vacuum. They typically are introduced to a gig opportunity by someone they know who already is working that gig or by hearing about it online.

Leaders of gig-providing companies that do not yet have significant numbers of women participating in their gigs would be wise to listen closely to the conversations that women are having today about work in general and about gigs specifically. By increasing their understanding, these companies can adjust their marketing and communication strategies to better appeal to a significant pool of potential talent. The companies even may find opportunities to tweak their business models to increase their relevance to this important market.

Gig economy executives also will find value in implementing the attributes taught in *Gracious Leadership*. That style of leadership defined so well by Janet Meeks lends itself to fostering a corporate culture that can attract and retain top talent. In gig-providing companies, the need for talent is magnified. These businesses require both full-time corporate teams, as traditional companies do, but also must attract their gig workforce. As more and more gig-providing companies enter the market, the competition will increase.

Change will continue to be the constant within the gig economy – and we see this evolution to be a positive for all involved. The vast array of choices has fueled the growth of the gig economy to date, and it is what will continue to drive its popularity among women moving forward. As you will see in the next chapter, the gig economy does not offer a one-size-fits-all solution for workers. Instead, each gig seeker can define his or her own path.

8

DEFINING THE ULTIMATE GIG

The definition of the ultimate gig is not universal because there are diverse reasons for embracing a gig. This is the beauty of this growing phenomenon. However, from our observations and interactions with those working gigs, we were able to identify standard gig components that lead to satisfaction. When a gig seeker finds a gig that includes each of these essential components, he or she may be inclined to feel they have found their ultimate gig.

That choice of an ultimate gig may change over time. There is high turnover in the gig economy, with the average person working a particular gig for months, not necessarily years. The reasons people choose one specific gig change over time. In other words, what may be an ultimate gig at a given period in time may not be the ultimate gig in a different period, and it does not matter. Turnover is not negative; it is the nature of the work and the beauty of the gig economy. Gigs do not require people to make permanent career-impacting decisions. Ultimately, the gig worker's selection is a result of a personal choice or perceived preference for a particular type of work at a specific moment in time.

We know that the motivation to seek and engage in part-time work is unprecedented. All of this is happening at a time when the US economy (pre–COVID-19) is experiencing the lowest unemployment rate in the past few years. However, as we know, the increases in those engaged in part-time work may also be a result of external economic-related forces, including underemployment. When economies are going through rapid change and transformation, some of those involved in part-time work may be in situations where they have been replaced or displaced and unable to find full-time work of preference. In previous chapters, we also learned that inflation over the past 20 plus years has negated much of the purchasing power associated with wage increases. The solution: find a gig that enables part-time investment of time and a return in income appropriate for time invested without disrupting what is most important: another job, the responsibility associated with family, or only the desire to make better use of one's time to enhance the quality of life.

The Ultimate Gig Checklist will help both gig providers and gig seekers. Working a gig can be more meaningful and rewarding when gig seekers apply a checklist to evaluate their choice of a gig. Gig providers can be more successful when they help people select gigs that best fit their needs. When a gig is easy to understand and easy to embrace, it is easier for the gig seeker to decide whether to pursue the opportunity, enhancing both provider and seeker's productivity and success. This can lead to the feeling that the ultimate gig has been found, at least for the moment the gig seeker may be experiencing.

Our checklist is created from personal experience and observations. Each component serves as a standard to be met. In using and completing the checklist, both gig providers and gig seekers are guided and assured that steps are being taken to support effective communication and understanding. A feeling of "no regrets" by the gig seeker is the objective.

Our Ultimate Gig Checklist is very logical (Fig. 8.1). These standards could apply to all forms of gig work. Many of the components illustrate why gigs are growing at an impressive rate and why the gig economy is appealing and meaningful to those who participate. The checklist serves to ensure success for both gig providers and gig seekers. Taking a few minutes to complete such a checklist will certainly help the gig seeker decide which gig to pursue. Gig-providing companies also can benefit from the checklist by helping gig workers gain clarity. This results in consumers receiving a higher quality of service and increasing the gig participant's lifetime value.

WHEN DESIGNING YOUR OWN GIG

If you love to make or create something that is marketable, the gig economy makes it simple to start a business. Taking this route may be a pathway to creating the ultimate gig. Work that you love

Ultimate Gig Checklist

■ Simplicity

Technology is once again a game-changer. What formerly required extensive research to find the answer can now be found through a few word commands spoken into our smartphones. Therefore, gig providers will benefit from clear descriptions of their opportunities to enable people to quickly understand the work and how the work can be done. Gig seekers who know how they will work and be rewarded will add to the value of the work and the customer experience.

■ Clarity

Gig income opportunities can be most enjoyable when they tie into the personal goals, values, interests, and the current skills a gig seeker may possess. Gig providers will benefit from a clear definition of what the gig seeker will do and why the gig seeker might select the gig opportunity inclusive of the types of skills that are important to achieving success and providing excellent customer satisfaction.

■ Easy to Engage

Fees and training requirements can be barriers to entry. Gig providers who keep it simple, make it easy to engage, and provide excellent support and guidance, appeal to a much larger segment of those seeking part-time income possibilities. Gig-providing companies that strive to reduce the often-perceived complexity of micro-entrepreneurship to simplicity in engagement will benefit both the gig provider and gig seeker.

■ Reasonable Return on Investment of Time

Gig seekers should be clear about what they are looking for in a gig. Research indicates the average gig worker earns $550.00 to $600.00 per month, depending upon the research sourced. Most gig workers are in pursuit of an incremental income of $500.00 to $1,500.00 per month. Quick pay for the work accomplished should also be evaluated and considered by the gig seeker. Timely rewards and evaluation of performance are considered essential when selecting a gig.

■ Enjoyable

Motivations can include more than the opportunity to earn money. Previous experience and skills should be taken into consideration as potential assets. Leveraging skills and experience makes sense, when possible, not that the gig seeker may be exploring something very different from what they already do in another form of work. When the gig selected is envisioned to be enjoyable at the start, the probability for succeeding and achieving objectives may be higher.

■ Customer Focused

Customer acquisition and retention are foundational to all business models, including gigs. Transportation gigs, for example, generally provide a gig participant with customers. Other gigs require an investment of time and effort into acquiring customers. Whatever your choice in gig selection, keep in mind that it is always about the customer. The customer acquisition strategy of the gig provider should be clear, easy to understand, and the digital tools provided should be intuitive.

■ Predictable Income

Gig seekers should do their homework when exploring gigs, as income predictability is essential. Every gig opportunity serving gig participants has a track record that can be researched by the gig seeker. The ability to foresee how the gig might work for the gig seeker and how income can be predicted is essential.

Fig. 8.1. Ultimate Gig Checklist.

unconditionally, which creates a monetary reward and offers the gratification of having created something that impacts others' lives, can deliver yields that go far beyond the amount of a commission.

Gone are the days when you needed to hire expensive experts, raise capital, risk your own capital, or have a facility and a small group of employees to start a business. Today, it is has become much easier to find and engage services that will provide you with all that you need to open a global e-commerce store and have an opportunity to promote your product or service to a broad audience. A subscription fee is often required to engage these types of resources; however, the costs are reasonable in comparison to what the costs of a business start-up were in the past. An excellent example of this type of service is Shopify. Shopify's services make it easy to create a website, use digital marketing tools, and have an online shopping cart to sell whatever you desire. The fee for the Shopify service is very reasonable, and the level of support is selected by the new microentrepreneur. The average person can be online, marketing, and selling a product within a few hours or days. For those who have a hobby, craft, or skill, there are many local ways to expose your products. These options include fairs and what we formerly referred to as flea markets, which are now very sophisticated point-of-sale locations.

Now that you are clear on how gigs are selected, you may be motivated to create your own gig. There is a lot of support available, and it is easy to explore the options. One step should include comparing and building your own gig with choosing an existing gig opportunity that may provide you with complete support, proven products or services, and identification with a brand already identified in the marketplace. When designing a gig, you will be the Chief Executive, Chief Marketer, and Chief Technology Officer. However, you can now take a hobby, product, or service and build your own brand with the new support available. There are several million people already experiencing success, having created their own gig.

The ultimate gig is ultimately the gig of your choice. Choose wisely!

TESTIMONIALS FROM PEOPLE WHO FOUND THEIR ULTIMATE GIG

I am an interior designer online for Havenly.com. I've worked with them for about five months. I had prior experience as an interior designer, just not as an online designer. I devote probably, on average, about 5 hours a day, including weekends. I also earn money through other jobs. I work for architects as just a draftsperson, and I am also an intern at a church.

My motivation for choosing to do gig work was to be able to work from home with flexible hours and making money doing something that I am familiar with, getting to do my own designs and not necessarily working directly under someone else. I really enjoy the creativity of it. That is what I enjoy the most about it.
— Cherise D., interior designer

I've hosted for almost a year, and I did not have any prior experience. I devote about an hour a week to this gig. Sometimes if I have a guest staying for a month, there is little to no time. In contrast, if I have seven different people staying in one week, there is going to be a lot of back and forth communication with each guest and potentially helping them find things or troubleshooting things or pointing them to local places to hangout.

I also earn money through another job, and that job is Stitch Fix. That is my primary employer. I work remotely for them, so it allows me to be able to interact with guests and be available for guests easily because of the flexibility of that job.

My motivation for working with Airbnb specifically was having really good experiences through traveling and staying at Airbnb properties and getting to enjoy downtown areas and getting to get more of a feel for the local landscape from an actual person/host that is there at a local level. So those good experiences were a huge motivation for working with Airbnb.

Probably the thing I enjoy the most would be the people I meet. I like to meet new people. It feels really good even if the guests don't want to interact when I know I'm providing them with a safe and clean space that they can stay in this area and make their travels more enjoyable. I really like to give local recommendations and being able to provide people with a quirky place to stay.

I plan to work my gig as long as I live in this house and for as long as I have a mortgage to pay. I know for each guest, my main goal is that they would have a safe and clean space to stay where they can feel like they are getting the experience of this local city. The goal is just to help pay the mortgage and meet new people.

– Abi S., home rental

We are four generations of independent beauty consultants. My grandmother, my mother, and I each started from other professional careers, on a part-time basis to supplement our incomes. As we discovered the power of empowering women by sharing the products and our company, our independent businesses grew, solely because of the hard work and attention we each put into our own businesses.

And now my daughter is the 4th generation! Her business is now her full-time career. She grew up watching me design my independent business around our family, mentor women to reach their potential, and enjoy my own success because of my hard work. She felt the company's enthusiasm and opportunity. And now, she has earned the use of her first career car!

I'm competitive. That is, I'm driven to achieve. I also know, as I pursue my business, I'm making a difference in the lives of women throughout my community and organization.

– Mary K., direct seller

My education, career, expertise, and professional joy for the last 22 years has been as a marriage and family therapist. A number of years ago, I had to listen to my own advice, and, with my husband, we made a conscious decision for the benefit of our family of five for me to adopt a home-based practice, and his career would continue on the traditional path.

As my practice time demands shifted, I was introduced to a direct selling company selling health and wellness products. I had some exposure to direct sales many years prior, so the concept of extra income representing a product that fits into my lifestyle and interest in overall well-being made sense. Then there is the added value and love I have for the proven science behind my company's product line.

Multiple sources of income have worked well for me and my family. My practice continues; we have land on which we board horses; we receive modest income and delight in working with the high school student exchange programs, and I am building residual income for retirement.

— Laurie A., direct seller

INSIGHTS AND UNEXPECTED LESSONS LEARNED

We approached this chapter with the thought that we would find the precise type of gig that might be considered the ultimate gig. As we researched the gig economy, we became more and more fascinated with the motivations behind the choices made and the types of gigs that are selected by those involved. The values associated with how we work are forever being changed. The gig economy represents a significant shift in how we define work and what we expect from our work environment. We doubt seriously that our grandkids will place a high value on a 9-to-5 job. They are already learning differently and no longer dependent upon the teacher at the front of the room; in fact, they may be more dependent upon their smart tablet or phone. Because we now have so much information available digitally, the need for physical presence is forever different; therefore, our values are changing. As a result of COVID-19, our understanding of the need for flexibility in how we work is forever changed.

We are working differently as individuals and as teams. The need for physical space is changing. The office-centric environment is quickly becoming a question mark in the business models of many companies. The virtual company may be the new reality in many cases. Company owners and executives are reevaluating the investments made in buildings that are no longer needed. What will the buildings be used for when a growing portion of the labor force works remotely or independently as freelancers and gig workers? What will the future of education look like if digital learning proves to be as effective as or more effective than classroom learning? As digital learning becomes more and more the norm, why would we expect those students to grow up to become workers who value the rigidity of a working model created over 100 years ago?

The questions we ask ourselves continue to reveal even more interesting questions. Our survey reviewed and discussed in Chapter 11 provides a contemporary, in-depth look at gig workers' points of view. We intend to continually provide you with information and ideas to keep you informed. As we have done, we encourage you to read. Search for the research and understand the findings, especially if you plan to be a gig provider. For those of you who are contemplating embracing gig economy principles, values, and business propositions, you must understand what is offered. The gig economy has reduced complexity in microentrepreneurship to simplicity. Traditional models will not benefit from merely changing labels and attempting to identify with the words "gig economy"; they must redefine, reposition, and possibly reinvent their models. There are many studies available beyond this book that will complement your learning. Simply search for them online, and you will be led in great directions. Take the time to explore. We loved many of the studies initiated by ADP and Deloitte.

Here is what we found: The ultimate gig is what you decide it to be! The power of labor, and how we choose to participate, has been transferred to the crowd, and we will never be the same!

9

MAXIMIZING THE POTENTIAL
OF A GIG

Most independent contractors get started in their gig of choice because of one primary objective: Earning income in a flexible, fun, and rewarding manner. They often overlook the basic principles associated with managing a good business, but they do so unintentionally.

When examining gig opportunities, we consistently find diversity in age, experience, and motivations. Therefore, gig providers will benefit from providing the guidance that gig participants need to manage their time, money, and expenses effectively. When these activities and management fundamentals are in place, the gig worker should have greater confidence that the work will be meaningful and tangibly rewarding.

Both gig seekers and gig workers will benefit from using a planning process to maximize their potential success. This is no different from the methods used by anyone seeking to build a business successfully. In this chapter, you will find a gig planning guide that is a terrific place to start.

Independent contractors, (the participants in a gig), enjoy the flexibility and freedom to work when they want, and we have been describing the many advantages of gig work and why gig work has become so appealing. Simplicity is replacing complexity in many ways; however, this does not mean that basic business-building principles are abandoned in the new form of work. In fact, we advocate that basic business principles become an integral part of the new work.

Gig workers are entrepreneurs, or, more specifically, a subsegment called microentrepreneurs. Microentrepreneurship is typically defined as a business that costs less than $35,000.00 to start and brings in a revenue of less than $100,000.00 per year. With the emergence of the gig economy, we now have microentrepreneurs who have virtually no investment in start-up costs and incomes generally far less than $100,000.00 per year. Despite the low start-up costs, we suggest both gig workers and gig providers take these businesses seriously. We also acknowledge that temporary gig work will remain the goal of many participants. However, our research indicates that there is a high degree of work satisfaction among gig workers; therefore, the original decision may extend to a more serious way of earning income. By providing coaching and guidance, we believe that the outcome will be a more successful work experience for gig provider and gig participant, resulting in higher productivity, quality of service rendered, and longer lifetime value for gig provider, gig worker, and consumer.

We advocate that gig providers should ensure that gig workers understand fundamental principles and guidelines and make it clear that they are indeed independent contractors – microentrepreneurs, with flexibility and freedom in how they work, not eligible for employee benefits, and responsible for compliance with all regulatory requirements including the payment of appropriate taxes on income earned. Therefore, a few goal setting and planning guides along with adherence to a few basic business principles can, we believe, make a significant difference in the outcomes of any gig worker.

GIG WORK CAN MAKE DREAMS COME TRUE

The phrase "making dreams come true" is a phrase that often triggers thoughts about such possibilities as new cars, homes, exotic vacations, or other desires that typically require hundreds or thousands of dollars to attain. However, our research indicates that such a description as "make dreams come true" can be applied to a gig income-earning opportunity, even if the income levels are modest. People can achieve their dreams when they take small steps that accelerate their quest to strike the work–life balance they desire.

The core research team formed to develop the Ultimate Gig project is convinced that the gig economy offers the types of opportunities that can help many in our society achieve more of their short-term personal objectives through the incremental income they can earn. Earning a few more dollars per month may be what it takes for an individual to pay the bill that often gets pushed to a later date, add a new luxury or experience to the household budget that could be as simple as a special night out for dinner, or to save and invest more. A part-time gig that one can enjoy doing is often viewed as the equivalent of giving oneself a raise without the stress of waiting for the next performance appraisal or the anticipated "cost of living" salary increase related to a regular job.

We also acknowledge that more income does not necessarily mean more enjoyment of life unless there is a plan. It would not make sense to be earning $100,000.00, spending $100,000.00, take on a gig and receive an additional $5,000.00 to $10,000.00 and then spend all the $5,000 to $10,000.00. To work and live this way does not, logically, improve the quality of life, yet many Americans live this way. The financial stats we have offered in previous chapters support the assertion. However, saving or investing a significant portion of the incremental income that can be earned through gig work, and using it purposefully, might tip the scales positively.

The current median savings account balances are quite low, no matter which age segment of the US population you examine. Yet, people can achieve meaningful financial goals with modest increases in personal income when they save or invest a portion of the new revenue (Figs. 9.1 and 9.2).

We believe gig-providing companies can reap more profits from the products and services they are bringing to market when independent contractors receive the necessary guidance to help them maximize their potential for the time and effort they invest.

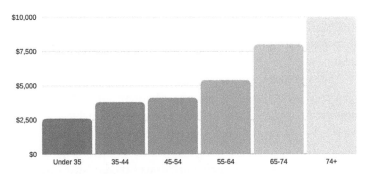

Source: Smart Assets smartasset.com.

Fig. 9.1. Median Savings Account Balances by Age.

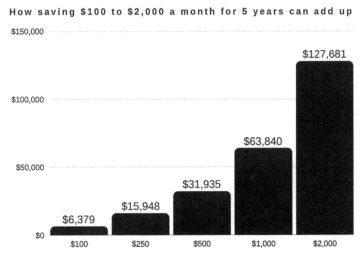

Fig. 9.2. The Compounding Effects of Increased Monthly Savings. *Note:*
The above calculations are based upon a 2.5% interest rate
compounded monthly.

Providing gig workers with planning support is just as important as
describing the gig. Our research discovered many gigs that require
workers to agree to a set of rules and policies. Still, we did not find
enough specific guidance on how to formulate a basic business plan.
This inspired us to provide more guidance on this subject later in
this chapter.

Business schools stress the importance of strategic plans. A tremendous amount of effort goes into the planning process in corporations, governments, and organizations all around the world each year. Often, organizations retain high-priced consultants whose only focus is to guide upper management through the planning process. It is doubtful that you will ever find a Fortune 500 company without an extremely detailed three- to five-year plan. In other words, no successful business will ignore the value of a well-thought-out and comprehensive plan for its operations for both the present and the future. We suggest that great principles and processes are not reserved for large businesses; they can be applied to the smallest of microenterprise – a gig. Direct selling models have generally provided some type of guidance to the new direct seller. How to generate sales is usually a part of the onboarding and ongoing training and development process. The more modern forms of gig opportunities have simplified microenterprise engagement; however, all models of gig work will benefit from providing more guidance without breaching the independent contractor relationship.

A successful income-earning opportunity is not based solely on sales and revenue generation. Everyone benefits from a clear understanding of the relationship between money earned and money spent. Making more than one spends is a fundamental principle of life that is foundational to the pursuit of a successful and rewarding outcome in any endeavor. Gig-providing companies that leverage the income-earning opportunities built upon flexibility and freedom in how work is done should not remove themselves from opportunities to contribute to the primary education that supports a more positive outcome for people who are investing their time and effort to achieve a better quality of life.

THE IMPORTANCE OF PLANNING

Teaching and coaching gig workers to understand the importance of planning should, we believe, be a prerequisite to doing the work or certainly complimentary to being able to maximize the potential of the work. Why shouldn't such guidance and suggestions be provided to every gig worker to help them more effectively optimize their potential? This type of advice would possibly increase success rates. Gig seekers and participants can find more information on this subject at the Ultimate Gig website, ultimategigresources.com.

There is another reason for our advocacy for encouraging planning. When we look at how we have worked from a historical perspective, we find that entrepreneurship declined from the beginning of the 1900s to date. As a society, we have gravitated toward a dependency on mega enterprises or corporations, which basically set the plans for workers through time requirements and job descriptions. In recent years, small businesses have provided more new employment than larger enterprises. The trends we see in the explosive growth of the gig economy could be contributing to what will be a very different type of workforce in the future, one in which entrepreneurship, once again, becomes more and more popular and possible for the average person.

While there are no guarantees for achieving success, understanding certain principles and concepts increases the odds. Doctors, teachers, auto mechanics, engineers, accountants, salespersons, gardeners, shopkeepers, clergy – you name the job, profession, or responsibility, and you will find a long list of white-collar and blue-collar workers who are working gigs. Regardless of past experience or inexperience, all gig workers will benefit from coaching and guidance. Simplicity can be maintained without adding complexity.

When we searched to find what type of guidance gig-providing companies were making available to gig workers to support maximizing the potential associated with the work, we found minimal and most often, no guidance. This is problematic because all work should be clearly defined. No business would hire a new employee without providing advice as to how the work should be done. Gig-providing companies are utilizing independent contractors, and some laws prevent the gig-providing company from setting expectations that interfere with the independent contractor's freedom to work when and how they desire. There can be no 9-to-5 type requirements or expectations as to how much time a person works or, specifically, how the work is done. However, there are always guidelines and best practices that support maximizing potential.

We share the following questions that gig providers and participants might consider using as a framework for a simple start-up plan. By answering such questions, the new gig worker would be starting with a clear understanding of why they have chosen to embrace a gig. This type of suggested start-up guide might enhance the motivation of the gig worker, help to clarify their expectations, and improve the satisfaction and success gained from work. The gig provider benefits as well.

Checklist of Questions to Support Quick Planning for Gig Workers

Note: We suggest the questions and responses be recorded via smartphone or notebook. By keeping a record of the questions and responses, the gig worker is developing a plan for success.

> ☐ Why do I desire to work a gig?
>
> ☐ Do I have the experience or skills I need?
>
> ☐ How much time will I invest, and when?
>
> ☐ What is the specific income goal?
>
> ☐ How will success be defined?
>
> ☐ Am I excited about doing the work?

Fig. 9.3. Checklist for Planning a Gig.

The above checklist (Fig. 9.3) can be expanded. The more detail an individual invests in the exercise, the higher the potential outcome. The preceding statement is our logical assumption; therefore, we were amazed when we did not find more specific guidance focused on supporting the individual and their successful outcome as a gig worker. Guidelines such as those proposed in our example do not interfere with laws and regulations that define independent contractors and the relationship with the company. A gig-providing company website could easily devote a section to "Our Guide to Support Your Success." Start-up guidance for every type of gig can also be simple and easy to design.

Suggested Start-Up Guidelines for Transportation, Service,
and Leasing Gigs

Daily checklist

☐ Only work when you are in a customer-friendly mood.

☐ Always present a professional presence.

☐ Always greet each customer cordially.

☐ Engage in cordial conversation when appropriate.

☐ Thank each customer for the pleasure of providing the service.

Fig. 9.4. Daily Checklist for Transportation, Service, and Leasing Gig Workers.

What would happen if each transportation gig provider driver followed such a list of suggestions? The quality of the effort might increase exponentially for both the company and the gig worker. The return on effort could impact the quality of service and lifetime value of both the gig worker and the customers served by the brand. Such a list is probably applicable to most gigs; however, as simple as a checklist can be, we did not find much guidance when researching several types of gigs (Figs. 9.4 and 9.5).

Suggested Start-Up Guidelines for Selling Gigs

Daily checklist

☐ Develop advocacy for the product or service through personal experience.

☐ Commit to a specific amount of prospecting time each day.

☐ Use company-branded scripts or tools for all prospecting efforts.

☐ Thank customers when they engage your products or services.

☐ Always seek referrals; satisfied customers are more likely to refer to others.

Fig. 9.5. Daily Checklist for Selling Gig Workers.

THE IMPORTANCE OF TIME MANAGEMENT

Gig workers who invest in a gig activity in addition to other activities such as a full-time job, caring for a family, or only working a few hours per week can benefit from scheduling their activities and managing their time wisely. To predict the amount of income a gig may yield, gig workers should determine the number of hours that will be invested in various activities associated with the gig. Gig workers will benefit from planning what specific days will be spent working the gig, the number of hours, and what times during the day. Daily, weekly, and monthly planning tools are easily accessible online. Depending on the detail desired, the tool selected should provide the ability to include all important responsibilities associated with the work and life balance. Sleep time is also important.

No business or organization would expect to operate without a plan as to how time will be managed. Time is considered one of our most precious assets. The gig economy provides opportunities to convert available hours into potential income, and gig workers will benefit from knowing exactly how much time they can realistically devote to the gig. Arbitrarily working a gig could lead to an attitude of "hoping" the gig will work versus planning to invest a consistent effort to ensure the gig provides a rewarding return on the time invested.

THE IMPORTANCE OF TRACKING EXPENSES

One of the first things many gig workers look at when starting a gig is revenue – that is, the money they receive for their work. Gig workers typically can start earning money quickly, which can be exciting because earning incremental income is the objective. However, if a gig worker fails to measure gig-related expenses, real income will be difficult to measure, and it will be difficult to tell if he or she has achieved a personal goal.

Gig workers may be amazed at what constitutes a legitimate expense when working their gig. For example, this book's purchase may qualify as a business expense if the purchase is related to gaining knowledge and understanding about the gig economy and the gig one has chosen. This is one small example of a much broader topic related to the responsibility of both the gig provider and the gig worker. Gig providers can help ensure that their gig workers use sound management principles and practices by making their gig workers aware. When gig workers choose part-time work as independent contractors for the first time, they may not understand the responsibilities associated with independent contractor status. In the United States, those who have only worked as an employee have been accustomed to receiving the familiar W-2 form, not the filing related to a 1099.

Delaying or improperly filing tax payments comes with stiff consequences. In addition to financial penalties, this often causes people to lose confidence in or motivation for their gig business venture. This lack of motivation can spiral downward, leading to premature abandonment of the income opportunity, an unfulfilling experience, and potentially, the loss of the very thing pursued: earning an income in a way that offers flexibility, freedom, and fair rewards for the work.

The good news is that technology, innovation, and creativity have provided tools that support income and expense management, and they are readily available. Some gig companies offer bookkeeping tools to their independent contractors at minimal costs or encourage their gig participants to seek the tools and services of simplified bookkeeping through one of the many apps now available. One need to only scroll an app store to discover a variety of systems. Most of these systems connect directly to bank accounts, credit, and debit cards, enabling the user to do what accountants once were required to do. These apps make it easy to track applicable business/gig related expenses, and the smartphone camera can be used to copy receipts when necessary. Accountants have not been eliminated from the process; however, the record-keeping tools available to gig workers have improved dramatically, making it much easier to prepare reports and tax filings quicker and more accurately. At the end of reporting periods, weekly, monthly, quarterly, and annually, detailed reports are no further than a click. Paying attention to recordkeeping and working in accordance with a plan increases the likelihood of not only successfully reaching the goals set, but greater confidence along with overachievement becoming a possibility.

EXCELLENT COMMUNICATION BENEFITS GIG PROVIDERS AND GIG WORKERS

The gig provider is challenged to communicate effectively with gig workers, and gig workers are challenged to communicate effectively with their customers when applicable. Transportation gigs set the standard by introducing tools that connected gig workers directly with customers. This form of communication changed the game, and the transportation sector has never been the same.

People also learn through communication, and this is another opportunity for gig providers, in particular, to explore. Historically, learning a new skill has required a significant investment of time into course work or hands-on training. Technology has changed the game in this area as well. We now live in a time when "instant" applies to almost everything we do. We can instantly find the weather report or the definition of a word. When driving, directions are easily accessed by just asking for directions, no need to put in the address manually. So, learning is often a shout away. "Hey, Google, tell me this. Siri, do this. Alexa, do this." And the list goes on.

Gig-providing companies, we predict, will begin to use technology to communicate more effectively when it comes to coaching or guiding gig workers without interfering with their independent contractor status. This will make the work even more attractive and more competitive. A motivational message could be sent each day to inspire the gig worker to look forward to a great day. Recognition might be extended for past performance; the ideas are limitless.

As reflected in Fig. 9.6, services like Quiq Messaging make communication and engagement with independent contractors and customers possible on the channels they prefer. Whether it is texting, web chat, Facebook Messenger, or several other channels, it is easy to share information.

We are communicating differently, and we are learning differently. No, differently than the customer who uses an app to arrange for transportation instead of using a telephone to call a dispatcher,

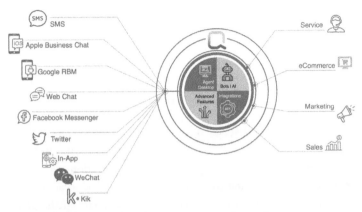

Source: Diagram created by Quiq Messaging. quiq.com/.
Fig. 9.6. Diagram of Digital Communication Tools.

customers shopping for products and services expect to communicate using the most-advanced systems technology can provide. Gig providers will be expected to provide the tools, and gig participants will expect to have the tools to support their businesses (Fig. 9.6).

Gig workers who have access to communication and information as diagrammed are more likely, we believe, to take their gig seriously and stay engaged for a more extended period. When a company uses multiple channels to communicate, it dramatically increases the chances the audience will receive the information – increasing the benefits to be derived by gig workers and their customers and impacting and supporting profitability for both the gig-providing company and the gig worker.

THE IMPORTANCE OF ADVOCATING PRINCIPLES AND VALUES

In our quest to find the right job, the right company, the right type of work to pursue, regardless of whether we are working for someone else or now exploring the many opportunities to work as a microentrepreneur, in our hearts and minds, we are subconsciously looking to align the principles and values associated with our work to what matters to us personally in life. We do not offer this position and advocacy to debate the value. We only share that it exists. It is seldom measured and quite often ignored when exploring the digital presence of companies.

During the days when I was working for Mies Van der Rohe, the world-renown architect, those of us working in the office had the pleasure, on occasion, to visit with Mies in his apartment. It was always after working hours and often on a Friday evening. We would sit around, on the floor, enjoying pizza and listening to one of the most influential architects of our time. You would think he talked mostly about designs, but it was mostly about philosophy, principles, and values. This is where I first learned the principle of "less is more." The principle is obviously in play when observing any building designed by Mies. What is not so obvious is the impact of the many principles we learned from Mies Van der Rohe that we have applied to our lives. The gig economy is a perfect example of a less is more philosophy in action. Less hassle, less stress, great products, and exceptional services made available to more people at a "click."

Another experience that profoundly impacted how I live and work may also be helpful to both the gig-providing companies and those who participate as gig workers. During my experience at Avon Products Inc., I became most impressed with the fact that vision and mission statements and principles guided the company, at least at that moment in time. *The Principles that Guide Avon* was presented to every officer in the company as a framed document. The principles that guided the company for more than 100 years are as meaningful today as they were many years ago. Our reason for sharing them in this book is directly related to the topic with which we started: *Maximizing the Potential of a Gig*. This chapter, as you now realize, applies to the gig worker, but it also applies to the gig-providing companies that offer income opportunities to independent contractors who are not bound by anything other than the performance of the work in an ethical manner. What is it that Avon, Amway, Mary Kay, Herbalife, and others provide their consultants and brand partners (all independent contractors) that serves to inspire and motivate them to do what they do? Here, we have another critical component of work that gig-providing companies can learn from direct selling companies: Remind those who are attracted to a particular gig opportunity that there is a purpose, a higher purpose, that is also a part of the brand with which one has chosen to affiliate.

Gig-providing companies will benefit from making their guiding principles very visible. If they do not exist, we suggest they be created and published. Your brand is about the products and services you sell and the people you serve. I chose the following example because I know the profound effect principles had on my life and the lives of those with whom I had the pleasure to work. Yes, I enjoyed a great career while at Avon Products Inc., but the principles changed my life. I also grew to believe in a philosophy that described "money" as being a result of the quality of the products and services rendered to the marketplace, not the cause.

The Principles that Guide Avon

To provide individuals with an opportunity to earn in support of their well-being and happiness.

To serve families throughout the world with products of the highest quality, backed by a guarantee of satisfaction.

To render a service to customers that is outstanding in its help-fulness and courtesy.

To give full recognition to employees and Avon Representatives, on whose contribution Avon depends.

To share with others the rewards of growth and success.

To meet the obligations of corporate citizenship entirely by contributing to the well-being of society and the environment in which it functions.

To maintain and cherish the friendly spirit of Avon.

David McConnell, the founder of Avon, incorporated the above principles into his business philosophy. The company was founded in 1886 and remains a brand recognized throughout many countries in the world 135 years later. Many other companies throughout the world are known for their principles and values as much as the products and services they make available. Principles and values can maximize performance. I committed to winning in work and life because I knew that I believed in principles and values beyond the opportunity to earn an income. This advocacy of principles and values will serve any company, especially gig-providing companies that depend on independent contractors, to build micro- and macroenterprises. When we believe in principles and values that guide us, we aspire to be good at what we do and better than we may have imagined. It is part of the secret sauce of companies that become legacy companies. Avon did become, at one time, the largest salesforce on the planet. Women from all walks of life were attracted, not solely by the products or the income opportunity, but by the principles and values that guided the company. Gig-providing companies can learn from this example, and gig workers can create their own principles and values if the company does not provide them. We have given you a guide. Principles and values are important!

THE IMPORTANCE OF ADOPTING A STRONG CODE OF ETHICS

A strong code of ethics is vital to every company. It serves as an essential guide for those who participate in work as independent contractors. Regulatory agencies expect to see an ethical code in place and integral to any agreement between a gig-providing company and an independent contractor. The gig-providing company is challenged to monitor and effectively manage adherence. Few realize that Amazon has an equal or higher number of independent contractors compared to their substantial employee base of close to 1 million. The independent contractors are referred to as Affiliates, and they promote the Amazon brand on blogs and websites for a commission on the purchases of customers they refer to Amazon. There are precise guidelines the affiliates must adhere to, and any misrepresentation or violation of their policies can lead to immediate termination of the relationship. Amazon has a reputation for not tolerating violations. This policy has been a brand builder for Amazon, resulting in the exponential promotion of the brand in a more personal manner.

INSIGHTS AND UNEXPECTED LEARNING

Maximizing the potential outcomes associated with gig work is dependent not only upon company guidance but also personal. With or without company guidance, gig workers will add value and potential to their efforts by focusing on serving customers' adhering to basic business building fundamentals. We have shared many business-building concepts in other chapters within this book. We believe gig work can be the link between creating a personal difference in the process by which companies serve consumers. The human link in the chain can be the strongest link especially when a human is the final link before the customer experience.

Direct selling companies, especially the legacy brands, emphasize the importance of culture and community and usually reveal their mission, purpose, principles, and values. When such guidance is provided, the independent contractor embraces the flexibility and freedom desired while gaining a sense of belonging to a community. Retention, self-confidence, and a sense of belonging to a community may increase lifetime value. Some gig-providing companies can undoubtedly enhance the value of what they currently offer by paying attention to what direct selling companies have focused on for the past 100 years.

Few business models focus on the personal development of the individual, which is a term related to education and learning beyond traditional and formal education and learning. Because we believe what credible research is stating: The gig economy is a labor revolution; we also advocate a stronger focus on the personal development of the gig worker. Gig workers will represent major brands and create brands of their own. They will often be the human link between the source of supply, client, and consumer purchasing. Gig workers who are motivated to perform at a high service standard, who build relationships with the consumers they serve, will also build consumer trust. This results in added value to the brands they affiliate or create, providing consumers with potentially the best products and services ever!

The personal growth and development of the gig worker should be considered as a critical component of the gig-providing company strategy. Personal growth and development are added value to the entrepreneurial spirit that attracts the gig seeker and gig worker. Gig-providing companies will be smart to better understand what motivates human behavior outside of traditional learning formats. Providing such guidance is not rocket science. The prerequisite is an awareness of the importance.

We provide an example of a short course in personal development that is another guide that companies can build upon. Gig workers will find the following guidance added value to how they are approaching current work and, most importantly, how they think about themselves and their possibilities.

A SHORT COURSE IN PERSONAL DEVELOPMENT

The One Course, *copyright 2008, authored by John Fleming and first published by SUCCESS Media in print format in 2008, is a foundational guide to how a life can be planned. Concepts and principles taught in* The One Course *were gained from the author's personal experiences and remain as relevant today as they were when first recorded and captured in writing by the author.*

No matter which path you choose in the way you select and work a gig, there are five critical areas of your life for which you must assume full responsibility. Those areas are your attitude, your health, your faith, your relationships, and your finances. While parents, teachers, and mentors can offer guidance and support, it is ultimately up to you to focus on these areas to create a solid foundation for the rest of your life, enabling achievement of the goals and aspirations you develop.

During my life, I have often relied on my architectural education and experience to guide me in building a successful life. Buildings are always the result of excellent design and adherence to basic principles of construction. Think about how a house, skyscraper, or football stadium is built. There is a science to the planning and development of any such project. Buildings must meet stringent tests of engineering principles and formulas to ensure they will withstand the elements. Ultimately, plans are developed, and construction begins. What we see in finished buildings and structures is the result of many successful processes that have been executed to perfection.

Like architecture, life is a science. In the process of designing the life we want to live, we, too, must follow time-tested principles for creating solid foundations. The selection of a gig opportunity may open a door for you to learn more about yourself, your self-confidence, self-esteem, commitment to goal setting, and planning. You are about to open a new door, as a gig seeker, participant, or microentrepreneur. You could be opening a new door to a new future. You are about to make choices that will impact your life for many years to come. This section of our book is devoted to you, the gig seeker, and the participant. It will show you how to think through some of life's fundamentals to make the best decisions possible. Most importantly, when you complete this portion of this chapter, you will be better prepared for whichever path you take, whatever gig you select.

Now is the time to prepare for your future, or the better phrase might be: Now is the time to design your future because it is always coming faster than we think. When an architect designs a building, the completion of the design enables the beginning of the construction process, and so it is with life. Good designs can be constructed. Poor designs are never built. It is possible to be the architect of your destiny.

If you are going to be the architect of your destiny, you must take responsibility for your attitude, health, faith, relationships, and finances. And often, what you do now may go unnoticed by your family, friends, teachers, or employers. However, these are critical elements for laying the foundation of your life and maximizing your gig's potential.

MANAGING LIFE

In simplest terms, creating a successful life is about managing the small details that might not seem so necessary to the overall picture – things like how much effort we put into the preparation for a task, how we interact with people, how we choose what we eat, and how we manage what money we have.

Managing the small details is what will ultimately determine the magnitude of success in life. Ludwig Mies van der Rohe, was known for saying that "God is in the details." He meant that the attention paid to the small details brings big dividends and big rewards. And if you can monitor and manage the small details in your life, you will see big rewards.

MANAGING YOUR MENTAL HEALTH

Has anyone ever told you that you have a bad attitude? You have most likely heard that phrase at one time or another from your parents, teachers, or even friends. Bad attitudes are just that – bad. They are bad for the people around you, who must cope with your negativity, and they are, more importantly, bad for you.

There is no such thing as a negative success!

The law of physics will tell you that positive energy and negative energy cannot occupy the same space. The same holds for your attitude. Positive and negative thoughts cannot coexist. To be successful at anything – whether you are taking an exam, learning a new skill at your job, or simply playing a new video game, working your gig – you must maintain a positive attitude. Always.

That might not seem so simple when you are faced with a challenging situation. But here is a sports-related example of how positive thinking can overcome seemingly insurmountable odds.

In Super Bowl LI, the New England Patriots were trailing the Atlanta Falcons 28-3 at halftime. By the start of the fourth quarter, the score was 28-6. No team had ever come back from such a large deficit. Most teams would have folded and accepted the inevitable. But not Tom Brady and the Patriots. They knew they had the tools to win. They knew they had to only play smarter and harder if they were to take home another Lombardi trophy. So, they remained positive and played on. And just a few minutes into overtime, they won the game, marking the greatest comeback in NFL history.

Maintaining a positive mental attitude can help you win games; it can help you overcome roadblocks that would stop most people in their tracks. That includes the negativity brought on by personal or professional rejection, physical limitations, failure, financial status, or disparaging remarks from others. Here are a few examples:

> *J.K. Rowling's first book was rejected by 12 publishing houses. That book, Harry Potter and the Philosopher's Stone, began the phenomenally successful series of fantasy books that are now the bestselling book series in history.*

> *Franklin D. Roosevelt was partially paralyzed from the waist down at the age of 39; 12 years later, he became our 32nd president, leading the country through the Great Depression and the early years of World War II.*

> *The inventor Thomas Edison was said to have made 1,000 unsuccessful attempts at creating a light bulb; when he finally succeeded, he remarked, "I haven't failed. I've just found 1,000 ways not to make a lightbulb."*

> *Liz Murray, the daughter of drug-addicted parents, was left homeless at age 15 but was determined to graduate from an Ivy League school; she graduated from Harvard University.*

The point is: Successful people remain positive no matter the odds against them. They see possibilities where others do not, and they take advantage of opportunities to learn from failures or negative comments or actions. Imagine what the world would be missing right now if Bill Gates and Steven Jobs had dwelt on their academic failures; if Steven Spielberg had given up his aspiration to be a movie director when he was denied entry into USC; if Oprah Winfrey had listened to all the people who told her she would amount to nothing. Not everyone you know is excited about the possibilities you envision for what you can accomplish with your gig. The most important person is you! You must believe in yourself!

To train your brain to think positive, consider these activities:

- Invest in personal development books or audiobooks that explain how to cultivate a positive mental attitude.

- Make a list of weekly goals and review them daily to reinforce a positive attitude.

- Avoid TV programming that presents negative attitudes about people and life in general.

- Read one inspirational book a month.

Reading is key to create a positive attitude. The person who reads one inspirational book each month, whether a biography or self-help book, is feeding his or her mind 11 times more than the person who reads only one book a year. When you read each day, you feed your mind with positive nourishment. This impacts what we refer to as "self-talk," which is essential to managing our attitude. Like our bodies, our minds need nourishment everyday. This component of life will have a profound impact on the outcomes you achieve in working your gig.

MANAGING YOUR PHYSICAL HEALTH

Can you imagine the swimmer Michael Phelps heading to the Olympics in anything less than the top physical condition? Or basketball star LeBron James not exercising in the off-season? How about a mountain climber scaling Mount Everest without first conditioning their body for the elements, or a marathon runner forgoing continuous training and attempting to run the race without preparation? None of that would make sense, would it? To achieve greatness, to give their personal best, athletes must continuously train and focus on physical conditioning.

Conditioning is also crucial for your success. Just as you feed your brain the right nutrition for a positive attitude, you must develop good habits when it comes to feeding your body. You must manage your nutritional intake, the amount of exercise you engage during the week, and yes – you must manage your weight. Your body is a precious asset, and you need it to be in peak performance condition for this one reason alone:

> *There is no such thing as a positive mental attitude in a tired body!*

If you do not have the energy required to achieve the goals you have set for yourself, how will you ever make your dreams come true? How will you manage to stay alert when working your gig? How will you put in the hours needed to accomplish a project if you lack the nutrition your body needs? How will you balance your work with your personal life if you are just plain too tired to do anything? When we do not leverage our experience and desire for more enjoyment, we could easily pass up the opportunity to work a gig and achieve more out of the great gift of life. We cannot work when we are tired.

The primary objective of your life should be to eat healthy foods that will sufficiently nourish your body and engage in some form of exercise. What we put into our bodies should be the nourishment we need to move through the day – not the sugar fix we want or the comfort food that will make us feel better. Regularly consuming fast food or processed foods will not allow our bodies to remain alert and energetic. If we do not exercise regularly, we will not have the stamina needed to get as much as possible out of each day. Eating healthy is important, and so is food supplementation. Good nutritional supplements provide assurance that we are getting balanced nutrition into our diets each day.

MANAGING YOUR BELIEF SYSTEM

Spirituality is the personal relationship between you and the god of your understanding. While your success in life is not dependent on participation in a church, mosque, synagogue, or other faith-based organization, it has been observed that most successful individuals have a strong belief system.

The sad truth is that, as you go through life, people will disappoint you. Even men and women with great qualities possess imperfections – moments of anger, hurt, or jealousy that are released and unfairly directed at others. You probably have had those moments as well. We all have. It is human nature to express our emotions, whether good or bad. We sometimes cannot grasp why these moments happen, why bad things happen to good people, why those we love are taken from us too soon, and why some people suffer as they do. Why the things we want in life never come to fruition.

To be successful in life, *you must believe in yourself.* Faith in your abilities and your contributions to the world is the stepping-stone to success. Without it, you may succeed; however, with it, you will achieve more than you can probably imagine right now. Your belief in yourself and the spiritual beliefs of your choosing can serve to protect you from those happenings in life that you cannot control from the newscast to the possibility of being exposed to the cynical attitudes of those around you. You will find it more difficult to overcome your current situation, whatever it may be, and move on to become the architect of your destiny. A strong belief system will enable you to be in better control of your most precious and personal asset: your mind.

MANAGING YOUR SOCIAL RELATIONSHIPS

As you head into your future, managing your social relationships becomes a critical aspect of your journey to success.

> *Your social relationships will either negatively or positively impact your ability to achieve your goals.*

What does that mean exactly? Social relationships fall into two categories: *socializing*, as with your friends, and *networking*. Socializing is important. We need that downtime to have fun and enjoy activities that we do not often have the chance to do. However, socializing can be a barrier to success if (1) you are always surrounded by negative people, and (2) if it is engaged too frequently without purpose.

Does that mean you must choose your friends wisely? In a sense, yes, it does. Your friends most likely exert some influence on you. It could be their comments on your clothes, your choice of work, or your physical attributes. Do you have friends that tease you? That teasing might be done in jest, but subconsciously their words may be planting seeds of negativity within you – seeds of doubt that you can accomplish what you want to do.

Think of your circle of friends. Who in that circle can you point to as one who has your back, who is there to support you no matter the occasion? Is it one friend? Two? None? Most people *think* they have a lot of friends. However, the friendships they have do not translate into positive, supportive relationships. In your circle, can you name five good friends whom you truly love, for whom you would do anything, who genuinely love you and would do anything for you? If not, then it might be time to redraw that circle and redefine your definition of friendship to include the quality of the relationship versus time spent.

That may sound harsh, especially if you have long-standing friendships. Still, you must surround yourself with supportive people who will buy into your plan for the future, who can look at the vision you have created for your life and wholeheartedly pledge their support. It may be that those friends might have other social connections that can help you along the way. And that is where networking comes into play.

You live in an age with unparalleled opportunities to instantly connect with people from all walks of life, from all corners of the world. The generations preceding yours spent years cultivating networks of people who could assist in their personal endeavors. You can now use social platforms and apps that can instantly connect you to people anywhere. There are no geographical barriers.

When we strive to build relationships through networking, we expand our network of resources and potential support. We make it possible to learn from others. In social settings, be conscious of the people there and who you can possibly meet through them. In doing so, you will develop a social network that is loaded with strong relationships and subject matter experts who have mastered their professions. Then, when challenged with difficult situations and problems, you will be able to contact someone who can offer advice on your dilemma immediately. Someone else may have already experienced a similar challenge, and the coaching they may be able to share will be based upon experience.

Having such networking resources that can help you solve problems and overcome challenges means less stress and confidence for you. That type of support can make a vast difference between a situation you quickly overcome or a situation that overwhelms you. Gig workers should remember that there is always someone else who has done or still doing what you have decided to do.

MANAGING YOUR FINANCIAL ASSETS

Let us examine some facts about the society in which we live. The basic needs of humans are food, water, clothing, and shelter. Without these essentials, we would be forced into despair, malnutrition, homelessness, and possibly severe mental and physical illness. We cannot exist as human beings without these basic needs being met. Therefore, we need money to obtain them.

With that said, let us add a word of caution about money: Do not ever buy into the concept that money is the root of all evil, or that love is more important than money. The lack of money can cause people to become evil, and love, no matter how strong, usually does not last when there is a shortage of available funds.

Money impacts every aspect of our lives, from what we eat to the clothing and shelter we have – all necessities for healthy, stress-free living.

You are looking at selecting a gig or working a gig because you are interested in earning more income on your terms. We are motivated to seek ways to make more because we need more, or we desire more. A few words of caution: Paying off debts may be a primary motivator for working a gig. If this is a motivator, one of the great lessons of life may lie behind this motivator. Credit can be the culprit that robs you of a successful life. By embracing the use of credit, you are embracing debt; and when you embrace debt to engage in necessities, food, clothing, entertainment, you become easily hooked. Credit is like a drug. Once you try it, you become a regular user. Two excellent sources of information are: buildfinancialfoundation.com/ and easethesqueeze.net/

> *Your credit card is not saving you from emergencies; it is creating them.*

Here is a startling truth: If you have $10,000 in credit card debt and make minimum payments each month (with no additional charges added to the card), it will take you 22 years to pay off the credit card. And in those 22 years, that debt will affect your ability to buy a car, buy a home, or obtain a personal loan. It could even impact your employment opportunities as employers now review financial data on prospects.

The point is, when it comes to managing your financial assets, be smart. Think of your future. Once you understand credit and debt, you will realize the importance of managing the financial part of your life. Then, you can begin your wealth accumulation plan. Wealth accumulation starts with a basic principle: Earn more than you spend. You must "cut the garment according to the cloth," which means you cannot spend what you do not have.

Along with credit/debit and wealth accumulation, there is another aspect of finance that you must embrace to secure a prosperous future: savings. You may have possibly heard the adage, "It is never how much you earn, but what you do with what you have." Sadly, most Americans are not taught the power of saving money early enough in life. You can easily assess a savings calculator online that will quickly calculate the result of your savings habits over a specified period. Knowing the power of savings will serve to be an excellent motivator as to why you are working your gig.

Just to be clear, we are not talking about smart investments, only smart savings.

BE THE ARCHITECT

Fig. 9.7. Architecting Your Life.

We have now examined five critical areas associated with managing our most precious asset, our life. We can summarize the five areas as components, and we can chart them into the familiar organizational chart as shown above, or we can visualize each component as links in a chain. When you apply each of the five basic areas to your life, you will realize that any weakness in one can quickly nullify your ability to achieve mastery over managing yourself. When we visualize each component being linked together instead of depicted in a typical organizational chart, we also realize that a chain is no stronger than its weakest link.

Being the architect of your destiny requires discipline and attention to detail (Fig. 9.7). It is your responsibility to ensure that each area of your life is healthy and sound. Continually inspect each area for weaknesses and make the necessary changes to guarantee that your future vision can become your reality. As a micro-entrepreneur, you can control the controls in your life. You have the flexibility to work as you desire and the freedom to set your goals as you wish. You are also responsible for managing your most important asset – yourself.

Be the architect of your destiny.

10

A PERSPECTIVE ON CHALLENGES
AND ETHICS

No matter how significant any aspect of life and work might be, there will always be challenges to face and overcome. Because the gig economy has grown in size and appeal so rapidly, it is causing policymakers to reexamine laws and regulations that were written to support and protect a very different labor force than what exists today. To help us understand the changing landscape, we invited an attorney – Kerry Tassopoulos, Tassopoulos Law Firm – who has an extensive background in corporate government relations in support of independent contractors to contribute to this chapter. His view is very candid, insightful, and informative.

The future of the gig economy and the laws applicable to independent workers were dramatically affected by two significant occurrences in 2020: the implementation of California Assembly Bill 5 and the aftermath of the COVID-19 pandemic. On January 1, 2020, employers in California faced the unenviable task of complying with a stricter standard in proving that a worker was an employee and not an independent contractor. Then, in March 2020, elected officials from Washington, DC, to state capitols quickly passed laws to stabilize the US economy by providing unprecedented economic support to millions of unemployed workers, in numbers that rivaled the Great Depression. The aftermath of these two events, combined with increased reliance on technology platforms, will impact workers' economic livelihood for decades to come and require a radical assessment of the laws and regulations that apply to the gig economy. New definitions of what it means to be an independent worker and further understanding among all stakeholders are needed.

Employment laws in the United States have typically focused on the employer/employee relationship. One example is the federal Fair Labor Standards Act of 1938, which was enacted to ensure employers properly addressed undesirable workplace issues such as child labor, low wages, and unpaid overtime. This legislation heralded the federal government intervention in the employer/employee relationship – some would argue in a paternalistic approach. In subsequent years, additional federal and state regulations were created, focused on either worker protections or employer rights. However, these laws now appear untenable as both employers and workers face an environment where a change in the way we work occurs more rapidly than ever.

Black's Law Dictionary defines an independent contractor as someone who is entrusted with undertaking a specific project but is left free to assign work and choose the method for accomplishing it. Conversely, it defines an employee as someone who works in the service of another person (the employer) under an express or implied contract of hire. The employer has the right to control the details of the work performed.

The foreseeable future will see continued unrest for workers caught in the turbulence of job elimination, life-threatening diseases, an aging population, and technological changes. The marketplace is responding by offering alternatives to the either/or predicament of employee/independent contractor in the form of opportunities to join the ranks of gig workers, roles in which people exert control over their time and income. This is not new. It has been traditionally seen in industries such as construction, real estate, sales, and professions, such as accounting and law. However, as salaried and hourly jobs shrink and the employee benefits of health insurance, pension or retirement instrument, vacations, etc., disappear, gig workers will expect similar access to traditional benefits, only in a different form but at realistic levels of investment.

At every level, policymakers must also deal with the reality that the either/or of employee/independent contractor may no longer be sufficient. Creating a new classification may be needed. Future evaluations of the challenges may impact the way taxes are generated and paid and how benefits might be addressed during the unexpected loss of income-earning opportunities. How much flexibility and control will independent workers have, and will their time and efforts be monitored by their gig-providing company? Many other issues will require an evaluation of the future of work.

In today's environment, the most successful approach is, perhaps, found in the direct selling model. Through direct selling, a gig worker can earn income; work when and how they choose; and benefit from the development of knowledge, experience, and skills transferable to other professional and nonprofessional endeavors. Direct selling companies are generally well experienced in engaging, supporting, and developing independent contractors without interfering with the guidelines and regulations relative to an employee versus independent contractor status.

In December 2015, Cornell University's Seth D. Harris and Princeton University's Alan B. Krueger shared a discussion paper as part of the Hamilton Project that proposed a new "independent worker" category. They suggested that independent workers work with an intermediary company that matches workers to customers. These workers have the flexibility to choose when they work, but, unlike pure independent contractors, they have to adhere to some intermediary company restrictions. The intermediary may set the fee structure, for example, or retain the right to refuse a worker access to the platform.

The proposal also called for this new class of workers to have the right to organize and collectively bargain, civil rights protections, tax withholdings, and employer contributions to payroll taxes. The gig company intermediaries would be allowed to pool independent workers to purchase and provide insurance or other benefits without having the workers be considered employees. Independent workers would not gain rights associated with hourly work, such as overtime or minimum wages. They would not have access to unemployment benefits.

Perhaps this was the impetus for enacting California Assembly Bill 5, popularly known as the "gig worker bill," a piece of legislation signed into law by Governor Gavin Newsom in

September 2019. This law codifies a ruling made in a case that reached the California Supreme Court in 2018, *Dynamex Operations West, Inc. v. Superior Court of Los Angeles*. The California Supreme Court overturned the longtime "Borello" test. It determined that a strict interpretation of the three-pronged "ABC" test was required to classify workers as employees or independent contractors. This test assumes that workers are employees unless the company that hires them can prove that the worker is free to perform services without the control or direction of the company; the worker is performing work tasks that are outside the usual course of the company's business activities; or the worker is customarily engaged in an independently established trade, occupation, or business of the same nature as that involved in the work performed.

The Dynamex approach created fear throughout the California economy, as businesses that had operated profitably in the past by using independent contractors would now be faced with the choice of hiring those workers, with the increased cost and administrative burden, or reducing the size and operation of their business. Specifically, if employers begin classifying gig workers as employees, they would be entitled to a minimum wage, expense reimbursements, employee benefits, rest breaks, and the other benefits for employees under California state law. In that sense, the bill creates a level playing field between those working in the gig economy and those hired as regular employees. The preceding was the perception of those who supported the bill.

The Dynamex decision was lauded by supporters of workers (such as labor unions) to protect against arbitrary firings, reductions in benefits, and arbitrary employee practices. However, the unintended consequence of the decision and Assembly Bill 5 was to turn the world of the independent contractor upside down. As is often the case, elected officials worked to pass the legislation without understanding how many sectors of the California economy would be affected. While the new law does not forbid the use of contract labor, the resultant obligation on employers to prove the status of its human resource has resulted in widespread job losses for freelance writers, photographers, sign language interpreters, and other moderate-income Californians who could not carve out exemptions for their particular industries. Other states, including New Jersey, New York, and Pennsylvania, are considering the enactment of similar laws. The likelihood that states across the country could enact similar legislation is considered rather high at this moment. It should be watched closely by gig-providing platforms.

Whether Congress will now address the independent worker/gig economy issue remains to be seen. Leaders in the US Senate and the House of Representatives realize that economic stability must occur in an environment that is future focused. As Sen. Mark Warner (D-VA) noted in 2019,

> *Changes in the nature of work mean that Americans are more likely to change jobs and be engaged in non-traditional forms of work than they were a generation ago – but our federal policies haven't kept up with those economic shifts. We can't and shouldn't try to regulate our economy into looking like it did 50 years ago, but we can and must do a far better job than we've been doing to prepare workers for economic shifts and changes in the nature of work. If we want to grow our economy and expand opportunity, Congress must take steps to increase access to skills training and support workers with access to flexible, portable benefits that carry from job to job.*

The impact of COVID-19 and the postpandemic world has prompted a bipartisan effort to address employee benefits' portability. As a result of tremendous job losses, Congresswoman Suzan DelBene (WA-01) and Senator Mark Warner of Virginia introduced a legislative proposal to establish an emergency portable benefits fund for states. Their plan would create a $500 million fund at the US Department of Labor to be administered to states. It will pay for the costs of modernizing state unemployment insurance technology systems and to create portable benefits programs. The Coronavirus Aid, Relief, and Economic Security Act is a recent example in the United States This new proposal would provide supplemental funds for states to update their unemployment systems for the twenty-first century to support long-term innovation and expanded eligibility.

The growth of the gig economy has revealed many issues that will need to be resolved moving forward. We have discussed a few in this chapter. We expect new rules and new regulations to become an ongoing conversation. We should expect this with any form of a business model that attracts those interested in income opportunities. While we may often feel that some types of business models have become overregulated, a concern with the gig economy is a lack of oversight. For example, Airbnb has led many property owners to now let out their spaces to short-term visitors. In effect, they have become freelance hotel operators. They do not have to adhere to the same laws or regulations applicable to hotels. Likewise, the widespread popularity of ridesharing has been dampened by reports of unregulated drivers assaulting passengers. These concerns are expected. They will trigger the right balance of regulation and support for much-needed flexibility in the way work can be done and assets shared and utilized to create income opportunities; therefore, the question is: How will these concerns play out?

It is helpful to review times when other new ways of doing business emerged. The franchise model has become very popular. Many business models use the franchise model to expand and grow the brand. The franchisor licenses business knowledge and proven experience to the franchisee, who is willing to pay specific fees for this intellectual property. The franchisees also agree to conform to guidelines and policies, all designed to protect the overall brand. As franchising grew in popularity and acceptance in the 1950s and 1960s, it began to attract the attention and scrutiny of regulatory agencies. Ultimately, the examination by consumer-focused organizations and regulatory agencies led to greater acceptance and greater use of the business model by more companies. Franchising is now a robust form of entrepreneurship that has changed the way consumers purchase many products and services.

The real estate industry is another example of a business model that utilizes independent contractors almost exclusively. It, too, faced regulatory scrutiny in years past, and we can clearly understand why. To be able to buy, sell, or trade real estate is one of the freedoms we now experience in free societies throughout the world. But that was not always the case. Such transactions as buying, selling, or trading real estate was once reserved for tribal leaders, kings, queens, and the selected few who became known as land-lords. Today, we have the power and opportunity to own our own homes, and this power has changed the way we live and the value we place on real estate ownership. This freedom to pursue owner-ship of land and structures had to be scrutinized and eventually regulated to protect the masses.

As in franchising, the regulatory oversight of the real estate industry led to vast improvements in the model. Regulatory authorities now license real estate agents. There are currently about 1.5 million to 2.0 million real estate agents representing more than $400 billion in transactional revenue per year.

The direct selling model has been under heightened regulatory scrutiny in recent years. The most damaging effect on the credibility of the direct selling business model is the occasional accusation of the model being a pyramid scheme. This accusation occurs when companies, posing as legitimate direct selling organizations, mislead prospective salespeople through recruiting practices where the premium is put on bringing more people into the company without an understanding that customer acquisition and retention are fundamental to building any form of business. Presentations that hypothesize what it may be like to build a large organization composed of other direct sellers sponsored directly and indirectly are being monitored carefully. From our perspective, authentic direct selling can be an excellent gig choice. A direct seller benefits from the aggregation of customers whom they acquire and retain as frequent shoppers and also benefits from the opportunity to engage others who also engage as direct sellers and replicate the same behaviors.

Compensation plans are considered an asset for direct selling companies and possibly a challenge for others. Complexity in the design of compensation plans often leads to misunderstanding, especially when reviewed by regulatory agencies. Simplicity and a "less-is-more" approach to design will support further reinvention and repositioning of a unique gig model. No different than the regulatory scrutiny applied to any other business model, direct selling companies will learn at a faster rate how to refine and, in some cases, redesign and reposition their models to ensure a clear understanding of how products and services are marketed and sold through independent contractors and ensuring a superb experience for consumers, independent contractors, and the company.

As we now realize, no business model is a panacea. The business challenges associated with a business model should not deter a quest to seek and find pathways that can offer solutions and the attainment of goals and pursuits. The gig economy is a new label applied to the importance of free enterprise concepts reduced to microenterprise opportunities that are forever changing the way we can work. The choices are many. The participants are the new pioneers who will, through experience, success, and failure, find ways to improve upon concepts that were hardly imagined or considered 20 short years ago. We have seen disruption initiated by gig models, and we will see more.

A PERSPECTIVE ON ETHICS

The growing market of products and services provided through gig economy platforms will require gig-offering companies to lead by their example as to the ethical standards expected of gig workers. Currently, it is difficult to find one set of definitions when looking to define the gig economy. The many labels being used and offered by academics who are beginning to conduct research, the community of business journalists and observers, and those responsible for regulation are often quite different and sometimes confusing. There is a need for collaboration and consensus. No different than any other business model, the gig economy, as a channel of distribution, will also attract those who use the model to avoid the regulations associated with a traditional business. Circumventing regulations, or finding ways to avoid compliance with regulations, and any exploitation of profit objectives in circumvention of regulations, will be detrimental to the overall good that both workers and consumers experience from this new method of connecting a product or service with a consumer need, cost-effectively and conveniently.

Ethics plays an essential role in building sustainable business models that contribute to the public good. Many businesses face challenges when it comes to agreeing to, adopting, and enforcing a specific ethical standard. The book *Business Ethics,* written by

Dr. Robert A. Peterson, the University of Texas at Austin, and Dr. O.C. Ferrell, the James T. Pursell, Sr. Eminent Scholar in Ethics and Director of the Center for Ethical Organizational Cultures at Auburn University, explores this perspective. As a precursor to the book, the professors organized a symposium on behalf of the School of Business at Colorado State University and the McCombs School of Business at the University of Texas at Austin that brought together internationally recognized business leaders, outstanding leaders of nonprofit organizations, and distinguished academics, including professors, philosophers, and university administrators. One of the perspectives, shared in the book *Business Ethics*, seems very appropriate today. Professor Patricia Werhane, the Wicklander Chair of Business Ethics and Director, Institute for Business and Professional Ethics at DePaul University, and Professor Emerita at the Darden School of Business, the University of Virginia, said:

> *Moral imagination, coupled with systems thinking, is necessary to understand, evaluate, and institute structural, organizational, and individual change. Organizations, institutions, and political economies are dynamic and revisable phenomena, created and changed by individuals. Only when the complexity of the systemic interrelationships is understood can the issues in question be successfully evaluated and changes made that are critical for the moral progress.*

In the same book, Ferrell stated:

> *Societal norms require that businesses assume responsibility to ensure that ethical standards are properly implemented on a daily basis. Such a requirement is not without controversy. Some business leaders believe that personal moral development and character are all that are needed for effective organizational ethics. These business leaders are supported by certain business educators who believe that ethics initiatives should arise inherently from corporate culture and that hiring ethical employees will limit unethical behavior within the organization. A contrary position, and the one*

espoused here, is that effective organizational ethics can be achieved only when proactive leadership provides employees from diverse backgrounds with a common understanding of what is defined as ethical behavior through formal training, thus creating an ethical organizational climate. In addition, changes are needed in the regulatory system, in the organizational ethics initiatives of business schools, and in the societal approaches to the development and implementation of organizational ethics in corporate America.

What we find to be most interesting in reading this book is the fact that it was published in 2009. Reading the book provides a feeling that the issues discussed and referenced are the issues we can expect to become even more important in a new labor economy where the majority of workers are in independent contractor status, not employee status. Everything mentioned in this book on ethics is considered 10x as important today. As Peterson notes later in the book in reference to Ferrell and the importance of ethics:

the complex, obtuse, and multifaceted nature of corporate ethics programs suggests the need for formal, structured ethics audits, similar to financial audits, management audits, and marketing audits, to sort out and investigate the explicit and implicit components and their elements. Unless the interrelationships and relative importance of the respective component elements are understood and appropriately managed, no corporate ethics program or ethics initiatives will be successful.

Gig providers must pay attention to the publishing and even marketing of a commitment to high ethical standards. In the employer/employee relationship, it might be easy to treat ethics as a training program conducted by the human resources department from time to time. In the gig economy, there is no human resources department, only independent contractors, and microentrepreneurs whose activities will reflect on and shape the corporate brands they represent. This new form of work deserves serious attention from all involved.

In our research, we reviewed many commercial and corporate websites of those who were making gigs possible. We found many great examples, and most notable was Etsy and the detail provided. This is another area where the direct selling model can be a benchmark because of its many years and experience with embracing independent contractors as the primary channel of distribution. Direct selling companies are supported by Direct Selling Associations that are members of the World Federation of Direct Selling Associations. This Washington, DC–based organization was founded in 1978 and advocates for a robust code of ethics among its members. This type of global guidance could be a model for gig-providing companies to pursue. These associations and organizations also offer a more formal way to negotiate with stakeholders, such as investors, suppliers, workers, consumers, and regulatory organizations, and provide an avenue to collectively conduct research in support of the channel.

INSIGHTS AND UNEXPECTED LEARNING

When we decided to create a chapter on challenges, we knew this perspective would be valuable. We also learned that embracing challenges is critical to innovation and creativity and essential to achieving a "win–win" for all involved in the equation. In our case, we sought to best understand the gig-providing company and their challenges in providing more gig choices for prospective gig workers.

Hopefully, our laws and regulations are always designed to improve the quality of life for all of society. We pay taxes and adhere to regulations for the benefit of all. The benefits we receive as citizens are in the form of conveniences such as roads, clean water, and public facilities.

The gig economy is more than a phenomenon. It has created more choices than we have ever experienced when it comes to how we work. This new way of work has attracted millions of people from all walks of life; therefore, new regulations that serve to guide and protect all involved are essential to the future we are creating. Gig-providing companies will improve their offers by providing more coaching and guidance to support ethical business practices by the gig workers they engage, including help to understand the applicable regulations and laws designed to support the business model utilized. The payment of taxes on income earned is essential to the future of work and why we included a chapter on *Maximizing the Potential of a Gig*. As a gig worker, you are responsible for understanding the attributes you have activated by becoming a microentrepreneur. They are, indeed, incredible! Work your gig as a small business owner, and the rewards will be beyond what you may have imagined at the beginning of your journey. We are living a revolution in the way we work.

Independent contractors also trade off access to certain employee-type benefits for the attributes of flexibility and freedom. They can shop for those benefits on their own. Employee-type benefits may be more expensive for independent contractors; however, new kinds of insurance and benefits are emerging as the marketplace demands that independent contractors be offered affordable products and services that are meaningful, affordable, and fulfilling of their needs. Gig-providing companies will not fulfill this new need. The new products and services needed will be provided by the same types of companies that provided the products and services, which met the needs of employers and employees, or they will be created and provided by a new breed of innovation and creativity.

One of the biggest needs that will continue to be important to all gig workers will be what we refer to as the "safety net" of products that will support retirement planning, health care, liability, cyber-security products – all of which will need to be easily accessible, understood, and affordable. We reached out to a good friend, advocate of the ultimate gig project, and subject-matter expert on insurance products designed for independent contractors. John Parks, John A Parks Company Inc., knows and understands the needs of independent contractors because of his years of experience with big brand companies that provide financial instruments and insurance products. Parks shared the following in response to our request for his insights:

> As the gig economy expands and adapts, access to
> quality insurance is just one of the many hurdles the

new gig entrepreneurs need to overcome. While the tradi-
tional insurance market is geared toward larger busi-
nesses, the gig entrepreneur needs innovative insurance
products, often on an "as needed" or "per transaction"
basis, enabling them to purchase protection or policies
that provide coverage for sometimes one day or even one
hour. These entrepreneurs need cost-effective, one-off
digital insurance policies designed specifically for the gig
economy.

The gig worker often moves from one job to another,
depending on their changing needs or gig. This could
leave the gig entrepreneur with coverages that don't
address their unique exposure or a policy designed for
a more traditional brick-and-mortar business model.
Each policy should provide coverage for the gig indi-
vidual's risk. The unique policies should provide
coverage for claims arising from short-term assignments
as well as gigs that could last a year or more.

With many gig workers finding their jobs via online
and/or mobile job sites, digital insurance policies are a
must, including immediate quotes, binders, and claims
handling. The understatement of the year is the gig
economy has changed the world and the way we do
business forever.

Big brand insurance companies must be realizing that as the
current employer/employee business model shrinks and the gig
economy continues to grow, there will be a shrinking base for
current products and services. These companies will have to
embrace the new gig economy phenomenon and design products
that fit a very different labor force. When we asked Parks to share
more of his personal perspective, he shared this:

In our 105 years of operating our family-owned insur-
ance agency, we have never seen these kinds of major
changes in protecting business and personal assets.
Individuals working from home and gig workers

building businesses are increasingly open to allocations
of losses from customers and client's personal informa-
tion and mishandling of financial data. Cyber lawsuits
are on the rise as both lawyers, clients, and part-time
employers sue for damages. Whether the lawsuits are
fraudulent or not, the out-of-pocket cost to defend an
uninsured loss to the gig worker could be disastrous.
Working with major insurance carriers, our agency is
adapting older insurance products and helping to create
new ones to safeguard individuals, consultants, part-
time, and full-time business owners as they navigate
and work in the new gig opportunity.

We are optimistic! We know companies that are already working on the products and services needed by the growing labor force
of independent contractors. The products may be different. However, we predict that more affordable health insurance, more
accessible savings and investment vehicles that encourage savings
and delay taxes, and lower cost liability coverage will soon become
available. Some of these new products are already being tested and
launched.

11

ULTIMATE GIG RESEARCH
FINDINGS AND INSIGHTS

When we started the Ultimate Gig project, I always envisioned writing a book on the subject. The gig economy was growing in its appeal, attracting gig workers from very diverse segments in the population, and I was personally fascinated. The group of people I was having conversations with were interested, which led to the formation of what I always refer to as the Ultimate Gig core team. We also had a lot of questions, and as we pursued answers, we did not find a lot of research on the subject. That does not mean that we did not find information to read; we found a lot of papers. I found the points of view expressed in the documents I studied to be very diverse and often biased toward what gig workers do not have versus what they do have.

As you have seen throughout this book, we wanted to focus on the incredible number of new work opportunities that have been created by the gig economy. I wanted to focus on what gig workers are achieving as a result of work being offered in a very different format under a very different set of rules from what the traditional labor force has been built for over 100 years. We covered the challenges faced in Chapter 10 because we would be remiss if we had not. But overall, our interest was in exploring those aspects of the gig economy that are offering innovation and new opportunities. In this chapter, we provide answers to the questions we developed.

In March 2020, I attended a meeting in Dallas, Texas, where I had the opportunity to renew a friendship with Dr. Robert A. Peterson, the John T. Stuart III Chair in Business Administration, The University of Texas at Austin, whom I have respected over many years because of his interest in the direct selling channel of distribution and his focus on the subject of ethics. After investing many months into reading papers written on the gig economy and a few books, I could not find the answers that I needed for some of my questions relative to the gig economy. Most of the information was a bit dated. It was Dr. Peterson who suggested that we do our own research for this project, and soon, the research project was underway. Dr. Peterson guided us through the process.

To obtain the data for our survey, a professional survey research firm contacted 2,210 members of the Dynata consumer panel, an internet panel consisting of some 62 million consumers. The survey was conducted from July 21, 2020 to August 1, 2020. The panel members were randomly selected and asked to read the following definition of a gig:

A gig is defined as a flexible work arrangement that allows people to work how, when, and where they want to work. Even full-time and part-time employees may sometimes work gigs in their free time. Typical gigs include the following activities:

- Manual skill-based services (such as home repair, yard maintenance, house cleaning);

- Personal assistance (such as pet care, childcare, eldercare);

- Professional services (such as accounting, law, consulting, graphic design, photography);

- Selling products through a direct selling or network marketing business;

- Selling products that you made yourself;

- Freelance computer work (such as data entry, website development);

- Short-term real-estate rental; renting personal property (e.g., car, boat, or RV);

- Ride-sharing, transportation services.

After reading this definition, panel members were asked whether they have "worked a gig in the past 12 months." A total of 1,001 panel members, approximately 45% of those asked, said they had worked a gig in the past 12 months. These 1,001 individuals constituted the survey sample. Forty-seven states and the District of Columbia were represented in the sample (Fig. 11.1).

WHO ARE GIG WORKERS?

This may seem like a simple question, but the answer has been difficult to find. From my perspective, I have always felt that women are underreported in the gig economy conversation. With so much of the conversation about the future of work dominated by discussions about Generation Z and Millennials, I also have been interested in what is happening with those who are being replaced or displaced in the current economy. The future of work also concerns those who are age 55+. Therefore, in our survey, we asked the questions that would provide a current sample of who is participating in the gig economy.

When we took our snapshot, we found gig workers represent all age groups yet generally have a high level of stability in terms of education, homeownership, and household income. They are also relatively stable with their gig work; 54% reported working their gig for more than one year. This is a profile that is very different from the gig worker often portrayed in media as being a person being taken advantage of by the gig-providing company.

According to our survey, gig workers are nearly as likely to be women (49%) as men (51%), and 26% are in the 55+ age segment. Gig work also has appeal across income levels, with 34% of respondents reporting annual household income of $100,000.00 or more. For most workers, gig earnings represent a small portion of their total household income: 45% responded that less than 10% of household income comes from gig work, and 38% indicated that the percent of earnings from gig work was between 10% and 49%. More than half (54%) are married, and 69% own homes.

Most surprising was the educational profile of gig workers our survey revealed. Marketers of gig opportunities should be aware that

Ultimate Gig Survey
The Highlights

35% were 18-34 years of age	47% want a home-based business
39% were 35-54 years of age	Gig workers responded with a 97.7% satisfaction score
26% were 55 years of age or older	Over half have specific goals
51% men and 49% women. 54% are married	74% preferred a gig over a full-time job or were neutral to the choice
Ethnicity: 28% people of color, 72% Caucasian	60% are looking to make better use of their spare time
69% own homes	51% are looking to develop new skills and develop personally
90% have education beyond a high school diploma, including 36% with at least some graduate work	Expectations and amounts earned were virtually identical
More than 200 gigs represented in our survey	90% have health insurance coming from outside of the gig experience
54% have been working their gig longer than one year	71% are currently saving for retirement
55% are working more than one gig	53% save through a 401(k) or similar plan from their non-gig employer
72% are working their gig(s) to pay household bills, student expenses, or to save and invest earnings. 16% are looking to improve their lifestyle	38% have engaged their own IRA-type plan
55% are desirous of being their own boss	19% save through a spouse plan
75% want to earn a little extra money	41% save via a savings account

Fig. 11.1. Highlights from the Ultimate Gig Survey.

many gig workers have completed some education beyond a high school diploma: 18% had completed some college, 35% had a college degree, 5% some graduate school, and 32% a graduate degree.

WHAT ARE GIG WORKERS DOING?

The general public perception of gigs tends to be one that is transportation-oriented. However, gig work is exceptionally diverse. Even within the categories that we used in Chapter 1 – transportation, service, selling, and leasing – are many subsets that result in hundreds, possibly thousands of opportunities that focus on specific types of gigs that are satisfying the diverse objectives and preferences of gig seekers.

In our survey, respondents cited more than 200 different types of gig work. Of those working a single gig, 6% reported being engaged in direct selling, one of the gig categories we have discussed at length in this book. We also found that many gig workers choose to work more than one gig: 24% worked two gigs this year, and 33% worked three or more gigs within the past year.

Our data confirm what had previously been more of a qualitative assessment: The vast majority of gig workers do not expect to earn thousands of dollars per month. In fact, 80% expected to earn less than $1,000.00 per month from their gigs. Some do earn significant incomes, and some work their gigs full time. Still, the gig economy is about making flexible work available to the masses.

We also wanted to know how many hours gig workers were working. We found 62% of gig workers work from 1 to 8 hours per week, 18% work 1–3 days per week, and 20% work 4 or more days per week. This confirms another feature of the gig economy that we have been advocating for many years; gig workers are not interested in full-time working hours. They are more inclined to flexible hours worked a few days per week.

Because of our hypothesis that women will play an increasingly important part of the gig economy, we were curious to see if there were significant differences among our male and female respondents. Gig economy participation is largely gender neutral, with no difference in the number of gigs worked, how long they worked in their gig, or the amount of time they spent working their gig.

PRIMARY MOTIVATIONS DRIVING GIG WORKERS

Survey participants were asked to think back to when they first started working their gig. They were then presented 16 possible reasons for entering the gig economy and asked the extent to which they agreed that each reason was important to them. By far the most important reason for entering the gig economy was, "I wanted to make a little extra money." Fully 75% agreed with that statement, with just 9% indicating that money was not a primary motivator and another 17% neutral. There was no difference in the responses of men and women to this statement (Fig. 11.2).

Most interesting, and supportive of our assumptions over many years, gig workers are also striving to make their lives better. Eighty-three percent primarily use their gig earnings for one of three basic purposes; they use their gig earnings to pay household bills (36.9%), save or invest (30.8%), and improve their personal lifestyle (15.6%) (Fig. 11.3). This information correlates perfectly with the motivations we described for working a gig in Chapter 3. You may wish to review the chapter again.

16 Motivations for starting a gig

The following lists all 16 possible reasons for entering the gig economy presented to our survey participants and ranked in order of percent agreement.

1	Make a little extra money **75%**	**9**	Wanted to work a short-term gig rather than a full-time regular job **46.7%**
2	Freedom to work from wherever I want **61%**	**10**	Started as a favor to a friend or family member **44%**
3	Enjoy both work and life more **60%**	**11**	More flexibility to work and care for my children or another family member **41.2%**
4	Something to do in my spare time **60%**	**12**	Build a business that would be my primary source of income **40.8%**
5	Be my own boss **55%**	**13**	Be a part of a supportive group/community **40%**
6	Specific goals that I wanted to accomplish with my gig **52%**	**14**	Wanted a bridge between my last full-time job while I search for my next full-time job **37%**
7	Learn new skills and develop myself as an individual **51%**	**15**	Was bored with my current job/career and wanted to explore something different **37%**
8	Have a home-based business **47.3%**	**16**	Receive a discount on products or services **31%**

Fig. 11.2. Motivations for Starting a Gig.

How do you primarily use the money you earn from your gig?

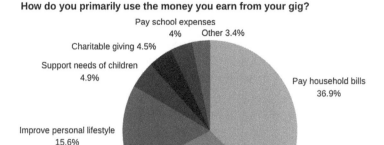

Source: Ultimate Gig research survey.
Fig. 11.3. Primary Uses for Gig Earnings.

Most respondents (55%) indicated, to some degree, a desire to be their own boss, and 47% stated a desire to have a home-based business. This confirms the entrepreneurial spirit that thrives within the gig economy. We now realize that Americans are not finding the traditional job to be enough. Some estimates indicate a contribution to the US economy above $1 trillion annually and growing. So, let us take a closer look at what has happened. As we explained in Chapter 5, gig-providing companies, through innovation and ingenuity, have offered new work opportunities based on the effective use of technology. One could easily argue that Uber and Airbnb were as much about software and technology as they were about driving cars and hosting people. Before the emergence of the gig economy and its innovative use of technology, it is improbable that a survey such as ours would reveal such keen interest in being the boss, having a home-based business, flexibly earning more money, or being able to work whenever desired.

Four in 10 gig workers also reported a desire to be a part of a supportive community. This was particularly interesting to us, as the vast majority of the gigs our responders listed do not seem to provide this feature. Direct selling is the only form of gig work that focuses on creating a community. Most direct selling companies are known for their incentives and recognition methods that shower their participants with praise and the opportunity to earn incentives that have been trips and experiences to various destinations in the country and around the world. For direct selling companies, this appears to be a clear indicator of the importance of community. For gig-providing companies of any type, recognizing this need through communications and other tools would appear to be an opportunity to create higher productivity and enjoyment of the gig.

SATISFACTION IN COMPARISON TO EXPECTATION

Gig workers are overwhelmingly satisfied with their gig experiences, so much so that our survey results were startling. Gig workers responded with a 97.7% satisfaction score, with 52% rating their overall experience working their gig as very positive. Another 35.4% rated their experience as somewhat positive and 10.1% were neutral. It would be hard to imagine evaluating job satisfaction within most companies and finding a dissatisfaction rate anywhere close to as low as 2.3%. This was especially impressive because we were polling gig workers across 47 of the 50 states who participated in a variety of gigs, not one particular type.

Part of this satisfaction, no doubt, comes from gigs meeting workers' expectations when it comes to earnings. We asked participants about both what they expected to earn when they started working their gig and what their actual earnings per month were. Within our sample, 39% expected to make less than $300 per month when they started their gig and currently do make less than $300. At the same time, 45% expected to make more than $300 per month and actually do make that much. That is an 85% match. Of the 15% whose earnings did not match their initial expectations, there was a pretty even split of 8% who expected to make less than $300 per month but made more and 7% who expected to make more but made less.

This high correlation between expected earnings and actual experience is a positive sign. It indicates that gig participants are able to accurately assess the income potential of the gigs they choose. They are not likely to go into a gig with high hopes only to be disappointed, and they can successfully use gigs to achieve specific financial goals.

There do appear to be some differences in earnings and expectations between males and females. Female participants reported beginning their gigs with lower earning expectations than their male counterparts, and they did, in fact, report lower actual earnings. We are interested in exploring this difference in more detail.

The high satisfaction rates also likely stems from the mindset of gig workers. Several years ago, I developed a course designed to help people with their personal growth and development, and I have been a student of the subject for many years. Based on my work in that area, I believe that less than 5% of the general population sets goals and creates plans to support those goals. Even fewer develop these plans in great detail. Among gig workers, however, goal setting seems to be more common. In our survey, 52% of gig workers said they had specific goals. When you have a goal and are taking action toward achieving that goal, you are more likely to say you are satisfied with what you are doing.

Gig providers can enhance worker satisfaction by emphasizing the aspects of their gigs that match people's expectations and desires. For example:

- 74% of respondents indicated a preference for gig work over a traditional job or being neutral about the two options when it comes to selecting future work.

- 60% are looking to make good use of available time.

- 51% are looking to learn new skills and develop as an individual.

By talking about these attributes in communication with gig workers, companies can highlight the areas that matter most to workers. In the gig economy, the gig worker is the primary asset in how a skill/service is connected with a client or consumer. By providing ancillary and complementary value to the gig worker's life and work, companies will improve their connection with consumers. Companies that offer encouragement, motivation, and recognition, delivered personally, will also see positive results in terms of worker satisfaction and, in turn, customer satisfaction.

Gig workers are responding with high satisfaction ratings because they are receiving what they value. They may not be receiving everything they want or need. Still, the model is working, and it is expected to continue to work, even better.

THE IMPORTANCE OF SAFETY NETS

One of the gig economy's frequent criticisms is that its workers lack health insurance, paid sick leave, and access to other safety-net services. While this may be true in some gig economy areas that were not well-represented in our survey, such as construction and domestic work, participants in much of the newer aspects of the gig economy do not seem to face this hurdle. In our survey results, 90% of respondents indicated they had health insurance, primarily from a nongig employer. Seven in 10 reported saving for retirement, with 38% reporting that they have retirement investments in an individual retirement account (IRA) or similar product.

Yet, there still are opportunities for innovation. With only 35% of responders preferring a traditional job over a gig when choosing work in the future, gigs that focus on treating the worker as a microentrepreneur are well-positioned for growth. What is needed to make these microentrepreneurial opportunities even more attractive are the products, services, and instruments long provided to employees through an employer's benefits program. The new products need to protect gig workers relative to liability, provide needed insurance and investment instruments, and provide encouragement, education, and support to help the gig worker choose, as best as possible, the right products to serve their needs. The products also need to be affordable, as the individual will be shouldering the cost. Gig workers are not seeking an employer, but they will increasingly seek affordable insurance, investment, and other products that create safety and stability.

As we complete this manuscript, Uber and Lyft are being challenged by the state of California to reclassify their gig workers as employees. This case's outcome will probably take many more months, even years, and other states may follow in the same pathway as California. The future of work is not envisioned to include the classification of gig workers as employees. Based on our survey results, we have to wonder if California gig workers really want to be classified as employees or if they are merely looking for the safety net of products they do not have. It is quite possible that California gig workers want to work their gigs more, not less. The sooner an affordable safety net of products become available to gig workers, the sooner some of the challenges we read about will be resolved. (As we reviewed the final manuscript, we now report that the proposed California law to reclassify independent contractors was voted down by Proposition 22 in the November 2020 election.)

One of the most significant findings in our survey was that more than half of the respondents indicated an interest in being their own boss. You cannot have both employee status and be your own boss. This mix has never been available in the past, and we should not expect it in the future. Perhaps, there is a new classification of workers that needs to be invented. In the meantime, we have a thriving and growing gig economy that is delivering what gig workers are seeking. More than 6 in 10 gig workers in our survey indicated they wanted to enjoy both work and life more, and a similar number stated that they wanted to work from wherever they want. They want flexibility and freedom. You can find that as a microentrepreneur but not as an average employee.

Notable in our survey results, and a bit concerning, only 34% of responders are using any kind of bookkeeping system to keep track of their income and expenses. This was anticipated when we started this project and why we included Chapter 9, "Maximizing the Potential of Your Gig." Tax compliance is critical to both gig companies and gig workers. Gig providers should not ignore the importance of reminding their workers of the potential benefits of an easy-to-access and easy-to-use online bookkeeping system. Using such a system makes tax compliance more manageable and can help individuals maximize the benefits of being a microentrepreneur. No entrepreneur would think of attempting to start, grow, and manage a business without a bookkeeping system, and neither should microentrepreneurs and gig workers. The bookkeeping system is considered a safety-net product. Yet, it is the gig worker's responsibility to explore and select one of the many systems available.

SUMMARY AND INSIGHTS GAINED

Our survey has provided a wealth of perspective into who gig workers are, what they do, what motivates them, and what safety net products and services are needed by this new breed of microentrepreneur. Our good friend, Dr. Greg Marshall, was the first person I had ever heard use the expression "the genie is out of the bottle" concerning the gig economy. He is right. This genie, the gig economy, is touching us faster than we may think. Why would we ever want to go back? The office-centric environment may indeed be over. When it comes to working, we will look at the need for real estate and the need for physical interaction differently. The need for physical presence was already changing due to incredible new technology and COVID-19 accelerated new norms. We are already communicating differently. We now communicate visually, and scheduling the virtual call is often assumed versus the idea of a regular phone call. Why just talk when we can interact more personally by seeing each other? We are not going back, only moving toward a future that is coming faster than we may think.

Our survey provides empirical evidence of the positive impact the gig economy is having on people's lives. It also provides direction to our continuing research and study. For example, we are intrigued by the finding that 32% of our responders worked three or more gigs within the past year. Suppose the satisfaction responses had not been as high as they were. In that case, we could easily assume that those who worked multiple gigs were, in some manner, dissatisfied with the results they were experiencing from any one of those gigs, thus the need to try a couple more. But since overall satisfaction is high, we are continuing to dig for more data and more understanding. There is the possibility that some of those working multiple gigs are simply not focused on mastering one of their gigs, and this could be an indication that gig-providing companies would be wise to invest more time into communications that help and inspire their workers to seek mastery of the gig they have chosen. It is also possible that some people just love the opportunity to bring variety into their lives. If this is the case, multiple gigs could mean the gig worker enjoys their gig so much they just have to work more than one. It is simply amazing how research can trigger our thoughts, which then trigger more investigation. It is the process by which we always get better.

The results of the survey confirmed much of what we have been advocating for several years. The gig economy and the innovations it brings to the world of work appeal to a wide variety of people. Men and women from all walks of life are working more, not less, and many seek more than what they can achieve in traditional jobs alone. The nine to five may be getting the pink slip. Gig workers are not attempting to earn incomes beyond realistic expectations; in our survey, what they earn is almost a match to their expectations. Working the way we desire and when we want is no longer a dream, it is a possibility.

In our next and final chapter, you will meet some of those who changed the game.

12

GAME-CHANGERS

This chapter is about a few companies we selected as game-changers that have contributed enormously to the disruption of the "status quo." These game-changers have provided us with choices in the way we can work, choices that were never imagined by the founders of industrialized society. These game-changers represent the ideas and businesses of many others who are charting the same pathways.

Many of our selected game-changers are companies that have pioneered gig work opportunities. The profiles and stories were developed by two outstanding graduate students that we were fortunate to work with on this project. Christina Schreiber and Christian Panier are enrolled at the Crummer Graduate School of Business at Rollins College, Winter Park, Florida. Both represent age and educational perspective that became extremely valuable to our work. Because of my great respect for the value I personally gained from the book, *Good to Great*, by Jim Collins, published in 2001, I quote the book often. I consider it to be one of the great books written in my lifetime, and I remain an advocate. However, we were reminded by Christina and Christian that the book was written about 20 years ago, long before they began reading business books. Their perspective was obviously a bit different than ours, and we are grateful.

We also conducted personal interviews with three C-level executives of direct selling companies. As we stated earlier, we take the position that direct selling was the first form of gig work even though direct selling companies did not use the term "gig worker." The more common terminology or labels used to identify those who worked when and how they desired were independent contractors, consultants, brand representatives, or distributors.

The following pages contain game-changing stories and insights. These profiles, stories, and personal interviews represent work that is impacting the lives of millions. The companies and individuals are extraordinary. This chapter is our salute to all who are on the pathways described. Work is being redefined, and the ownership of the work is moving toward the crowd. This means more people within the masses of society will be in control of the quality of products and services provided, creating a robust, growing, and appealing way to work as a microentrepreneur.

Gig-providing companies represent a new competitive group of innovative businesses that effectively use technology and the power of human resources. The companies, their founders, and those who are leading these companies today see work differently. As a result of great vision, innovation, and creativity, the gig economy has become a phenomenon. Participation in the gig economy is not restricted by age or résumé, only by personal restrictions. People from all walks of life are grateful for the disruption and shift in how work can be accomplished. Desire is the new prerequisite to becoming a part of this new economy.

Meet some of the game-changers.

COMPANIES CHANGING THE GAME

As we searched to identify companies that would fit the category of "game-changer," revenue was not the only criterion. Innovation and creativity were considered essential. In all cases, the gig-providing companies mentioned have contributed to new ways to work. In some cases, traditional forms of work have been reinvented to be more appealing to both gig workers and consumers.

You have heard us describe the gig economy in four facets: transportation, services, selling, and leasing. Now, we look at each one of these gig categories for our game-changers. As we describe some of what we discovered, you will also find a few gig-providing companies you may not have heard of before. There are a few hundred million people worldwide working some type of gig every day impacting over a billion lives, and much of the gig phenomena started with a few companies and their founders who saw things differently.

Transportation Gigs That Changed the Game

Uber Technologies has become synonymous with ridesharing; the market leader is currently valued at almost $62 billion. Since 2009, Uber has expanded to 63 countries through innovative platform design and brand recognition. Uber contracts local drivers to use their personal vehicles to transport passengers and has been able to expand its offerings based on demand. In addition to base-level service, Uber offers premium, luxury, and large SUV vehicles to customers, even offering a hybrid and electric green option in Europe.

Thanks to their focus on innovation and convenience, Uber also expanded into the food delivery market. Uber continues to explore innovative ways to leverage the time cars sit unused, all while providing attractive opportunities to drivers.

While Uber gained notoriety early on as the market leader, Lyft has grown quickly. *Lyft Inc.* has gone toe-to-toe with the industry leader and survived, even carving out almost 30% market share. Available in nearly 650 US cities, their coverage competes effectively with Uber domestically but has no meaningful international presence.

Uber and *Lyft* have successfully claimed the US market, but the international market remains up for grabs. Giants like *Ola Cabs* and *Didi Chuxing* have achieved a dominant presence in India and China, respectively. By offering an even more extensive range of services to match different price points and customer preferences, both have become key players in the two most populated countries in the world. Didi Chuxing became so successful in China that it acquired Uber China in 2016 for $35 billion and became the global industry leader. *Ola* has grown to incorporate traditional taxi services and food delivery, as well as expanding to Australia and the United Kingdom. This success has led to a $10 billion valuation as of October 2019. Most American consumers will name Uber and Lyft as the leading players. Still, competitors like Ola and Didi Chuxing are expanding worldwide despite the considerable resources of the two familiar names.

Ridesharing differs from ride-hailing in one significant way. While ride-hailers can call a car to take them anywhere at any time, regardless of the driver's plans, ridesharing puts the power in the driver's hands. For ridesharing, drivers offer their extra seats to passengers going to the same places they have already planned to visit themselves.

BlaBlaCar (France) – one of the major players in the ridesharing industry – provides a platform for users to post a planned drive and connect with passengers willing to chip in for travel costs. By promoting a sense of online community, BlaBlaCar has served over 70 million passengers across its services. Available in over 20 countries, BlaBlaCar offers a more affordable option to other ridesharing and rental services. By receiving a 10–15% commission for each booking, they have been able to profit from an innovative service and expand into flat rates for bus services. While other platforms can connect passengers heading to the same destination, BlaBlaCar's success has gained global notoriety.

Service Gigs That Changed the Game

Service gigs have become a great way to outsource labor. From programming to graphic design, companies in need of a little help can connect with professionals, assess their experience level, and work together remotely. Over 90% of US workers would consider freelancing, and major companies like Bank of America, FedEx, and Verizon are increasingly seeking out freelancers, meaning demand for freelance gig workers will only increase. Also, around 24% of small businesses outsource for increased efficiency, meaning opportunities will spring up everywhere, not just with big corporate players.

Some of the most attractive opportunities can be found through *Upwork, Toptal, Freelancer, Fiverr,* and others. Upwork aims to connect companies with the best talent – no matter where they are. The company serviced over 30% of Fortune 500 companies in 2019, and their clients even include other gig companies, such as Airbnb. Toptal has a similar mission, and in 2020, they became the world's largest fully remote company, launching The Suddenly Remote Playbook to assist companies and employees unexpectedly working from home during a pandemic. Freelancer, an Australian competitor to Upwork and Toptal, boasts the world's largest freelancing and crowdsourcing marketplace by number of users and projects, connecting over 46 million employers and freelancers across 247 countries, regions and territories.

For example, while Fiverr can link you to professionals nearby, it is also a platform for any tedious task. It is the perfect place to find help with shopping, arts, crafts, and even assembling that challenging IKEA furniture. It's the ideal place to find help with anything someone would do for a "fiver," as the name implies. These types of gigs are incredibly flexible and allow workers to choose what services they are willing to provide. This idea of being your own boss is appealing to many workers across the globe. Another service that might surprise you: dog walking. Man's best friend is making a lot more friends. What used to be an extremely niche profession is now an accessible side gig for thousands of dog lovers.

Meet *Rover and Wag!* These two applications allow local animal lovers to connect with dog owners who need help walking their dogs daily. Rover promises to offer local pet sitters and walkers who will care for pets the way their owners would. The service provides dog boarding, house sitting, dog walking, doggy daycare, and drop-in visits. Wag offers on-demand dog walking and gives owners the flexibility to manage everyday life and instant access to experienced and trustworthy dog walkers, boarding hosts, and sitters in their communities. They offer daily walks, drop-in visits, boarding, sitting, and daycare services. They take a pet-centric approach to their businesses.

So how does it work? With Wag, all you have to do is create a profile and then accept walks as they pop up. You must be the first to accept the walk because it's open to any available walkers in the area. For Rover, you create your profile and set the hours you would like to work, along with any preferences regarding dog breed or service type. Whether you are looking for a part-time gig during your free hours or want to make dog walking a full-time job, Rover and Wag are great places to start.

For example, we found the story of Kiki M., a full-time sitter who started her business with Rover *and* Wag. "*I honestly didn't intend to grow this into a business*," she said. "*It just kind of...happened. I started doing it in the evenings after my day job because it improved my mental health and made me happy. When people started giving me really great feedback and requesting me, I realized I could make a job out of it*." After just six months walking with Rover and Wag, Kiki quit her job and moved to pet sitting full-time – and she has never been happier.

Both platforms allow sitters to set their schedules and prices. Rover takes approximately 20% of sitters' profit, while Wag takes about 40%. Wag also donates a portion of each walk to help feed local shelter dogs. Sitters can earn in accordance with the time they invest with local dogs and other animals in need of the company. We found that some sitters, like Kiki, earn up to and over $1,000.00 per month doing what they love to do. Both companies provide background checks on their walkers, and every walk is insured.

Eliminating Everyday Inconveniences

A classic inconvenience well-known to homeowners is finding professionals for domestic projects. Instead of being relegated to endless phone calls or word of mouth, customers searching for high-rated professionals can now use convenient online services to schedule projects with ease. Homeowners search through vetted and qualified professionals with customer reviews to find the best fit, a task that would have taken days only a decade ago. Depending on the platform and desired task, homeowners can find a solution to any home improvement need in a matter of minutes.

One of the names recognized by homeowners in the United States is *TaskRabbit*. TaskRabbit markets its close connection to customer needs to stand out. According to their website, they believe in "providing users with an amazing experience, which means finding and building new and improved ways to support them." This has proved invaluable in building a close network of users and professionals, even leading to expansion into France and Germany in 2019 to meet their high demand for outsourcing.

Some of the most successful gig companies in the service category are those that eliminate the inconveniences of everyday life. From planning a nice meal for one to feeding the family last minute, multiple platforms now take the hassle out of eating and cooking. Some focus on your meal needs while others save you the trouble of a lengthy grocery store trip, but all of them offer a convenient, easy-to-use service that benefits customers and the gig worker providing the service.

ChefsFeed, which acquired Feastly in 2018, connects an expert community of chefs with new diners and moneymaking opportunities with brands. The company has a digital reach of over 100 million people and a network of over 5,000 experts contributing to date. Hire-A-Chef is affiliated with the United States Personal Chef Association and helps bring affordable yet high-class meal and dining experiences to your home. They also publish the magazine "Your Personal Chef Business."

Looking for a child, adult, or senior home care? Check out *Care.com*, which has been endorsed by USA Today, Mom.com, Fortune, Real Simple, CNBC, and Bloomberg for their network of providers. Whether you need someone to tutor your child, help care for someone with special needs, or even simply check in on your pets, Care.com has the resources you need.

In the food delivery space, qualified drivers can seamlessly jump into high traffic areas and deliver takeout and groceries from millions of restaurants and stores, while getting paid through fees, mileage, and tips. Restaurants are benefitting from significantly increased marketing and a workforce of independent drivers, rather than having to hire employees to deliver. Grocery stores can reach customers on days when going to the store feels like a chore.

These expedient and accessible delivery services are saving customers time and offering them a wider variety of goods, expanding retailers' customer bases, and providing gig workers with an easy entrance into the gig economy. Additionally, through the lens of COVID-19, demand for delivery has skyrocketed and shows no sign of slowing down.

Several big players have grown from the seemingly limitless potential of the food delivery industry to cover millions of restaurants and stores worldwide. The key players include *Postmates, DoorDash, GrubHub, InstaCart,* and *Uber Eats,* while popular but niche services include *GoPuff, Drizly, Caviar,* and more.

Postmates enjoys a significant presence in around 3,500 cities, with about 170,000 drivers. The company was founded in 2012, setting out to answer a simple question: "why can't I have delivered what I really want?" Eight years later, they serve 80% of the US households across all 50 states. *DoorDash,* recently valued at $16 billion, positioned itself to deliver from "any" restaurant, expanding to 3,300 cities to reach 80% of Americans in 2018. DoorDash has also launched Project DASH, which aims to tackle the problems of hunger and food waste in the local communities they serve. On average, one restaurant can produce 100,000 pounds of food waste every year, which only 1.4% of that is donated. Project DASH aims to fix that through 1:1 donations that reduce food waste.

GrubHub is a longtime player in the industry, boasting 17.7 million users and 436,000 average daily deliveries in 2018. GrubHub has been on the delivery scene since its inception in 2004, aiming to connect hungry diners with great, local restaurants. They now feature over 300,000 restaurants in over 4,000 US cities. *Uber Eats* benefits from the massive user base of its sister ridesharing platform and can attract large partnerships with McDonald's, Coca-Cola, the Golden State Warriors, and more. *GoPuff* even offers any snack you could find at your local gas station.

For online grocery shoppers, *Instacart* has become a national leader. Their mission is to create a world where everyone has access to the food they love and more time to enjoy it together. Though relatively new to the scene, they now boast over 200,000 shoppers in over 5,500 cities, and while 5% of households currently buy groceries online, that number is expected to quadruple in the next five years. *Drizly* is a leader in alcohol delivery. Drizly only connects the customer with a local liquor store, but they have raised over $30 billion to date and bring consumers their favorite libations in over 100 markets across the United States and Canada. On the higher end of food delivery, *Caviar* focuses on catering large functions or businesses. This allows drivers to make substantially more in base pay and tips for objectively swankier service.

Similar services can also be found around the world running on similar structures. For example, *Grab*, *Just Eat*, and *Deliveroo* are not currently available in the United States but operate in 7, 13, and 14 different countries, respectively. *Grab* has 2.7 million drivers in Southeast Asia. London-based *Deliveroo* operates in 500 cities around the world and was considered Europe's second fastest growing company in 2019 by the Financial Times. On top of a recent round of funding led by Amazon, *Deliveroo* is poised for growth.

New Ways to Access Funding Are Changing the Game

Gone are the days of pleading with the bank for a loan. Thanks to the explosion of the gig economy, online services now connect lenders and borrowers from all walks of life, from startups and small businesses to individuals looking for some assistance with costly ventures. Many platforms worldwide offer personal loans, business loans, auto refinancing, patient loans, and more, with each category broken down further.

For example, *Upstart* focuses only on personal loans but breaks down the category 16 ways. Each company positions itself differently to attract new users by changing their interest rates, expected returns, loan size, and which loans they support. Additionally, while the industry has issues with its terminology, it comprises both direct person-to-person lending and mass crowdfunding. Each is best suited for different offerings, but popular crowdfunding platforms offer the bonus of a chance at virality.

Services like *Kickstarter* and *GoFundMe* gain international attention regularly due to trendy or wacky products like professionally shot cat calendars, sleep masks for inducing lucid dreaming, and a 50-foot rideable snake. Yes, you read that correctly. All in all, these services provide reliable funding for anyone unable or unwilling to fundraise through a bank and give individuals a chance to invest in worthwhile projects without jumping through financial institutions' hoops.

Several popular platforms have emerged in peer-to-peer (P2P) and crowdfunding sectors that support individuals, small businesses, and startups. While each has slightly different attributes, they all provide an unconventional and attractive path to funding. US-based *LendingClub* boasts over 3 million customers and $50 billion borrowed through the platform since its founding in 2007. Considering itself the "first P2P lending marketplace in the United States," *Prosper* has facilitated more than $17 billion to over a million users since 2005. Meanwhile, *Funding Circle* supports the United States, United Kingdom, Germany, and the Netherlands. While only offering business loans, they have managed to invest over $11.7 billion in businesses worldwide. Each of these is also providing COVID-19 relief and support for small businesses. Each provides easy-to-use services for both lenders and borrowers alike, supporting those creating their own gig businesses.

Selling Gigs and the Platforms That Changed the Game

As the gig economy continues to swell, creators' opportunities to monetize their hobbies and their desires to build businesses will only grow. There are so many resources out there for creators to launch their businesses that the hardest part might be figuring out which platform best meets goals and objectives.

Etsy and Shopify provide platforms for creators to set up shop – literally. Each platform aims to make it easier for dreamers to become entrepreneurs. It's a popular idea, and it's working; take a look at some of the numbers (Table 12.1):

Table 12.1. Overview of Etsy and Shopify.

Etsy	Shopify
2.4 million active sellers	1+ million active sellers
1,240 employees	5,000 employees
$5 billion in revenue (2019)	$1.578 billion in revenue (2019)

These are models people believe in and flock to – and it's a lucrative business for those managing the processes behind the scenes. Etsy and Shopify provide the platform and help their community members with their marketing needs.

Etsy was founded in 2005 and is a global marketplace for unique and creative goods with no warehouses, does not ship products, but connects effectively, the creators and sellers of the products with consumers. They operate on five guiding principles: Committing to their craft, minimizing waste, embracing differences, digging deeper, and leading with optimism.

Etsy embraces diversity by promoting genuinely unique products on its site, and all products are made or offered by a micro-entrepreneur. This takes quite a few forms on the Etsy platform:

- featuring Editor's Picks from black-owned shops

- running special promotions, like #StandWithSmall

- endorsing small businesses

- encouraging people to buy essential items (like government-mandated face coverings) from the microentrepreneurs they support

Most notably, Etsy now has a visible advertising presence on television networks in the United States.

Where Etsy truly shines is in supporting their sellers. Michael S. launched his business on Etsy in January of 2020. Michael produces mainly custom wooden creations – charcuterie boards, cutting and serving trays, and drink coasters, just to name a few.

"Like many people, I have always dreamed of starting and owning my own business, and Etsy provides the steppingstones to do so," Michael said. "It allows me to build my own business while simultaneously serving as my creative outlet."

"The process of setting up my shop [with Etsy] was very easy," he said. "Ironically, the hardest part was coming up with my shop name and logo! Etsy provides a simple step-by-step process to get everything created and keep everything organized. I truly believe that anyone who is interested in setting up their own shop would be able to do so."

Michael was most surprised by the ease with which anyone can launch their shop. Starting a business may seem simple on the surface, but there are a lot of moving parts that Etsy helps manage, including shipping, tax tracking, data analytics, marketing, and more. In short, they do the tedious work for you. For someone who draws inspiration from everything around him – whether that be interesting design elements found online or contemplating ways to upcycle his coffee grounds – Michael loves that he can focus on what he loves: creating (or as he calls it, tinkering) while the Etsy platform does most of the marketing and selling.

"I underestimated how satisfying it would be to fulfill orders," Michael said. "Since an Etsy shop is a direct reflection of the owner, it truly feels spectacular when someone orders one of your items. It means they appreciate and value what you are doing and that all of your hard work has paid off in the end."

Shopify is another major player in providing support for microentrepreneurs. Shopify was founded in 2004 by Tobias Lütke, Daniel Weinand, and Scott Lake. Their mission: *Make commerce better for everyone by helping individuals start, run, and grow their own businesses.* They have certainly lived up to their mission statement, and they continue to break down barriers associated with starting, managing, and growing a business. We discussed Shopify in Chapter 4 as a gig-supporting company that is redefining free enterprise. Now we recognize Shopify as a game-changer.

While Etsy provides a platform and brand to market products created by microentrepreneurs, Shopify approached their model differently. Shopify supports the entrepreneurial desire to be a store or shop, not simply sell on another branded platform. Shopify enables the building of an independent online brand. An example would be the quote we found on the Shopify website about a branded online store that used Shopify for all of the needed support: "We've been able to build something in 3 years that a lot of brands haven't actually gotten to in 10 years."

Shopify is an innovator in the way they introduced tools to support microentrepreneurs. The tools are creative and very professional. They help to market the products, find customers, drive sales, and manage day-to-day business responsibilities. Reports are provided on all essential activity which brings a sophisticated level of analytics to the microentrepreneur; therefore, Shopify is actually an example of one platform with all the e-commerce and point of sale features you need to start, run, and grow a business. Built into the platform are tools to help take the guesswork out of marketing with the ability to execute and analyze digital marketing campaigns. Shopify also provides many themes for entrepreneurs, eliminating the need for investment in branding and strategy that often is beyond the budgets of the new microentrepreneur.

Etsy and Shopify have distinguished themselves through the resources and support they provide to their community members and the resulting brand power that flows through a network of the millions of microentrepreneurs they serve. Etsy and Shopify have paved the way for many other gig-supporting brands. They are real game-changers.

While platforms such as Etsy and Shopify make it easier than ever for people to sell physical products, the gig economy has also opened up new possibilities for content creators to sell digital products online. Content creators might be your neighborhood artists, the contributing writers in your local newspaper, or your favorite musicians – but they can also be your go-to podcasters, your how-to YouTubers, or your preferred gamers. There are two primary ways that content creators earn money; they either charge consumers for their content or they allow advertisers and sponsors access to their audiences for a fee. Both methods have picked up speed with the rise of the gig economy.

One of the first organizations that come to mind when discussing content creators is *YouTube*. YouTube was founded in 2005 and has grown immensely in popularity. As of 2018, 90% of Internet users in the United States access the site to watch online videos. In 2019, the net advertising revenues for the site exceeded $3.4 billion. While YouTube does offer subscription services, the primary method for content creators to create a steady flow of income is to build an audience large enough to catch advertisers' attention.

Generating revenue on YouTube is akin to becoming a social media influencer; some might even argue that popular YouTubers should be considered influencers. When a certain celebrity or social media mogul gains an online following, particularly when that following is made up of a certain demographic, companies will pay the influencer to promote their products on their social media platforms. For example, an athletic wear company might pay a well-known fitness instructor with a good following on YouTube to promote their new line of workout clothes. In this instance, the fitness instructor is not selling their training services to their audience, but rather they are selling their audience to the athletic wear brand.

Creators on YouTube have the opportunity to turn their channels into businesses. Simone Giertz is a notable example of this. Giertz began by making elaborate robots to perform simple tasks – poorly. The alarm clock that wakes you up by slapping you repeatedly, the machine that pours milk into your cereal (and all

Table 12.2. YouTube Creator Awards Levels.

Level	Subscribers
Graphite	1 to 1,000
Opal	1,000 to 10,000
Bronze	10,000 to 100,000
Silver	100,000 to 1 million
Gold	1 million to 10 million
Diamond	10 million +

over your counter), and the drone that gives you the world's worst haircut are just a few examples of her early work. Giertz's robots may have been completely useless, but they were funny, and they gained traction across the Internet. Giertz's channel now has over 2.2 million subscribers, enough to earn her YouTube's Gold Creator Award. (See Table 12.2) She has spoken at technology conferences around the globe, collaborated with today's most well-known inventors (such as Adam Savage), created content to promote popular shows like Westworld, and even co-hosted a TV show – all thanks to her YouTube success.

Video content is one of the most popular ways to generate partnerships with advertisers and sponsors as a way to generate income. While YouTube is the most well-known, there are other sites that offer more niche content, such as *Twitch*. Twitch, which was acquired by Amazon in 2014 for $970 million, is primarily used for streaming video games, and it allows for both advertising-supported and subscription-based channels.

The personal education market is another sector undergoing great change in the gig economy, thanks to the emergence of eLearning. Companies such as *Thinkific*, *Kajabi*, and others allow individuals to share their expertise on any subject by creating digital courses or learning communities and selling them to their target audiences. The content people are making available through these and other similar platforms is virtually limitless. You can find courses on budgeting, gardening, healthy living, playing guitar, meditation, painting techniques, photography, writing, yoga, and more. Thinkific reports that its users have made over $200 million so far. According to Kajabi's website, its customers have made over $1 billion on the platform to date. Kajabi also has a program titled Kajabi Heroes that incentivizes its users to grow their businesses.

Affiliate marketing is fairly simple. An affiliate earns commission for helping to market and sell a product for another person or company. Affiliate marketing as a practice has potential to make a big difference for those earning a commission by promoting and selling products they already enjoy, and many companies provide opportunity for people to participate.

Amazon Associates is the affiliate marketing program associated with Amazon – one of the largest affiliate marketing programs in the world. The Amazon Associates Program helps content creators, publishes, and bloggers monetize their traffic by offering easy link-building tools to direct their audience to their recommendations, earning from qualifying purchases and programs. Walmart has a similar program, titled the Walmart Affiliate Link. Their program allows affiliates to display banner ads or text links on their websites, earning up to 4% on qualifying purchases driven by their promotions. Their program is free to join. Affiliate marketing has gained traction in many of the world's largest companies, including *eBay*, *The Home Depot*, and more.

The gig economy also now includes a number of companies that support people in building a business through affiliate marketing. *Alibaba* is China's biggest e-commerce company. As the leading platform for global wholesale trade, they are taking advantage of affiliate marketing and expanding their global reach. Their mission is to make it easy-to-do business anywhere by giving suppliers the necessary tools to reach a global audience for their products. *Wealthy Affiliate* is another example of this. Wealthy Affiliate helps users build their own online businesses, providing an estimated 600 million products for users to sell. They boast over 1.4 million members and help build over 10,000 new business monthly.

The way we buy and sell has changed the game, and gig workers are benefitting.

One Leasing Idea That Changed the Game

The idea behind Airbnb pioneered many other stories that now make it possible to lease unused assets. We mentioned this story in Chapter 4; now, we recognize Airbnb as a game-changer. To date, the company has raised over $5 billion in venture capital and served over 750 million guests in more than 1,000 cities around the world.

As the company advertises on its website, "Airbnb is one of the world's largest marketplaces for unique, authentic places to stay and things to do, offering over 7 million accommodations and 40,000 handcrafted activities, all powered by local hosts." Airbnb hosts make a profit by renting out any living space they have – including apartments, houses, boats, treehouses, tiny homes, and more.

Airbnb hosts do more than providing a space for guests to stay; they help create memories. Hosts offer a unique and authentic view of the local scene in many of the world's greatest cities. A Paris host can teach you the ways of the Metro so you can avoid scams and pickpockets. Looking for a bookstore to visit during your time in Mexico City, your host will probably know of the perfect hole-in-the-wall. A New York City host can tell you what is worth seeing. Imagine you are planning a trip to Italy. You will be staying in Florence, taking day trips to tour the wineries of Tuscany, and enjoying the rich culture that the city has to offer. You want to see the Ponte Vecchio, climb the 463 steps to the top of the Duomo, and of course, see Michelangelo's David. But where else should you go, and what else should you see? A hotel concierge might tell you to visit the Piazzale Michelangelo, the Giardino di Boboli, or the Uffizi Galleries.

What the concierge may not be able to tell is that next to the Piazzale Michelangelo is the Giardino delle Rose – a stunning garden full of roses and many other flowers with a breathtaking view that is free to the public or about the locals' favorite pizza shop around the corner from the Giardino di Boboli. The concierge may not know about the small restaurant run by culinary students at the Florence University of the Arts in the same piazza as the Uffizi. These are things that an Airbnb host might know to share, and this is one reason why, on any given night, over 2 million people choose to stay in an Airbnb.

Staying in an Airbnb can be a rewarding experience. Hosting can be as well. Airbnb boasts over 650,000 hosts who earn from leasing unused assets and space. There is no minimum or mandatory time for hosting, so hosts have complete flexibility on when they can rent out their space. Hosts can set a minimum or a maximum number of nights a guest can stay and set their own nightly prices. There's even a House Rules clause that protects hosts' preferences; if guests break the expectations set at the time of booking, the host can cancel the reservation without penalty.

Airbnb automatically scores reservations for risk and cancels any bookings that seem suspicious. They also provide free protection of up to $1 million in property damage for every booking, as well as liability coverage of up to $1 million. This protects hosts from any guests claiming bodily injury or property damage that occurs on the host's property or during the guest's stay. There are no startup fees associated with listing your property on Airbnb, but the company does charge a 3% fee on all transactions to cover the cost of payments.

It's no secret that the COVID-19 pandemic of 2020 has immensely disrupted the global economy. Among the hardest-hit sectors are travel and tourism. In response to global shutdowns, Airbnb expanded its extenuating circumstances policy to protect their community and provide peace of mind. Any reservations booked before March 14, 2020 and scheduled to occur before the end of May 2020 were covered by the policy.

Guests received a variety of cancellation and refund options, and hosts were able to cancel without charge or impact on their Superhost status. Proof of COVID-19 impact was required for full eligibility. Any reservations placed after March 14, 2020 were subject to the host's specific cancellation policy. The extenuating circumstances did not apply to any reservations already underway. Airbnb also curated several articles provided to the community through the Resource Center, encompassing the company's response to COVID-19.

While Airbnb works hard to protect its hosts in times of distress, it also works hard to promote the biggest travel trends in times of peace. According to a recent survey commissioned by Airbnb, 57% of Americans prefer to spend their money on experiences rather than things. The company identified five major trends in travel this year: nature trips, historical experiences, disconnecting, minimalism, and eating clean. Each of these is a reflection of trends in guest bookings, searches, and preferences – but Airbnb creates trends as much as they monitor them.

Many individuals have built businesses for themselves using the Airbnb platform and other gig-based rental services like *Home-Away*, *VRBO*, and *Homestay*. Some hosts manage multiple properties putting their affinity for customer service and hospitality to good use. It's become such a phenomenon that short-term rentals have permeated popular culture. The Netflix original show "Stay Here" aired in 2018, and it features designer Genevieve Gorder and real estate expert Peter Lorimer, who teach property owners how to optimize their space for short-term rentals. Netflix also picked up "Instant Hotel," an Australian show in which homeowners who have transformed their properties into hotels judge each property to declare an overall winner.

This increase in focus on short-term rentals reflects a larger trend in global travel. Over the last 10 years, the short-term rental industry has exploded, particularly in significant tourist destinations such as major cities in Europe and the United States. There is a blossoming market of third-party companies that help monitor trends in short-term rentals and a thriving online community of hosts sharing tips and tricks to create the best space to attract guests. In addition to Airbnb's tools, hosts have access to thousands of articles on best practices for creating short-term rentals. If you have space and you are willing to share it, Airbnb and other similar gig-providing companies offer a great way to earn money on underused assets with the potential to grow into a full-time gig.

INDIVIDUALS WHO ARE CHANGING THE GAME

For this section of the chapter, we went to the direct selling channel, the original form of gig work, to better understand how direct selling companies may be responding to the new gig economy phenomenon. The early pioneers of the direct selling model recognized the value of using people in the distribution channel to handle most of the marketing and selling of the products and services direct selling companies provided. As we conducted our research and reflected on personal experiences, it is easy to imagine that the original direct selling companies may have selected a product or service that they wanted to market and then made the decision to use direct selling, with its use of independent contractors, as the preferred channel of distribution. In the case of Avon, David McConnell started as a book salesman who used the gift of a small bottle of perfume as a "door opener" because he knew women would be opening most doors. Once he found his fragrances to be more interesting to women than his books, at that time, he decided to make perfumes his primary product and then he decided to build a salesforce focused on women as the sellers, not just the potential customers. Of course, we will never be able to prove whether this hypothesis is accurate or true. The same hypothesis may have been in the foundational strategies of other direct selling companies. However, we also know that there are brands that use direct selling as their channel of distribution because the founders believed that direct selling would be a more personable selling and consumer experience. People who are intricately connected with the consumer also become a source of continuous education and information. Consumers benefit, and so does the company that prefers to compete with a focus on quality and value, not price.

We know that direct selling has evolved over the years, and new strategic priorities are supporting original direct selling concepts. People remain the focus, but the way people participate is vastly different in a world connected with technology and consumers empowered by technology. The connection between the company providing the products and services and the consumer is still the direct seller, a gig worker, and sometimes a microentrepreneur, who is building a serious business.

To best understand how direct selling companies are innovating and applying creativity to their models, we talked personally with the CEOs of both Amway and USANA Health Sciences. Both CEOs bring a new vision to their respective companies – so does Sheryl Adkins-Green, the chief marketing officer (CMO) at Mary Kay. Each of these individuals is a game-changer because of his or her individual responsibilities and the impact their company has on the lives of millions throughout the world.

Milind Pant, Chief Executive Officer, Amway Corporation

As of this writing, Amway is a leader in health and wellness and the largest among companies that utilize the direct selling channel of distribution. Founded by Jay Van Andel and Rich DeVos in 1959, Amway is a privately held corporation and a family-owned business. Van Andel and DeVos were lifelong friends who believed in the idea that owning a business could "help you reach your full potential and provide a better life for yourself and your family." It was a simple vision executed by two adventurous, daring, and committed individuals. The company does its own research, manufactures, and distributes nutritional supplements, beauty, personal care, and home care products. In 2019, the company reported over $8 billion in sales through more than 1 million Amway Independent Business Owners in more than 100 countries. Since 1959, Amway has paid out more bonuses and cash incentives to its distributors worldwide than any other direct sales company.

The entrepreneurial focus and spirit, displayed and advocated by the Amway founders, drew our attention to selecting Amway as one of the three direct selling companies we wanted to focus on in our research on the subject of the gig economy and our quest to define the ultimate gig.

Most who have studied the direct selling channel would agree that Amway disrupted and revolutionized the business model known as direct selling because of the company's focus and advocacy of the importance of entrepreneurship, making an entrepreneurial opportunity based on flexibility available to people, at a microlevel, in free societies throughout the world. Included in the focus on flexibility in being a part of Amway is a unique approach to how those who participate are rewarded and recognized for successfully acquiring and retaining customers and building communities for those customers and for other Amway Business Owners (ABOs) who also would like to build businesses selling Amway products to customers. Today, we find Amway using language and making statements such as: "Today we're still disrupting the retail industry by empowering Amway Business Owners to be leaders in social commerce."

Throughout Amway's 60-year history, the company has always been led by members of the founding families who were responsible for the positions of CEO and president of the company. In 2019, that history changed when the board of directors decided to go outside of the family for its next CEO. The Amway board of directors chose Milind Pant, a seasoned, talented, young executive who had global experience with major retail brands. The family remains active in many ways through children and grandchildren who are involved in the company, and the family remains in control of the company's board of directors. However, Pant's hiring was a considerable departure from the traditional succession plans, and his selection signaled that something different might be in the air for the world's largest direct selling brand.

When we spoke with Pant, we found a blend of tradition, respect, and acknowledgment of Amway's foundation and a strong passion for what will propel Amway as it formulates new strategic plans and executes upon bold new visions. There is a 10-year vision and plan in place to "unleash entrepreneurship with an online and offline platform that amplifies communities through social channels, turning passions into profit."

These plans are being fueled by megatrends that are happening across the world. Pant was quick to point out these trends in our conversation, and he identified them especially noting that these trends are quite apparent in countries like China, India, Russia, Japan, Thailand, Korea, and, of course, North America. Pant described the megatrends as follows:

1. Explosive growth in the gig economy

2. The emergence of online social communities that connect people with common purpose and passion

3. The growth of a "health and wellness" consciousness and the trend toward more plant-based diets

Our motivation for writing this book was directly linked to the explosive growth of the gig economy and why we have described gig economy growth as a phenomenon. Now we were talking with the new leader of the world's largest direct selling company, and he shares that the first described megatrend was one that Amway is paying close attention to. These three megatrends link to new Amway strategies; however, these new trends also link directly to the founding concepts expressed by the founders of Amway 60 years ago. Pant reminded us that the founders of Amway were passionate advocates of making entrepreneurship more available to all people, that freedom and flexibility should be the primary enablers of a business opportunity that could support individuals and their families, and that this personalized form of entrepreneurship would ultimately build better communities. "*These concepts are as relevant today as they were 60 years ago,*" he said. "*Amway's 'why' will never change, but the 'how' and 'what' associated with Amway is changing. These three trends are close to our purpose and our why. How we support our independent business owners as we address these megatrends will change significantly.*"

As our conversation with Pant continued, he often used language that we were not accustomed to hearing from direct selling executives. He described Amway as a platform, which is another label used to describe gig economy opportunities. Pant shared: "*Amway is a platform; Uber is a platform. A platform connects people with quality products and quality services and with customers. Going forward, we want to support our Amway independent business owners, both offline and online, as they build their businesses.*" In online language, a platform permits entrepreneurs to connect consumers to quality products and services. "*Going forward, Amway will build our online platforms as a primary way to build a business, always offering freedom and flexibility in how much time a person wants to invest."*

As our conversation reached this point, we knew we were talking to a transformational leader who saw the opportunity for Amway to be far beyond what this great company had been; it was more about what Amway could be. Our research had led us to a place where we observed the direct selling model and its annual rate of growth, overall, to be less than it had been in past years. Direct selling companies undoubtedly recognized the acceleration of innovation and creativity and new competition. From our point of view, the direct selling channel of distribution will be recognized as a unique form of gig work as competitive advantages are effectively leveraged. Amway intends to leverage its competitive advantages fully.

Pant shared: *"We want to help people pursue their passion, their purpose, and help them connect that passion to profits, whether it be in beauty, health, adventure, cooking."*

Amway realizes that to attract the next generation of entrepreneurs, the experience has to be easy and flexible for both the business owner and their customers. Earnings must be easy and early. Recognition and providing our participants with a sense of identity in a shared community is also very important.

Pant's comments had just helped describe why direct selling, as a form of gig work, is worth exploring in more detail. It includes a focus on passion and purpose, two elements that are not universal in work.

"No e-commerce platform – be it Amazon in the US or Alibaba in China – has the secret ingredient Amway has: the entrepreneurial spirit of our business owners leveraging their own passions and drive for flexibility, freedom and personal success. Our competitors in the gig economy don't have that secret ingredient either," Pant said.

The gig economy is known for quicker pay once the work is performed, and it is one of the key drivers of growth. When we asked the question as to how important paying quicker was for the future of Amway, Pant reminded us that the question about pay should also be about "return on effort." *"Frequency is one thing, but the return on the investment is the bigger thing. We must be competitive with what a gig economy participant expects, but return on effort is also a measurement."*

Amway has also introduced new incentives to address important learnings from the gig economy, such as a focus on customer acquisition and retention and paying ABOs quicker for their efforts in acquiring and retaining customers. The company has named this new incentive COREPlus+, referring to Amway's core methods of recognition and rewards plus incentives built for new ABOs to earn more meaningful income more quickly through sales to customers. Amway founders were known to have always stressed the importance of customers. Rich DeVos has been quoted as saying: *"When you focus on customers, you do not have to worry about the rest of the business."*

When we asked Pant about the impact of Amazon on the marketplace, the learning for direct selling models, and the new benchmarks Amazon has established relative to customer service, he quickly acknowledged that Amazon is a reminder to us that customers are the name of the game. One could easily derive from our conversation that Amazon had inspired Amway when Pant acknowledged, *"Amway is making it ten times easier for Amway Independent Business Owners to acquire and retain customers."*

Our next objective in our conversation with Pant was to get a better understanding of what Amway perceived its strengths to be. Pant had already talked about the importance of passion and purpose, but we wanted more insight from Amway's new leader. As the largest direct selling company in the world, we believed that Amway's strengths would probably provide us with greater insight into the direct selling channel's strengths. Pant was just hired into his role at Amway in January of 2019; however, when in discussion with him, one gets the feeling he has been around the Amway business model and culture for many years. His background included companies like Pizza Hut, Yum brands, and Unilever. As we continued to talk about the future and how Amway will compete, through its ABOs for even greater market share, he described Amway strengths as follows:

"1. The entrepreneurial spirit of ABOs

2. Expertise and experience in "seed to supplement" farming and supply chain transparency

3. Vibrant communities built by ABOs both offline and online

4. Partnership with ABO leaders."

Each of the strengths describes a company positioned to compete and even lead in the new gig economy. Amway's entrepreneurial spirit is nothing new. It started with the founder's vision, and it remains foundational in all strategies. What is very different in an Amway that has recently celebrated 60 years as a successful business are the accumulated assets and the expertise gained. Amway's Nutrilite brand is now the world's leading brand of nutritional supplements supported by research in their laboratories and products grown on their farms throughout the world. Amway is also made up of vibrant communities offline and growing online, led by ABOs. The community culture of Amway rewards and recognizes ABOs who build successful businesses through tiered compensation and incentives that can be earned for sustainable business building based on sales to happy, loyal customers. Consequently, those recognized as ABO leaders are also recognized as partners in the common purpose of helping people live better and healthier lives.

As a result of our research, we have predicted that the future of the gig economy will be more inclusive of women. Direct selling historically has been approximately 75% women versus 25% men, so we wondered what the Amway outlook might be. Pant shared that Amway is for everyone but that he, too, expects women to play an even greater role in the future. Currently, in Korea – a billion-dollar market for Amway – 90% of Amway IBOs are women. In Russia, 80% are women.

As we concluded our conversation, Pant shared his enthusiasm for what the gig economy represents, how Amway is planning to be a major player, and how Amway supports entrepreneurial education through other organizations and programs throughout the world. Pant's most recent experience in India was a great cap to our conversation. He told us a story about a young woman who entered an entrepreneurial education program through a nongovernmental organization, or NGO, that Amway had helped to fund. The program focused on teaching basic skills associated with being a successful entrepreneur. Through the program, this young woman overcame shyness and self-doubt, gained the self-confidence she had lacked, and started her own business. Her business concept supported her passions and her goals. Pant said that making this kind of education available throughout the world is part of Amway's 10-year vision to be the change for a better world, empowering women and increasing economic opportunities for everyone – in other words, living Amway's decades-old purpose to help people live better, healthier lives.

Interview With Kevin Guest, Chief Executive Officer, USANA Health Sciences, Inc.

Kevin Guest, CEO of USANA Health Sciences, has attracted our attention on many occasions. Guest is humble when it comes to talking about current USANA success. The USANA brand is one of the few direct selling brands to exceed a billion dollars in annual revenues. Guest is also the type of chief executive who does not mind sharing his personal thoughts about his company's future. For a couple of years, probably more, Guest has been talking about change, becoming an easier to understand and more appealing business model. He openly talked about the gig economy. When we interviewed Guest for this book, as expected, he was ready to talk.

The following text is all a reflection of the ideas shared by USANA's CEO in an interview that lasted about one hour. The thoughts shared provide an example of innovation and creativity called into action quickly as a result of external influences. In some cases, we may have slightly rephrased a statement or parts of the story to enhance clarification.

Guest said: "*USANA has been working on the future for quite some time; however, COVID-19 hits and suddenly, we are faced with a different reality relative to our entire business model. What it did catapulted us into either sink or swim mode. Luckily, we were already somewhat on the runway when we had to make a shift and a change. We went from a person-to-person model to a technology-based model very quickly, and it has been a good thing for USANA.*

The entire team at USANA embraced change very quickly, streamlining our distribution channels, evaluating our supply chain challenges, eliminating redundancies, keeping our customers supplied with products, and our associates throughout the world paid for the work they do. The process of adapting to sudden change is complex when dealing with different governments and different issues in different parts of the world; however, our success is a testimony to the USANA organizational structure and the talent and commitment of our people.

USANA employees were also forced to work from home, and the experience provided another positive for us. The experience gave them a much better understanding of what our home-based independent business owners experience every single day; therefore, we are now shifting our culture from having everyone come into the office to allowing people to work how they want to work and how they are most productive, which is very counterintuitive to traditional business. This has been new learning for me personally, and I have totally changed my mind about how employees can do the work. I've seen productivity go up ever since these decisions were implemented, and I totally expected the opposite. It's been a very pleasant surprise."

When we asked Guest about the new marketplace and the new competition for those companies who utilize the direct selling channel of distribution and direct sellers themselves, we found another interesting response. Specifically, we asked Guest how he viewed competition such as Amazon, and he responded:

"Amazon is an interesting strategic question. They have established new benchmarks for customer service, and we talk about Amazon frequently. From a strategic point of view, you could take one or two different approaches. They can be viewed as a competitor, especially when your products show up on Amazon. However, the Amazon interaction with the customer experience is, in my opinion, second to none. So, at USANA, we do not view Amazon as a competitor; we view them as a partner. The question becomes, how can we leverage Amazon as a distribution channel while not competing with our sales channel and enhance our value proposition?

By becoming the authorized seller of our products on the Amazon platform, we can set the price level. Amazon is also a search engine, and people use Amazon frequently to locate products for which they are looking. If your business does not come up on Amazon from a business perspective, it directly affects your credibility with the end buyer. At USANA, we are choosing to look at Amazon from a different perspective, not as a point of sale perspective, but to control the channel from a partner perspective so that we become more relevant in the digital world."

We asked Guest about the importance of how direct selling models have been described and how they will be better described in the future. Once again, Guest provided insights helpful to all using the direct selling model.

"*We are changing the language we use because language is important. We must stay relevant. Our business model has been around for many years. Many of the old terms and phrases we once used are no longer relevant in today's world and society. In the direct selling world, we have been good in the use of acronyms, terms, and descriptions that we learned very well. The new challenge: the layperson and the masses out there, don't understand a lot of what we have said about how our business model works. There is a new speed associated with decision making that goes against the speed that people want to receive information. In other words, we no longer have time to explain. If we don't change our language to be relevant to the person who knows nothing about what we do or how our businesses work, we'll miss the opportunity to attract so many more to our business model.*

One of our more recent examples of how our language and behaviors are creating new opportunities for USANA Associates is the story of a former Fortune 500 company executive who has been involved as a USANA Associate for over 20 years. He is considered a senior baby boomer who has figured out how to use the language of today to optimize search engine results, which bring people to his personal USANA platform. With a new language, he has reinvigorated his entire business. He is one of our new rock stars. He has developed several hundred customers, perhaps many more. Just last week, I know he attracted more than 50 people to our preferred customer program. This is an example of how our USANA Associates can build a very profitable business focused on customer acquisition and retention.

In support of customer acquisition and retention, we encourage our USANA Associates to add value beyond just the transaction of buying a bottle of vitamins from us. Our associates are learning to take the digital support we offer and add value by offering a personal touch. Some offer personal information, free classes, sharing recipes, or whatever they might be doing that is value-added to a person's life. The sale, when it happens, becomes much more than just a transaction. It becomes more of a relationship, and the opportunity to build a relationship with the end-user is one of the attributes we offer our independent business owners. The opportunity to build relationships with consumers is an asset to our business model. When customers do not find more than the sales transaction, they will try something else, perhaps something cheaper."

In this book, we have taken the position that gig-providing companies are expected to provide their gig workers with excellent support, including guidance in how to do the work without jeopardizing the workers' independent contractor status. Because direct selling companies have typically provided specific onboarding guidance, we wondered what else might be important from USANA's perspective.

Guest said: *"From a company perspective, we are now very conscious about leading by example. We must be an example of what we expect from our independent salesforce of USANA Associates in everything that we do, inclusive of our social presence and the tools we provide. What we do must also be shareable by our associates. Therefore, we consider who our associates are in everything we do. The questions are many. The housewife with three small children, who is trying to build a part-time business in her neighborhood, must be understood. We must also understand that the shareables that we create must be customizable so that our independent associates can add some of their own images and their own language. This will certainly become one of our most important competitive strengths."*

Game-changers are usually newer companies with innovation and creativity that tend to disrupt the more traditional models. USANA was founded over 27 years ago by Dr. Myron Wentz, a PhD, visionary scientist, philanthropist, and entrepreneur. The company also has a track record on ongoing success, so it would be easy to understand a status quo stance and strategy.

Guest shared the challenges of being successful and needing to change: *"One of our greatest struggles and challenges lies in the fact that we are a 27-year-old company, and we have been very successful over those 27 years and continue to be. We cannot fall into the 'if it's not broken, don't fix it space.' As a direct selling company, we were accustomed to a selling process, in which the direct seller would meet personally with a prospect, give a presentation, and answer questions about everything pertaining to the products. But in today's world, we must think like the retail competition. The new retail competition thinks in 30-second sound bites, and they assume that the person considering their product, or their offering, knows nothing about it. Within those 30 seconds, a message has to be conveyed.*

Today, the selling process has to be so simple that a person can either enroll or buy products with one touch from their smartphone. If it is too complicated, we risk losing that transaction. We're not there yet as a company at USANA, but that is our end goal. We see a different future, and it is one of more simplicity."

We asked Guest about the role and importance of women in USANA's outlook and growth strategies. *"One thing that will not change at USANA is the role we see women playing in the future of our business. Currently, women represent 75–80% of USANA Associates and customers. We find that women are the ones who make most of the household decisions, especially decisions relative to how money is spent, and how best to support the family's concern for health and fitness. Previously men dominated the recognition of our top-performing independent business owners;*

however, that is changing. Our top-performing independent business owners are now becoming more women than men.

The gig economy is attracting those primarily interested in supplemental income that offers flexibility, and the possibilities are very appealing to women. USANA provides flexibility, the ability to work from home, and the ability to engage the business opportunity for a modes investment in a starter kit. The entry-level investment is low and includes support from the company. It works beautifully for the woman who wants to supplement her family income. The company handles all the logistics and details as far as shipping the product to customers, and we pay our associates weekly for their successful efforts."

As Guest concluded, he acknowledged that non–direct selling companies known for their innovation and new models of customer service have served to shape the thinking at USANA. He also provided the following outlook for the future of direct selling.

"My outlook for the direct selling model is: we are perfectly positioned to move into our next wave of growth in our next iteration of what this business model can be if we are open-minded and willing to change. And if we're willing to be disruptive, disruptive in our innovation from a business model perspective, as well as a product offering perspective. And I believe that direct sales will come up with some innovative ways to move the gig economy even further along. It can't be business as usual or more of the same.

The direct sales model has something that companies like Wayfair and Amazon don't have. We literally have tens of hundreds of thousands of distribution points all over the globe in the form of people who love our products, buy our products, consume our products, and use them frequently. That is a powerful army, and as we continue to leverage that army in a new disruptive way and look at this army from a distribution perspective, that's very powerful! The direct selling model has millions of people involved around the world, more than any retailer has stores. This is huge power and one of our greatest assets. We also, as a distribution model, focus on developing personal relationships. Technology can try to emulate this quality through different computer algorithms, which we will also use; however, our personal connections with people is really the gas in the engine. It's the fuel and power that's going to drive this model into the future."

Sheryl Adkins-Green, Chief Marketing Officer, Mary Kay Inc.

Sheryl Adkins-Green, Mary Kay's CMO, is a game-changer because of the enormous responsibility of her position. As a CMO, Adkins-Green is responsible for the brand and its many products in the cosmetics category. However, Mary Kay is a different kind of cosmetics company. The products are only sold through independent direct selling consultants. The brand is also composed of the story of Mary Kay Ash and her reasons for starting the company. Founded in 1963 with four products, Mary Kay Inc. is now a global brand recognizable in over 40 countries through millions of independent consultants, achieving several billion in annual revenues.

Changing the game was what Mary Kay Ash set out to do when she founded the company, and she did. When we recently reviewed the Mary Kay website in preparation for the interview with Adkins-Green, we found descriptions of the founder that concisely describe her motivations. The following is reprinted from the Mary Kay website:

> *For Mary Kay Ash, it was always mission possible. After experiencing inequality in the workplace, she knew she had to make a change, not only for herself but for all women. In 1963, Mary Kay Ash launched her business and disrupted the idea of "business as usual", turning the male-dominated workplace on its head in the process. A change champion and ground-breaking businesswoman, Mary Kay Ash dedicated her life to empowering women and putting them in control of their own futures.*

Mary Kay Ash always believed that the right values could carry you all the way to the top. She remained faithful to the life lessons that shaped her as a person and used the Golden Rule to guide her, making sure she was always leading by example and lifting others up along the way. She often told others, "Never, absolutely never, compromise your principles." Her unwavering integrity has inspired millions of women and made her one of the world's greatest entrepreneurs and leaders.

When Mary Kay Ash was a young girl, her mother always told her, "You can do it, Mary Kay!" From onstage recognition to electrifying speeches, Mary Kay Ash shared this same encouragement with millions of women. She imagined everyone wearing a sign that said, "Make me feel important," and she made it part of everything she did. With these simple words of inspiration, Mary Kay Ash connected a community of women who found confidence through encouragement and grew it into a global empire.

As a CMO, Adkins-Green brings a wealth of global sales and marketing knowledge to her role. She joined Mary Kay Inc. in January 2009 as the Vice President of Global Brand Development and was named CMO and executive team member in July 2011. Her goal is to strengthen Mary Kay's position as an irresistible beauty brand around the world. Prior to Mary Kay, Adkins-Green held executive positions with Alberto-Culver, Cadbury-Schweppes, Citigroup, and Kraft Foods. She has significant experience in business development, strategic thinking, and high-level negotiations.

Closely aligning with Mary Kay's focus on improving women's economic independence, Adkins-Green is actively involved in the community through the Mary Kay Foundation's mission to find a cure for cancers affecting women and stop the incidence of violence against women. In addition, she is a Trustee of Texas Christian University, and she serves on the board of the Dallas Museum of

Art. She received a Bachelor of Science, cum laude, from the University of Wisconsin and a Master of Business Administration from Harvard Business School.

Our first question for Adkins-Green: Could you describe the differences in Mary Kay today versus the company founded over 50 years ago? Her response was indicative of a company that consistently finds ways to reinvent itself while staying true to founding principles and values.

"The fundamental drivers of the Mary Kay business, both in terms of how Mary Kay supports the independent salesforce and in turn, how they support and serve their customers, remains focused on golden rules, providing products and services focusing on building relationships, not just selling. That's not going to change, and it hasn't changed for 55-plus years. Our use of technology and tools have obviously changed, and they will continue to change in the future but always with a goal of building and maintaining value, building loyal relationships, between Mary Kay and the independent salesforce, as well as the independent salesforce with their customers."

We also wanted Adkins-Green to describe her role and responsibility. We knew that it would include more than a traditional approach to marketing and our assumption was correct: Here is how she described her role: *"My role is really about supporting the success of the independent salesforce, making sure that I'm helping them represent themselves, the products, and Mary Kay opportunity in a manner that is relevant to what people are looking for today. For example, we have certainly seen, over the last five-plus years, the rise of social influencers. An independent beauty consultant is very much an influencer because she is knowledgeable and becomes a trusted advisor to those she serves. So maintaining the relevancy of our brand image – our products and opportunity – requires modern tools, and that is part of my responsibility, making sure that our marketing materials, social content, apps, all keep her and her image modern and relevant."*

So much of the popularity surrounding the interests in gig economy opportunities grew out of the use of technology and the easily accessed app we can download onto a smartphone. As we expected, Adkins-Green had more to say about apps and the importance of the Mary Kay beauty consultant. "*I think we were on the leading edge, particularly in the direct selling industry, with some of the apps we first developed. We could not pull them off the shelf or just put our branding on something that came out of a box. The value adds to our apps is the independent beauty consultant being able to add her experience and advice. So in other words, you can try to program what the right shade of lipstick might be for my skin tone, but it's not going to do as good of a job as someone who actually knows me, that has seen me at church, or seen me in the grocery store. Our beauty consultants will always do a better job of guiding me, even if we're leveraging technology and keeping a safe social distance.*"

We talked with the CEOs we interviewed as to how Amazon had impacted any of their plans or outlook for the future, and we asked Adkins-Green the same question. Her response: "*Well, I'm proud to say that great customer service, including timely and convenient delivery, has always been part of our model. Around the world, delivery options can take different forms, and in some cases, we leverage third parties. I would not single out Amazon, but we certainly cannot ignore the fact that for many people, Amazon is their benchmark experience. We look to the best of the best across e-commerce and other retail experiences. Our goal is to bring the best practices together for the independent beauty consultant so that she will have the best options and support for her customers.*"

We also wanted to know if Mary Kay was encouraging any new language and behaviors of beauty consultants that may have changed over recent years as the marketplace changed. Direct selling has always been focused on a method of selling that required personal interaction, one-on-one, or in small groups. The party plan or home party method of selling has long been the Mary Kay preferred method. Beauty consultants who took their knowledge and expertise, along with adding innovative ways to bring fun and enjoyment into the home party experience, created one of the most respected cosmetics and skincare brands in the world. Adkins-Green acknowledges that some things have changed, but some things are also the same: *"As I think about the language and vocabulary of Mary Kay, in broad strokes, the vocabulary has always been around sharing, not selling. Not that selling is not important; it is just not part of the primary vocabulary. It has always been about 'try before you buy,' and 'here is what I can show you.' This whole notion that when you help others achieve their goals, you will achieve your goals, is very much a part of the Mary Kay DNA, which originated with our founder. Now, of course, we have millions of independent beauty consultants, and I will never know what's in every dialogue or conversation, but I can speak very confidently that our DNA is the same in terms of the communications and guidance we provide our beauty consultants, the vocabulary of creating value and serving others is predominant. These are the things that remain the same and distinguish Mary Kay as a culture, as a brand. And I don't imagine any of this will change going forward. If anything, I think this is a time when empathy and humanity is front and center .... Why would we ever express ourselves differently, particularly at this moment in time?"*

Knowing that the emergence and growth of the gig economy have been thriving due to effective use of technology and reducing complexity to simplicity while emphasizing flexibility, freedom, and fair rewards for the work – traditional attributes of the direct selling model – we wanted Adkins-Green to share thoughts relative to the importance of customer acquisition and retention in the Mary Kay model. Adkins-Green shared:

"Customer acquisition and retention have always been important, and we are always striving to help the independent salesforce build a loyal customer base. When she has a loyal customer base, her business is better. It's more productive for her. In other words, when she has a loyal customer base that she's maintaining, as opposed to always needing to find a new customer, her business is usually better. Maintaining a strong base of loyal customers is usually the result of building strong relationships. The importance of loyalty and relationships is important, and it always has been."

Mary Kay was one of the original champions for women in business, and their beauty consultants are mostly women. Adkins-Green fondly spoke about the needs of women:

"Certainly by nature of what Mary Kay established and what we focus on, we know and understand how important the flexibility of the opportunity is to a woman. Community is also important, and so is culture. Women are often the primary caregiver, the primary breadwinner in their family; therefore, they need choices and flexibility to be able to balance family goals, their personal, professional goals, and their financial goals. These are challenges that women have always faced and will continue to face. Going forward, because of the pandemic, the need to be able to be home to care for, even educate, children, make sure that other relatives in the family network are getting the care and supplies they need, becomes even more important. In my opinion, gig opportunities will be important for women."

As the CMO of one of the world's largest direct selling companies, we wondered if new innovative companies like Shopify, known for making business simpler for microentrepreneurs, had impacted the marketing strategies or the support a company like Mary Kay provides its independent salesforce. Adkins-Green spoke to the importance of the support Mary Kay provides:

"I think any technology that makes it easy and convenient to conduct your business basically from anywhere, anytime, is always going to be relevant. And so in that respect, we are always looking at our tools, our platform, our technology, to provide the convenience, the speed, the mobile-friendly applications needed to make it convenient for the independent salesforce. So yes, I think Shopify is one of those competitive benchmarks, but we're always going to be looking around the world for the best practices."

We asked Adkins-Green what she felt to be most important about the direct selling business model:

In my opinion, it's the individual, the independent business owner. They are the brand. Direct selling is more than direct to consumer. Direct selling offers the opportunity to build relationships with consumers, which is about more than the transaction between seller and buyer. Just because one person transacts with another individual is not a relationship. Relationships are built over time. And, for me, that is what distinguishes direct selling. When done right, direct selling is about the relationship and the value that an individual can bring to a transaction. Caring about the customer being satisfied with the products or services is the added value a direct seller brings, and that, to me is unique, and probably the most important and sustainable element of direct selling. Relationships are important, and you cannot put relationships in an app. You can't use artificial intelligence as effectively; you got to come back to a human being, a human being who's inspired, and a human being who does care about the customers with whom they're doing business.

Everything my team and I do, and really all that we all do at Mary Kay, is centered around our independent salesforce of Mary Kay beauty consultants, and how do we elevate her value and her importance. We always think about the service we provide, the tools she must have, and the corporate resources we must make available. She must spend some time becoming knowledgeable, confident in the quality of the products that she is representing and be able to answer questions or know how to get to the right information quickly. We are always thinking about how to make sure that she is confident and credible as that value-added resource to her customers.

SUMMARY

This chapter has served to highlight gig-providing companies and individuals who have changed the game. Gig-providing companies are noted for their contributions in support of an estimated 60 million gig workers in the United States alone. It is because of these

> Mary Kay is a unique way of life that provides the brushes,
> the oils, the pigments, and the canvas on which you can paint
> your life as you really want it to be. You choose your own
> colors, your own design, and your own pattern. It's a place
> where you can reach higher, think bigger, grow greater, and
> live deeper than anyplace else on the face of the earth.
> — Mary Kay Ash, Founder, Mary Kay Inc.

companies, and the visions and innovations of their founders, that
we now have work opportunities available to the masses in a
flexible manner. In this new economy, the worker actually decides
how and when they will work their gig.

Unlike the position many journalists take when writing stories
about work opportunities outside of the traditional formats, we
chose to focus on the positive attributes gig-providing companies
bring to a labor force that is challenged by shrinking wage
increases, the possibility of being replaced or displaced by artificial
intelligence, aging, and the need to be retrained to maintain value in
a competitive world dominated by the use of technology and new
efficiencies. The gig economy provides new hope and, more
importantly, new work opportunities available to the broadest
segments in the marketplace, perhaps ever. This is of utmost
importance because part-time, flexible work opportunities are
important to a growing segment of Americans.

The US Department of Labor continues to forecast growth of
the gig economy. This, in itself, is a significant data point. The
American dream of attaining the desired work and life balance will
always, we believe, be in the DNA of free people in free societies
throughout the world. People from all walks of life are not
attracted to gig opportunities because they are already earning
enough; they are looking for more, enough to make a difference in
their lives.

A gig can be that ray of hope. Gigs, as we now know, are engaged by both the younger generations and the more mature. A résumé is not needed to participate. Neither age nor other traditional job requirements are a barrier to entry. Most interesting for us was the discovery in our research results, of the amount of education the majority of gig workers have. (See Chapter 11 for more detail.) Gig workers are smart.

Gigs are not perfect, but they are incredible. We are compelled to use the descriptor "incredible" because gigs are helping those who are willing to work to have the opportunity to meet and overcome challenges, pay off bills, possibly eliminate some debt, care for their family while they work, and enjoy a bit more of the great gift of life. Gig workers need more support. Those who provide safety net products and services need to step up their games. It is not the worker's fault that they do not have access to affordable safety net products and services, nor is it the responsibility of gig-providing companies to supply them. This is not intended to be a political statement, rather only recognition that there is a new force of workers who are having a profound impact on the future of work. The gig model works for gig providers, workers, and consumers. These new workers need new products relative to their needs at affordable costs.

We also interviewed leadership from three direct selling companies for this chapter, very intentionally. We took the position earlier in the book; from our perspective and knowledge of work history, the direct selling model was the first form of gig work. However, today's direct selling company is very different from the days of the "Yankee Peddler." Direct selling companies are more of a platform being utilized by independent contractors to exponentially expose the band/platform in a more personal manner to friends, family, social contacts, and new prospects. Direct selling is a sub-set within the gig economy. Collectively, the gig economy supports hundreds of millions of customers being served by the products and services provided by gig providing companies (Table 12.3).

This chapter has been about game-changers, and there are many more!

BRIEF SUMMARY OF GIG-PROVIDING COMPANIES CHANGING THE GAME

Table 12.3. Profiles of Companies Changing the Game in the Gig Economy.

Company	Bus. Model	Description	Founded	Headquarters	Funding	Public/Private	By the Numbers
Airbnb	Property rental/ management	Platform allowing property owners to market and rent underused properties	2008	San Francisco, CA	$5.4 billion through 16 rounds[a]	Private	>650,000 hosts and >750 million guests to date
Angie's List	Home services/ contractor referral	Platform connecting users with licensed/vetted professionals for long list of services	1995	Indianapolis, IN	$182.6 million through 9 rounds[a]	Public (NASDAQ: ANGI)	2019 revenue: $1.3 billion (parent company)
Bark	Home services/ contractor referral	Platform connecting users with licensed/vetted professionals for long list of services	2014	London, England	–	Private	5 million users; 2019 revenue: ~$25,500,000

BlaBlaCar	P2P ridesharing	P2P ridesharing that expanded to bus and train lines, major acquisitions	2006	Paris, France	$448.5 million through 6 rounds[a]	Private	70 million passengers across all services in 2019; 2019 revenue: est. $92.5 million
Care.com	Home services	Platform connecting families and local caregivers for child, senior, or pet care, as well as special needs, housekeeping, and tutoring services	2006	Waltham, MA	–	Public (NYSE – CRCM)	$499 million market capitalization (8/20), $192.2 million in 2018 revenues
Caviar	Food delivery	Platform connecting customers, businesses, and independent contractors for delivery with a focus on higher-end meals and restaurants that typically would not deliver	2012	San Francisco, CA	$15 million through 3 rounds[a]	Private	Acquired by DoorDash in 2019

Continued

Table 12.3. (Continued)

Company	Bus. Model	Description	Founded	Headquarters	Funding	Public/Private	By the Numbers
ChefsFeed	Home services	Platform allowing chefs to showcase their meals and connect with users for a tailored dining/pop-up experience	2011	San Francisco, CA	$8.5 million through 7 rounds[a]	Private	Expanded into 24 US cities with 1000 "experts" by 2013
Deliveroo	Food delivery	Platform connecting customers, businesses, and independent contractors for food delivery	2012	London, England	$1.5 billion through 8 rounds[a]	Private	~30,000 drivers (2016); 2019 revenue: est. $605 million
Didi Chuxing Technology Co.	Ridesharing/ ride-hailing	China's largest ridesharing platform	2012	Beijing, China	$21.2 billion through 18 rounds[a]	Private	10 billion+ trips/year

	Industry	Description	Year	Headquarters	Funding	Status	Metrics
DoorDash	Food delivery	Platform connecting customers, businesses, and independent contractors for food delivery	2013	San Francisco, CA	$2.5 billion through 11 rounds[a]	Private	340,000 stores; 2019 revenue: $900 million
Drizly	Food delivery	Platform connecting customers, businesses, and independent contractors for delivery with a focus on alcohol	2012	Boston, MA	$119.6 million through 8 rounds[a]	Private	est. 2019 revenue: $50 million–$100 million
Etsy	E-commerce/marketing	E-commerce platform for sale of variety of creative goods	2005	New York, NY	$97.3 million through 9 rounds[a]	Public (NASDAQ: ETSY)	2.8 million active sellers; 47.7 million active buyers; 2019 revenue: $818 million

Continued

Table 12.3. (Continued)

Company	Bus. Model	Description	Founded	Headquarters	Funding	Public/Private	By the Numbers
Fiverr	Home services/ Gig outsourcing	Outsourcing for any service imaginable, competes with Upwork, Freelancer, TaskRabbit	2009	Tel Aviv, Israel	$111 million through 6 rounds[a]	Public (NYSE: FVRR)	2.27 million annual customers as of Q3 2019; est. 2019 revenue: $107.1 million
Freelancer Technologies	Gig outsourcing/ staffing	Platform connecting potential employees with companies addressing staffing issues	2009	Sydney, Australia	A$37.5 million through 4 rounds[a]	Public (ASX: FLN)	More than 46 million users
Funding Circle	P2P lending	P2P lending	2010	San Francisco, CA	$746.4 million through 10 rounds[a]	Public	More than 100,000 global investors; est. 2019 revenue: $219.6 million

Company	Category	Description	Founded	Location	Funding	Status	Notes
GoFundMe	Crowdfunding	Crowdfunding platform for all kinds of projects, includes separate charity platform (GoFundMe Charity)	2010	Redwood City, CA	–	Private	50 million donors; est. 2019 revenue: $50 million to $100 million
GoPuff	Food delivery	Platform connecting customers and independent contractors for low-cost good delivery	2013	Philadelphia, PA	$866.8 million through 5 rounds[a]	Private	3,000+ products in regional facilities, 200+ facilities, flat delivery fee, 500+ cities, $1 billion valuation
Grab	Food delivery/ ride-hailing	Platform connecting customers, businesses, and independent contractors for food	2014	Houston, TX	$10.1 billion through 31 rounds[a]	Private	60% market share in Southeast Asia, forecasted doubling of revenue in

Continued

Table 12.3. (Continued)

Company	Bus. Model	Description	Founded	Headquarters	Funding	Public/Private	By the Numbers
		delivery, while also featuring ride-hailing functions					2019, valued at $10 billion, Uber holds 28% stake, growth spurred on by Uber resources
Grubhub	Food delivery	Platform connecting customers, businesses, and independent contractors for food delivery	2004	Chicago, IL	$284.1 million through 8 rounds[a]	Public (NYSE: GRUB)	>300,000 restaurants; 2019 revenue: $1.3 billion; approximately $6 billion in gross food sales to restaurants

Handy	Home services	Standard Home Services platform focused on handyman tasks	2012	New York, NY	$110.7 million through 7 rounds[a]	Private (subsidiary of ANGI Home Services)	est. 2019 revenue: $33.4 million; 1 million bookings as of 2015, 80% of bookings are repeat customers, value based on type of service, acquired by ANGI Homeservices in 2018
Home Advisor	Home services/ contractor referral	Platform connecting users with licensed/vetted professionals for long list of services	1999	Lakewood, CO	–		~100,000 professionals as of 2015; 30 million homeowners

Continued

Table 12.3. (Continued)

Company	Bus. Model	Description	Founded	Headquarters	Funding	Public/Private	By the Numbers
Homeaway	Property rental/ management	Platform allowing property owners to market and rent underused properties	2005	Austin, TX	$510.3 million through 7 rounds[a]	Public, Delisted (NASDAQ: AWAY)	Phasing out brand to promote VRBO, acquired by Expedia Group in 2015 ($3.9 billion)
Homestay.com	Property rental/ management	Platform connecting live-in hosts with traveling guests	2013	Dublin, Ireland	$3 million through 1 round[a]	Private	est. 2019 revenue: $9.5 million
Houzz	Home services/ contractor referral	Platform connecting users with licensed/vetted professionals for long list of services	2009	Palo Alto, CA	$613.6 million through 6 rounds[a]	Private	>17 million annual customers; est. 2019 revenue: > $500 million

InstaCart	Full-service shopping	Platform connecting users with those willing to shop on their behalf at grocery stores and other popular outlets	2012	San Francisco, CA	$2.2 billion through 13 rounds[a]	Private	~130,000 full-service shoppers; ~12,000 in-store shoppers; ~50,000 users
Just Eat	Food delivery	Platform connecting customers, businesses, and independent contractors for food delivery	2001	London, England	$122 million through 4 rounds[a]	Public (LSE: JE)	est. 2019 revenue: $1.27 billion; acquired GrubHub, merged with Takeaway.com in 2020
Kajabi	Content creation	Knowledge commerce platform for sharing any category of knowledge	2009	Irvine, CA	–	Private	Focus on online business creation, empowered 60 million students in 120 countries to date to make over $1.5 billion in sales

Continued

Table 12.3. (Continued)

Company	Bus. Model	Description	Founded	Headquarters	Funding	Public/Private	By the Numbers
Kickstarter	Crowdfunding	Crowdfunding platform for creative projects	2007	New York, NY	$10 million through 1 round[a]	Private	17.462 million users; $4.8 billion pledged to date
Lending Club	P2P lending	Platform connecting lenders and borrowers with attractive interest rates and low barriers to entry	2007	San Francisco, CA	$392.2 million through 14 rounds[a]	Public (NYSE: LC)	2019 revenue: $188.5 million
Lyft	Ridesharing/ ride-hailing	Main Uber competitor in ridesharing/ride-hailing	2012	San Francisco, CA	$4.9 billion through 20 rounds[a]	Public (NASDAQ: LYFT)	1.4 million drivers; 23 million users; 2019 revenue: $3.6 billion

Ola	Ridesharing/ride-hailing	India's biggest ridesharing company	2010	Bengaluru, India	$3.8 billion through 25 rounds[a]	Private	1.5 million driver-partners; > 1 billion rides/year; est. 2019 revenue: $364.8 million
Patreon	Content creation	Platform connecting artists/content creators with fans and sponsors willing to support them on a monthly basis	2013	San Francisco, CA	$165.9 million through 5 rounds[a]	Private	150,000+ creators; 5 million monthly active patrons, $1 billion paid out to date
Porch	Home services/contractor referral	Platform connecting users with licensed/vetted professionals for long list of services	2013	Seattle, WA	$119.9 million through 5 rounds[a]	Private	>8,000 companies; 65% of US homebuyers; est. 2019 revenue: $50 million to $100 million

Continued

Table 12.3. (Continued)

Company	Bus. Model	Description	Founded	Headquarters	Funding	Public/Private	By the Numbers
Postmates	Gig food delivery	Competes directly with Grubhub, DoorDash, other food delivery gigs	2011	San Francisco, CA	$903 million through 13 rounds[a]	Private	
Prosper	P2P lending/ funding	Platform connecting lenders and borrowers with attractive interest rates and low barriers to entry	2005	San Francisco, CA	$415.5 million through 16 rounds[a]	Private	$17 billion borrowed to date
Rover	Pet services	Service connecting pet owners with sitters/ walkers	2011	Seattle, WA	$310.9 million through 10 rounds[a]	Private	>300,000 sitters; ~10.5 million customers/year

Shopify	E-commerce/marketing		2004	Ontario, Canada	$122.3 million through 4 rounds[a]	Public (NYSE: SHOP)	2019 revenue: $1.578 billion
TaskRabbit	Home services/gig outsourcing	Similar to Home Service gigs but with wider variety of services	2008	San Francisco, CA	$37.7 million through 7 rounds[a]	Private	>140,000 Taskers in North America; est. 2019 revenue: $25 million
Thinkific	Content creation	Platform enabling entrepreneurs to create, market, sell, and deliver online courses	2012	Vancouver, BC, Canada	–	Private	6 million students in 2019
Thumbtack	Home services	Platform connecting local professionals with customers	2008	San Francisco, CA	$423.2 million through 7 rounds[a]	Private	est. 2019 revenue: $170.6 million
Toptal	Gig outsourcing/staffing	Platform connecting potential employees with companies addressing staffing issues	2010	San Francisco, CA	$1.4 million (seed)[a]	Private	$100 million revenue in 2016

Continued

Table 12.3. (Continued)

Company	Bus. Model	Description	Founded	Headquarters	Funding	Public/Private	By the Numbers
Twitch	Content creation	Social video platform for gamers	2007	San Francisco, CA	$35 million through 3 rounds[a]	Private	Acquired by Amazon in 2014 for $1 billion, $300 million generated in advertising in 2019
Uber	Ridesharing/ ride-hailing		2009	San Francisco, CA	$24.7 billion through 26 rounds[a]	Public (NYSE: UBER)	2019 revenue: $14.1 billion; 1.7 billion trips in Q1 2020; 111 million active users FY 2019
Uber Eats		Platform connecting customers, businesses, and independent contractors for food delivery	2014	San Francisco, CA	–	Private	

Upstart	P2P lending/funding	Platform connecting lenders and borrowers with attractive interest rates and low barriers to entry	2012	San Mateo, CA	$144.1 million through 6 rounds[a]	Private	>490,000 customers; est. 2019 revenue $15 million
Upwork	Home services/gig outsourcing	Online platform matching users with freelancers across different categories	2015 (1999 as Elance-oDesk)	San Francisco, CA	$168.8 million through 12 rounds[a]	Public (NASDAQ: UPWK)	2019 revenue: $302.6 million; 12 million registered freelancers and 5 million registered users as of 2017
VRBO	Property rental/management	Platform allowing property owners to market and rent underused properties	1995	Aurora, CO	–	Private	Recorded $267 million in revenue in the first quarter of 2019
Wag	Pet services	Service connecting pet owners with sitters/walkers	2015	Los Angeles, CA	$361.5 million through 8 rounds[a]	Private	>300,000 caregivers

Continued

Table 12.3. (Continued)

Company	Bus. Model	Description	Founded	Headquarters	Funding	Public/Private	By the Numbers
Wealthy Affiliate	Affiliate marketing	Community platform for marketing education, online business development, and mutually beneficial reviewing	2005	—	—	Private	Over 750 training updates per year, 1.5 million entrepreneurs helped, can build an online business "in 29 seconds"
YouTube	Content creation	Video sharing platform for any kind of content	2005	San Bruno, CA	$11.5 million through 2 rounds[a]	Private	2 billion monthly active users; $15.1 billion in ad revenue in FY 2019

[a]Retrieved from Crunchbase.com.

EPILOGUE – GLIMPSE OF THE FUTURE

REDEFINING WORK TO INCREASE VALUE

The gig economy can be viewed as the gasoline that hit the fire of change in mature economies throughout the world. Flexible work grew out of a cultural shift in how we defined and desired how we wished to work. The gig economy also grew out of a need, a need to earn more to keep pace with the inflation that nullified expected gains in purchasing power as wages increased. We no longer define work as related to the brick and mortar buildings that housed the traditional 9-to-5 job. Work from home is no longer a wish. It is a reality, and the gig economy has been the fuel that has helped companies realize new and better ways to engage labor and serve consumers.

Traditional forms of work still exist in manufacturing facilities, office buildings, and schools throughout the world, and we do not expect these critical components of an advanced society to disappear completely. We do expect artificial intelligence and robotics to change job descriptions and, in some cases, eliminate some types of current jobs. We are also experiencing, perhaps, the redefining of the need for an office-centric environment to accomplish work. The same thought applies to education as well. The need for classrooms and large events will be defined differently.

New efficiencies will embrace the use of more outsourcing. More companies will explore alternative work possibilities. The gig economy – and the opportunity to participate as a gig worker or

267

under a newer label that may be the outcome of more innovation – will offer more choices. High school and college graduates will spend as much time preparing for the possibility of alternative work as much as they prepare for more traditional jobs. They understand that there may be no such thing as a "traditional" job as we continue to invent the future.

Companies that attempt to utilize the popularity and attractiveness of engaging independent contractors to reduce benefits and other employment costs may find the effort, and any success gained, to be short-lived. Becoming more profitable in the short term by reducing the number of employees without a solid plan for future growth is not a growth strategy.

THE GIG ECONOMY WILL SPARK MORE INNOVATION AND CREATIVITY IN HOW WE WORK

The Federal Reserve has a broad definition of people working in the gig economy. The Fed says gig workers could be anyone from a babysitter to an Uber driver. According to that definition, Forbes reports that as many as 75 million gig workers work a gig in the United States alone. When we look at mature markets worldwide, the number is growing and on pace to reach more than one billion workers in the future. Globally, there are double-digit increases in the number of people working in the 55–65 age segment, according to a 2018 report by Morgan Stanley, *The Gig Economy Goes Global*. That is a clear indication that we have a mature global marketplace that is redefining work and its importance to living the lifestyle desired. Why else would an older segment in the population be looking for flexible work opportunities? There is always much discussion about the importance of appealing to millennials because they do represent the future. The older segments remain important, and the gig economy is positioned to provide much-needed opportunity and choice. Age is not a handicap to income opportunity pursuits when pursuing a gig. In fact, it makes no difference.

Global organizations such as the World Bank and International Monetary Fund are paying attention. The future of work is different, and the future is always coming faster than we think.

What we have described as the gig economy in this book will also evolve quickly over the next few years. Pioneering gig-providing companies such as Amazon, Uber, Shopify, Etsy, and others are continuing to innovate and are expected to be disruptive again and again. When Uber disrupted the transportation industry, they did so by using advancements in technology in an innovative manner to engage thousands of drivers who would use their own cars to provide others with transportation. Uber did not want to own a fleet of vehicles; therefore, people from all walks of life benefited from a new flexible work opportunity. We also know that Uber is experimenting with driverless cars. Skeptical thoughts could easily predict that Uber will eliminate its drivers at some point; however, we see it differently. Uber does not appear to be interested in owning physical assets, so we expect a company like Uber to possibly offer leasing opportunities. Those who lease their cars will benefit from leasing without doing the driving. This creates an even greater choice of opportunity for people from all walks of life, and it will not stop there.

The emergence and popularity of Amazon Prime is also a disruptive business model. By offering customers free shipping via a subscription to Amazon Prime, the subscription segment became very profitable for Amazon (over 100 million subscribers). Customers benefit from free shipping and fantastic service. Ironically, customers who pay the Amazon Prime subscription fee may be more inclined to make purchases through Amazon consistently. As a result of this one innovative and creative approach to the business challenge of how to transfer shipping costs to the consumer, Amazon eliminated a barrier that had begun to impact consumer preferences as to which company they choose for online purchases. All companies now work to handle shipping and handling costs innovatively and creatively.

GIG-PROVIDING COMPANIES WILL ADVOCATE AN ADHERENCE TO HIGH ETHICAL STANDARDS

The gig economy does not have a national association or universal body that advocates on behalf of all gig-providing companies or all gig participants. We predict the gig model will begin to adapt and advocate for basic principles and values that are common to all successful business models. Some gig-providing companies are already doing this. Because the gig economy has grown so rapidly, it is clearly understood why there is no one-stop source of information or advocacy. This is where trade associations can be helpful as intermediaries when addressing challenges and the need for advocacy of the business model. However, because the gig economy is growing at such a robust growth rate, new companies are creating more platforms, and more gig workers are being attracted. Gig-providing companies should not wait to adopt and advocate good business practices, including the expectation that all gig workers engaged will always perform at a high ethical standard of expectations.

Without a commitment to high ethical standards, the gig economy could become vulnerable to bad actors no differently than any other model. In our chapter on "A Perspective on Challenges," we identified franchise models, direct selling models, and real estate models as business models that have always relied on independent contractors to do the work of representing the brand, attracting, and retaining customers.

A Universal Code of Conduct for gig workers that could be quickly agreed upon by gig providers might focus on three key points:

1. The importance of delivering an excellent customer experience.
2. Adherence to a high standard of ethics and a no-tolerance policy for unethical behavior.
3. Compliance with all local, state, and federal guidelines, regulations, and tax codes.

When the above three suggested areas are incorporated into company communication, reinforced in ongoing communication, and enforced, directly and indirectly through those who are a part of the crowd involved, all stakeholders win. The primary stakeholders are gig-providing companies, gig workers, consumers, and regulatory bodies.

OTHER INSIGHTS GAINED FROM ULTIMATE GIG PROJECT

The Work and Life Relationship Is Changing

People are increasing their focus on the relationship between work and their quality of life. When we are involved in a traditional type of job that requires a fixed set of hours, we manage our life according to the requirements of the work. Unless we arrange to take time off, we do not schedule a time to shop, attend our children's activities, or even make medical appointments without gaining the proper approvals. However, when the worker determines the type of work and the amount of time invested, work is more likely to be integrated into the person's quality of life. In this scenario, a person can engage a gig and schedule other aspects of their life to work best for them. They can work as many hours as they desire per day and per week.

Gigs Can Be Bridges

The loss of a job may not be as detrimental as in past economies built upon traditional structures, both organizational and physical. The enormous choices in gig work opportunities can be the bridge needed between jobs. They also can provide a chance to explore skills that might be further leveraged into a microenterprise opportunity. In our traditional industrialized society, job loss could be devastating, a fact that helped spark the existence of safety nets. Job loss can occur when the demand for a product or service may diminish. This condition arises from many factors, including seasonality, reduced demand, and or diminished profits. The primary safety net has been unemployment insurance, which is not always available to those who have been eliminated, replaced, or displaced or professionals earning significant income.

Gigs and freelance opportunities can be excellent bridges. These opportunities can be activated immediately, while the job search can last for weeks or months. When we review what we have learned, a gig itself is a safety net. It can be much more powerful and meaningful because the individual controls engagement.

Gig Workers Own Their Work, and They Perform the Work

Employees perform the work, but they do not own the work. Employees generally work for a company, and that company has much higher visibility than the individual contributor. The same could be said for many of the gig-providing companies; however, the consumer or client gets to know the gig worker who is the product or service provider. Because the gig worker owns the product or service and is the person who delivers the product or service, it has become easy for us to predict that quality and consumer value will also increase as the gig economy continues to grow as a channel of distribution. Gig workers are typically rated immediately upon delivering the product or service. The rating is an immediate evaluation of the product or service rendered, which becomes the gig worker's résumé. The difference is that this form of evaluation rates real-time performance, not historical performance. Quality and value are expected to increase for all stakeholders. This is another reason for describing gigs as an economy.

Gender Inequality Has Been a Part of the Labor Discussion for an Entire Century

It remains a debate and will continue to be a debate well in the future as traditional organizational and corporate structures remain the primary distribution methods for products and services. In the June 25, 2019, *Harvard Business Review* issue, Jack Zenger and Joseph Folkman wrote an article entitled *Women Score Higher Than Men in Most Leadership Skills*. It is a fantastic article. Organizational and corporate structures are dominated by men at the top, and women represent about 30% of all senior management positions. Zenger and Folkman stated the following:

> *Still, the disturbing fact is that the percentage of women in senior leadership roles in businesses has remained relatively steady since we conducted our original research. Only 4.9% of Fortune 500 CEOs and 2% of S&P 500 CEOs are women. And those numbers are declining globally.*

.... Women were rated as excelling in taking initiative, acting with resilience, practicing self-development, driving for results, and displaying high integrity and honesty. In fact, they were thought to be more effective in 84% of the competencies that we most frequently measure.

The gig economy model is not based on hierarchy. Therefore, women start any form of gig work as equals. The technology used to identify the talent or provider of the service is not dependent upon who but upon when. My purchases through Etsy are not about who but more about what I desire to purchase and the quality and value the vendor provides. The same is true when I use any of the many apps I enjoy. It is not about who but when if I am seeking a service. The gig economy and its use of technology will continue to level the playing field. We predict the future of gigs will be much more inclusive of women, as more women begin to realize the enormous number of choices available regarding how work can be done on their terms. Gigs empower women and can potentially shift the world of work toward greater equality.

Relationships Can Create Community

Technology is the wonderful connector between products and services, and gig workers connect the dots. However, in our interview with Kevin Guest, CEO at USANA Health Sciences, he emphasized the following particularly important fact: *"You cannot build relationships into an app."* This reaffirmed our observations and previous experiences with the direct selling business model. People make the difference. Independent contractors, from all walks of life, are the critical link in the supply chain that uses people to connect a product or service with a consumer. Airbnb founders, and many others who have pioneered the gig economy popularity, disrupted business models that had been in place for a century. Direct selling companies, along with real estate and insurance companies, were among the first to understand the independent contractor model's value. The older models realized that recognition is often as important as wages. Direct selling companies do this more effectively than any other model that fits a gig economy definition. Direct selling companies are known for their events, which gather people personally and now virtually. Gig-providing companies can learn from the direct selling models and possibly increase productivity by providing more sense of community. It could be accomplished with simple tools such as newsletters and blogs. The tools are available.

The Word Freedom May Need a Broader Definition

We do not tend to think of using the word freedom when describing work. From the traditional perspective, work has generally implied that we are giving up something (time) and providing something (expertise) that will be considered valuable to an employee. The entrepreneur has always viewed work differently.

Our dictionaries typically define freedom from a point of view relative to laws, regulations, and governance. The following type of phrase is typically included regardless of source used to find a definition of the word freedom: "absence of undue restrictions and an opportunity to exercise one's rights and powers." We now apply the word freedom to a new way of working that is inclusive of more than the word flexibility, which is a primary attribute associated with gig work according to our survey and the research conducted by others. Gig work attributes go beyond the word flexibility. Future research will explore this thought more extensively, but it is well worth noting. The growth and popularity of gigs, working when and how one desires to work, means a new type of freedom is being extended to the worker. The employee was the one making the types of decisions discussed. The worker can now make these most important decisions, meaning the worker now has the freedom to determine how and when they will work. This also translates into the amount of money one desires to earn for their efforts. This asset is beyond the asset of flexibility. We call it freedom.

Microenterprise Income Opportunities Will Have a Positive Impact on the Quality of Work!

The industrial revolution provided us with processes that improved the quality of the products and services manufactured for distribution to consumers. Until recently, those who manufactured or provided the products and services depended upon distribution systems that did not rely solely on the participation of individuals. As artificial intelligence and robotics take over more of the functions previously handled by humans, the quality will continue to improve. What is also changing and contributing to even more improvement is the change in how we utilize distribution channels. The gig economy is a new form of distribution.

When fixed stores or online platforms are utilized to connect with consumers, the enterprise controls the distribution channel's critical components. In the gig economy, individuals are now at the center of the distribution channel and closest to the consumer even though technology is the connector. It may appear to the customer that they are connecting directly with the company brand; however, they are not. Amazon utilizes many brand affiliates who direct potential shoppers to Amazon sites. Those affiliates have an opportunity to earn when customers they encourage to visit an Amazon site make a purchase. The affiliate is now a part of the distribution channel, even though the affiliate may be invisible to the consumer.

In most aspects of the gig economy, including direct selling, the gig worker is not invisible. They serve as an actual host, driver, taskmaster, software designer, craftsman, lessor of assets, and provider of products and services that would be unlikely to be found in the traditional marketplace. We could continue to name the thousands of roles a gig worker can play in this new gig economy. The gig worker is not only being held accountable to high performance standards (they are usually rated immediately upon delivery of service), their continued existence and sustainable success are contingent upon a process of continuous improvement. The motivation to improve is huge, and the consumer will continue to befit from greater and greater quality and value because gig workers own the work, the product, and/or the service rendered.

Gigs Provide a Sense of Ownership, or at Least They Can

Ownership changes the game. Workers who contribute to the enterprises they work are known to be more productive when the enterprise recognizes and rewards performance beyond the paycheck. However, when employees complete their contribution, on any given day, they are not expected to take the challenges associated with the work home to their families. Those who own the work, its quality, and the value others receive are expected to give the work the attention it deserves because that is what entrepreneurs do. Based on the research we have conducted, many gig workers do not see themselves as microentrepreneurs. When they recognize themselves as microentrepreneurs, pride in the work will increase, and a sense of ownership will prevail. Gig-providing companies will benefit from a better understanding of this key driver of performance long understood by those companies who utilize the direct selling channel of distribution.

The previous thought reminded me of my best Uber experience. The car was immaculate. The driver got out to open the door for me, offered a bottle of water, and thanked me for choosing Uber before we started the journey. I immediately complimented him and spoke of his attitude, energy, and detail associated with how he cared for his car. I could sense a slight fragrance that was just enough to let me know that care was extended to please the client. My last question to my driver was: What motivates you to provide this type of service? His response: "This is my business, and I am here to serve and please." Wow, what a refreshing ride with this entrepreneur. My continued use of Uber is more about the memory I have of such an extraordinary transportation provider. The tip I included exceeded the cost of the ride. As more gig workers understand their gig as their own businesses, the quality improves for everyone, and the brand also benefits. The gig worker, in many cases, will benefit immediately in forms that may not be immediately tangible, but the impact of the relationship and experience will be realized. This may sound philosophical; however, life seems to promise that what we hand out does come back. Of course, we are referring to the positive attributes of quality as it relates to service rendered.

Gig-Providing Companies Must Support and Protect Their Human Resource

This thought became obvious as we grew to realize the significance of gig work as being the beginning of a new economy – the gig economy. As we started our research, we used the words gig economy a lot. Our conversations and presentations were more focused on the attributes of work that could be embraced with flexibility and the freedom to make important decisions as to how and when the work would be done. What we learned along the way is that the gig economy is, in fact, a new form of economy. As we mentioned earlier in this book, gig workers were recognized in the language used by national governance as our country took steps to protect those whose work was suddenly disrupted by COVID-19. It was a very revealing moment as the government had now recognized the value of a channel of distribution built upon the use of independent workers who work in accordance with the hours they choose, not the hours associated with the traditional job.

Never before had this type of work been recognized from an "unemployment benefit" point of view. This moment of recognition was huge! It does not mean that such benefits should be expected in the future, but the landscape of protective or safety net products that gig workers need should rapidly increase. Gig-providing companies are not expected to provide these benefits, but they should encourage the innovation and creativity needed. They have the clout to be effective accelerators who already represent a new economy contributing over $1 trillion to the US economy.

Gigs Can Provide Serious Income!

Our focus has always been about the incredible choices now available through gigs to earn what can be the difference between earning more than one spends during a month. Most gigs certainly satisfy this need providing income possibilities that probably fall between $500.00 and $1,500.00 per month. However, much more is possible. For those seeking to test themselves in a more entrepreneurial environment, a gig can be the perfect laboratory. A gig or several gigs could grow into a small enterprise. Direct selling companies are known to boast some extraordinary examples of those who have turned a part-time income opportunity into a full-time career granted it is a small percentage of participants. When we look at the distribution of income in any society, it is always a few who earn the lion's share. What we observe to be different from the emergence and growth of the gig economy is that more people can test themselves. They can also opt to test themselves in a variety of ways, not one way. The job restricted the worker to specific lanes. There are no restrictions relative to gig work or the number of gigs one might try. With so many people participating as microenterprise participants, the chances of more people breaking their own glass ceilings may increase. There are neither age restrictions nor résumé requirements when engaging gig work. If more people are able to break their own glass ceilings, and we believe this will happen, the gig economy may actually have a significant impact on the way wealth is distributed but certainly a positive impact on the overall quality of life. When we can earn more than we spend, regardless of income level, we are happier.

Wage Inequality

Gig workers generally earn in accordance to a set of rules, not the résumé or amount of previous experience. Gig opportunities are also easy to explore, and potential compensation is basically the same for everyone who chooses to engage. Jobs have never offered equal pay to every participant. The gig economy, unintentionally, is providing something valuable – the potential elimination of wage inequality or at least the perception. If a microentrepreneur chooses to use a platform like Etsy to sell their creation, they will find it difficult to blame Etsy if the marketplace does not respond. If they are good at providing uniqueness to the extent the marketplace does respond, it is more a result of the quality of the product they are delivering and their own personal marketing efforts. The same can be said for any gig worker who delivers excellence in the work they do. I have experienced a gig service provider who delivered poor service. I doubt that they will succeed. I also doubt that they realized that they were the problem.

Through my many years of working with direct sellers, I always observed that some would find a way to succeed regardless of experience or inexperience. Some would not succeed, but wage inequality was never the reason. The gig economy is providing many more choices where wage inequality is never the issue. The outcome of the work is performance based.

Positive Social Experiences

Because of the flexibility of gig work, participants determine not only how the work will be done but also what types of social interactions they prefer within their gigs. These social interactions can provide fulfillment beyond the income earned. The traditional job environment does not offer choices relative to where the work is done and the social experience gained. In fact, the work is generally done in the same place, every day, around the same people. The social experience is not diverse. Gig work, in many cases, offers a social experience that possibly changes daily, and it is more controlled by the worker versus the traditional employer. For those looking to bring a more diverse social experience into their life and work, choosing to do gig work could be a dream come true, especially if one finds their ultimate gig.

Participation in Personal Development Education Should Be Encouraged

The independent contractor is an independent worker who can benefit from encouragement and nurturing. The nature of independence in a work relationship should not be misunderstood as meaning "leave them alone and let them do it the way they desire." Based upon what we have learned, this perception would nullify much of the tremendous potential of the gig economy to redefine the future of work. We take the position that human ingenuity is best served and nurtured when we are encouraged to grow in self-esteem, believe in our possibilities, and challenged to be the best that we can be. Traditional educational curricula and the traditional workplace have often overlooked this component of what is often referred to as "personal development." In architectural school, we learned how to design buildings, but the curricula did not include one course on designing, planning, and living life. It was my first experience with a direct selling company, as an independent contractor, where I first learned the importance of "me" in the work/life equation. Gig-providing companies will serve their gig workers and themselves well by encouraging participation in personal development guidance. Some may find ways to provide such guidance themselves. They only need to take a page from the direct selling playbook.

Financial Education Also Is Important

Just as gig-providing companies should encourage gig workers to participate in personal development, they would also be wise to support financial education. One of the major reasons most people seek a gig is to earn more money. Yet, financial literacy rates remain quite low. In addition, becoming an independent contractor through a gig opportunity can add a new level of financial complexity to a household. Gig workers who learn the basic skills of money management and how to navigate microentrepreneurship will be more likely to meet the financial goals that caused them to seek a gig than those who do not. Gig-providing companies should see this as an opportunity to stand out from the crowd. Companies that point their gig workers to tools and resources that support financial literacy will likely see a positive return.

Business Ethics Are 10x More Important in a Gig Economy

The ethical standards of a business have always been important, but they are rarely discussed unless the business runs afoul of laws or regulations. When this occurs, the subject of ethics rises toward the top of a priority list. However, we learned in our reading and study in preparation for the writing of this book that a company's adherence to high ethical standards should warrant audits no differently than the audits regularly done on the business components of finance, marketing, compliance with laws and regulations, customer service, supply chain, and other components considered critical to the success of the enterprise.

Human resource departments are generally responsible for the ethics of the corporate culture when the business model depends on employees. When the workers are gig workers, and they are projected to become the majority of the workforce, this new independent contractor labor force also needs to adhere to a high ethical standard. Adherence cannot be assumed; performance and adherence to a high ethical standard will need to be marketed, promoted, and integral to the new culture of independence, flexibility, and freedom in how the work is done. Communication of these ideals must be embraced by the new culture.

There Are No Excuses

As we travel life's journey, most of us experience challenges, especially financial challenges. The current enormous debt faced by those who had to borrow their way through college seems almost unfair. Then we discovered the statistics about household debt and savings levels, and it became easier to understand why the gig economy has grown in its appeal. People need to find ways to earn more. Traditionally, this was not easy to do. Who wants to really get excited about a part-time job that requires the same rigidity associated with the traditional full-time job? During the research for this book, I remembered several close friends who worked two traditional full-time jobs at a point in their lives. When they finished the work at one job, they immediately went to the second job.

I also remember when it was rather easy to succumb to despair when a bill could not be paid because the money had run out before the month. The gig economy provides more choices than ever when it comes to finding ways to earn additional income. Whatever our circumstance, regardless of age or résumé, the gig economy has created an opportunity. Anyone interested in earning more, paying off debt, saving and investing more, or simply doing more of what is most enjoyable should explore the possibility of a gig.

Trust Is a Valuable Commodity

The gig economy, if taken seriously by gig workers, is an economy built upon the value of trust. Trust is available to anyone who wants to embrace and leverage it as a primary tool. By extending the best of service, the best of professionalism, regardless of the type of work being performed, the client and customer will take notice, and the development of a trusting relationship will most likely lead to satisfied clients and consumers who may continue to embrace the brand and/or the products or services rendered. The gig economy makes it possible to leverage the value of trust.

Gigs Unleash Talents, Grow Confidence, and Enhance Self-Esteem

The gig economy makes it easier than ever before for people to explore microentrepreneurship. With a low cost of entry and a high probability of at least modest income, people from all walks of life are experiencing how it feels to be their own boss, even if it is only for a portion of their total household work. When people have more control over their finances and can see a direct correlation between their efforts and the rewards, they tend to feel more optimistic about the future and begin to dream bigger.

The exceptionally high satisfaction scores workers gave to their gig experiences in our survey showcase the positive experience people are having within the gig economy. Feeling good about your work tends to have a halo effect on other aspects of your life. We hope to explore this idea more in future research.

REFLECTIONS

We became excited about the gig economy phenomenon several years ago. It has been wonderful to observe and research and exciting to participate in work such as this. Our society is forever grateful for the inventions and utilization of technology that puts the control of so many products and services into devices that fit the palm of a hand. We are also excited about the freedoms being created by the gig economy, possibly leveling the playing field of income opportunities like none other. Of course, this would not be noteworthy if consumers were not benefiting, to a higher degree, from the quality and variety of services offered with an appealing price/value relationship.

Of all the gig types, direct selling appears to be positioned for a new period of appeal and growth within the gig economy context. We expect even easier entry and a greater focus on customer acquisition, retention, and sponsorship of others who duplicate customer acquisition and retention behaviors to support brand-building strategies. Direct selling models are also expected to attract a much higher percentage of those who seek gigs simply because direct selling companies approach selling, customer service, rewards for sharing and involving others, recognition of performance, and providing a sense of community a bit differently.

The future has arrived! The marketplace is favorable to new ways to purchase products and services. Gig opportunities will continue to grow as a viable distribution channel and a meaningful way to earn income. The ultimate gig is ultimately the one that best matches the gig seeker's definition of what matters most.

Our ultimate motivation for taking on the work of this book, this research project, is rooted in a belief that the gig economy is helping to define a new reality; flexibility and freedom in how work is done can be achieved. We believe in the free enterprise system. We believe that by taking the time to create this book, we spark or join conversations that impact lives, which is always appealing to those of us who focus on contribution. When we focus on contribution, we best explore the possibilities that improve the quality of any product or service and the quality of all the lives we touch.

What we found in researching the gig economy convinces us that most of the workforce is going to be working differently. Therefore, it is easy for us to predict that the gig economy will continue to grow, and the choices will be even more numerous than they are today. Gig-providing companies can expect a marketplace that will continue to be favorable to part-time work opportunities. Each sector or category of gig work will become competitive for the gig-providing company as more players enter the game. The competitive spirit of free enterprise is expected to yield more benefits and better service for consumers and more income opportunities and choices for gig seekers.

REFLECTIONS FROM TWO OUTSTANDING GRADUATE STUDENTS

We were honored to work with Christina Schreiber and Christian Panier, MBA students at the Crummer Graduate School of Business at Rollins College, Winter Park, Florida, on the Ultimate Gig. We asked them to share their conclusions as we wrapped up the project.

As we came to the close of the *Ultimate Gig* project, things felt bittersweet. This project morphed and twisted and grew in ways we never could have expected at the onset, and we are very grateful to have been a part of it. We moved from a more logistical, facilitating role to one that was much more hands-on. Our work on the *Ultimate Gig* project was not our first exposure to the literary side of business, but it was the most primary research we have done as graduate assistants so far, and we have learned a lot.

Our biggest takeaway: there is an entire hidden world of people working to make their dreams a reality and helping to reduce the monotony of day-to-day life. This world is extremely pervasive, too. Just within our own networks, we had our pick of contacts who were involved with some gig company or other – those with Etsy or Shopify stores, those who walk dogs after work, those with Twitch channels, those who drove for Uber, and the list goes on.

More than that, people were interested! Friends would ask us about the gig project, send us interesting articles from the local paper, or offer up their favorite experiences with gig companies. It is difficult to keep up with the changes in the gig economy that are being wrought by the pandemic, but we have seen people come together in new ways and have no doubt that this transformative time will inspire innovation from the farthest corners of the world. We are looking forward to seeing how companies can continue helping people connect and reach for their goals.

One of the primary reasons we applied for graduate school was to open doors and build relationships. We did not realize just how impactful that would prove. People want to help people, and people particularly want to help students. We are grateful for the friendships and relationships that have blossomed through this process. We are impressed with the team's dedication to getting the project done, even in the midst of global change.

We would like to say thank you to all of the executives, press teams, and other employees who took the time to chat with us about the book and about the future of the gig economy. We are inspired by the gig workers we talked to, some of whom are just starting out and others who have turned their dreams into a reality, working full-time on their gig-based businesses.

Thank you, most especially, to Dr. Greg Marshall, Lauren Lawley Head, and John Fleming for the opportunity to be a part of this project. We have always maintained that we are lucky to have a graduate assistantship that allows us room to be creative, collaborative, and inquisitive, and you have given us the room to participate in a larger conversation regarding the world we are diving into. We look forward to continuing that conversation in the future.

SUMMARY/OUTLOOK

As we arrived at this point in the work, we were both sad and glad. To conclude work such as this is also to begin a new quest to learn even more. We approached the work that went into this book intending to serve three audiences of readers:

1. The general marketplace of readers who are continually exploring possibilities because they are dissatisfied with the status quo. This is an essential segment in our society, and they read many books. They continuously drive innovation and change within their jobs, in the activities they pursue outside of their primary jobs, in their personal lives, and their families' lives. They love change and believe that life can always offer more. To this audience, we have consolidated thoughts and insights learned from experience and observation. We believe gigs should be explored by anyone capable of investing a few more hours in a day simply because we can. There is so much more that we can do with our time today than we could 25 years ago. In many ways, the gig economy is sending a message; no more excuses

because we can now be more in control of some portions of our income possibilities. Some will find ways to make a gig their full-time way of working. A gig can convert underutilized time into an asset.

2. We also knew we wanted to produce a body of work that could be embraced and used within the academic community. The classroom combination of professors and students is where innovation and ideas are often birthed. The brave, courageous, and brilliant students who are molded, shaped, and led by professors' wisdom and experience create new forces that enter the marketplace with every graduating class. It is truly a phenomenal process, probably why I tend to "tear up" every time I hear the song *Pomp and Circumstance*. A new graduating class means new brilliance is being unleashed into our society. We wanted this work to be appealing to the academic community because, if used there, it would be like having the best laboratories in the world validate and perpetuate the information and ideas within. Because of our second defined targeted audience, we invited many of our academic friends to advise, share, or participate in the work.

3. The business and regulatory communities are important. We wanted our work's outcome to be valuable to the decision-makers in companies, who are already changing the landscape of the future of work, and those who have regulatory responsibility who seek information and understanding, so crucial to the decisions they will make.

Regulatory personnel also benefit from knowledge and insights that may help to better understand the positive aspects of new phenomena that disrupt traditional practices, especially work models that can shift a tax base or redefine long-standing rules and regulations.

This book has been focused on each of the audiences we just described, and we hope that each has benefited. The future of work defines the future of the world!

RESOURCES & REFERENCES

The following are resources and references for material in Ultimate Gig or which influenced the Ultimate Gig team's thinking throughout the project. They are organized below based on the first chapter to which the item most closely aligns.

2018 Amway global entrepreneurship report. (2018). Amway.

2018 APAC workforce insights: Q1 report. (2018). Persol Kelly.

2019 Global Human Capital Trends. (2019). *Deloitte Insights.* Retrieved from https://www2.deloitte.com/content/dam/Deloitte/cz/Documents/human-capital/cz-hc-trends-reinvent-with-human-focus.pdf

2020 Global Marketing Trends. (2020). *Deloitte Insights.*

A significant number of Americans are interested in flexible, entrepreneurial opportunities. (2020, March 3). *Ipsos.* Press Release.

Abraham, K. G., Haltiwanger, J. C., Sandusky, K., & Spletzer, J. R. (2018, August). *Measuring the gig economy: Current knowledge and open issues.* Cambridge, MA: National Bureau of Economic Research. Retrieved from http://www.nber.org/papers/w24950

Accelerating our unprecedented growth. (2019). DoorDash. Retrieved from https://blog.doordash.com/accelerating-our-unprecedented-growth-e5c9eb343ce8

Bahney, A. (2018). 40% of Americans can't cover a $400 emergency expense. *CNN Money.* Retrieved from https://money.cnn.com/2018/05/22/pf/emergency-expenses-household-finances/index.html

Bajwa, U., Knorr, L., Di Ruggiero, E., Gastaldo, D., & Zendel, A. (2018, April). *Towards an understanding of workers' experiences in the global gig economy.* Global Migration & Health Initiative. Toronto, Ontario. Retrieved from https://www.glomhi.org/uploads/7/4/4/8/74483301/workers_in_the_global_gig_economy.pdf

Barnett, C. (2013). Top 10 crowdfunding sites for fundraising. *Forbes.* Retrieved from https://www.forbes.com/sites/chancebarnett/2013/05/08/top-10-crowd-funding-sites-for-fundraising/#6cb4f2623850

Barzilay, A. R., & Ben-David, A. (2017, February 16). Platform inequality: Gender in the gig-economy. Retrieved from https://poseidon01.ssrn.com/delivery.php?ID=702000084013069001075107029068029065061037007020071061119066029014064125077103117101058020007125050109119004019122001125117015030071029038092102112007123001070024038040202209609602002408108602509300808800300600708908906611509612408102908900050670711068&EXT=pdf&INDEX=TRUE

Beres, D. (2017). 6 weird kickstarters that actually got funded. *Reader's Digest.* Retrieved from https://www.rd.com/list/weird-kickstarters-that-actually-got-funded/

Boulton, R. E. S., Libert, B. D., & Samekl, S. M. (2000). *Cracking the value code.* New York, NY: HarperCollins Publishers.

Bracha, A., & Burke, M. A. (2014, December). Informal work activity in the United States: Evidence from survey responses. Federal Reserve Bank of Boston (No. 14–13).

Brockland, B., Garon, T., Dunn, A., Wilson, E., & Celik, N. (2019). *U.S. Financial health pulse: 2019 trends report.* Financial Health Network. Retrieved from https://s3.amazonaws.com/cfsi-innovation-files-2018/wp-content/uploads/2019/12/16161507/2019-Pulse-Report-FINAL_1205.pdf. Accessed on September 18, 2020.

Brzezinski, Brzezinski, M., Ginny, B. (2020). *Comeback careers.* New York, NY: Hachette Books.

Building a 100-Year Company. (2020). *Shopify's 2019 sustainability report.* Shopify. Retrieved from https://cdn.shopify.com/static/sustainability-report/2019%20Shopify%20Sustainability%20Report.pdf

Caruso, J. (2020). Coronavirus and the gig economy – tensions grow between grubhub and restaurants. *The Daily Caller.* Retrieved from https://daily-caller.com/2020/04/26/coronavirus-gig-economy-grubhub-price-restaurants/

Charan, R., & Bossidy, L. (2002). *Execution.* New York, NY: Crown business, division of Random House.

Charan, R., & Tichy, N. (1998). *Every business is a growth business.* New York, NY: Times Books, division of Random House.

Clement, J. (2019). U.S. user reach of leading video platforms of 2018. *Stat.* Retrieved from https://www-statista-com.ezproxy.rollins.edu/statistics/266201/us-market-share-of-leading-internet-video-portals/

Coca-Cola, Uber Eats partner to combat hunger. (2020). Beverage Industry. Retrieved from https://www.bevindustry.com/articles/93244-coca-cola-uber-eats-partner-to-combat-hunger

Collins, B., Garin, A., Jackson, E., Koustas, D., & Payne, M. (2019, March 25). Is gig work replacing traditional employment? Evidence from two decades of tax returns. IRS SOI Joint Statistical Research Program.

Collins, J. (2001). *Good to great.* New York, NY: HarperCollins Publishers.

Contingent workforce: Size, characteristics, earnings, and benefits. (2015, April 20). Washington, DC: U.S. Government Accountability Office.

Creating value and impact through the alternative workforce. (2019). *Deloitte.* Retrieved from https://www2.deloitte.com/us/en/pages/human-capital/articles/alternativeworkforce.html

Dautovic, G. (2020). 15 must-know outsourcing statistics (2020 update). *Fortunly.* Retrieved from https://fortunly.com/statistics/outsourcing-statistics

Delaney Thomas, K. (2018). Taxing the gig economy. *University of Pennsylvania Law Review, 166,* 1415–1473. Retrieved from https://ssrn.com/abstract=2894394

DeSilver, D. (2018, August 7). *For most U.S. workers, real wages have barely budged in decades.* Pew Research Center. Washington, DC. Retrieved from https://www.pewresearch.org/fact-tank/2018/08/07/for-most-us-workers-real-wages-have-barely-budged-for-decades/

Diamandis, P. H., & Kotler, S. (2015). *Bold.* New York, NY: Simon & Shuster.

Diamandis, P. H., & Kotler, S. (2020). *The future is faster thank you think.* New York, NY: Simon & Schuster.

Dillet, R. (2019). BlaBlaCar to acquire online bus ticketing platform Busfor. *TechCrunch.* Retrieved from https://techcrunch.com/2019/09/24/blablacar-to-acquire-online-bus-ticketing-platform-busfor/

Direct Selling News. (2018). Dallas, TX: Direct Selling News. Monthly Publication. Print & Digital.

Drop, D. (2020). How twitch streamers make money. *Dare Drop*. Retrieved from https://daredrop.com/blog/index.php/2020/02/27/how-twitch-streamers-make-money/?gclid=CjwKCAjwrcH3BRApEiwAxjdPTemhcPtVGhmtZI smAgqrfHBjhaVQ_raTa49kL7v_wHIFW4pt.03Bw2hoCynYQAvD_BwE

Eddington, J. (2016). Ride-sharing vs. Ride-hailing: What's the difference? *The Zebra*. Retrieved from https://www.thezebra.com/insurance-news/2811/ ride-sharing-vs-ride-hailing/

Farrell, D., Greig, F., & Hamoudi, A. (2018). The online platform economy in 2018: Drivers, workers, sellers, and lendors. JP Morgan Chase & Co. Institute.

Federal Reserve Board. (2017, June 14). *Report on the economic well-being of U.S. Households in 2016 - May 2017.* U.S. Federal Reserve. Retrieved from https://www.federalreserve.gov/publications/2017-economic-well-being-of-us-households-in-2016-economic-preparedness.htm. Accessed on September 10, 2020.

Federal Reserve Board. (2020, September 8). Consumer credit – G.19: Consumer credit outstanding (levels). U.S. Federal Reserve. Retrieved from https://www.federalreserve.gov/releases/g19/HIST/cc_hist_memo_levels.html. Accessed on September 10, 2020.

Federal Reserve Board. (2020, May). *Report on the economic well-being of U.S. Households in 2019, featuring supplemental data from April 2020.* Retrieved from https://www.federalreserve.gov/publications/files/2019-report-economic-well-being-us-households-202005.pdf. Accessed on September 9, 2020.

Fidelity Viewpoints. (2020, July). How much do I need to retire? *Fidelity*. Retrieved from https://www.pymnts.com/gig-economy/2018/hyperwallet-tilr-digital-marketplace/. Accessed on September 18, 2020.

Galarza, D. (2017). McDonald's doubles down on food delivery with Uber Eats. *Eater.com*. Retrieved from https://www.eater.com/2017/10/24/16453444/ mcdonalds-doubles-down-on-food-delivery-with-ubereats

Gansky, L. (2016). The life & times of we the people in the age of distributed power. *Instigating.co.*

Georgieva, K. (2019, November 14). Measuring the informal economy. Washington, DC. Retrieved from https://www.imf.org/en/News/Articles/2019/11/14/sp111419-the-informal-economy-and-inclusive-growth. Accessed on September 10, 2020.

Gessner, K. (2020). Uber vs. Lyft: Who's tops in the battle of U.S. rideshare companies. *Second Measure.* Retrieved from https://secondmeasure.com/datapoints/rideshare-industry-overview/

Gig Economy Index. (2019, January). Hyperwallet and PYMNTS.com.

Gig economy: A boon for women. (2019, May 24). *Entrepreneur.* Asia Pacific edition.

Gitis, B., Holtz-Eakin, D., & Rinehart, W. (2017, January). *The gig economy: Research and policy implications of regional, economic, and demographic trends. Future of Work Initiative & American Action Forum.* Retrieved from https://www.americanactionforum.org/research/gig-economy-research-policy-implicationsregional-economic-demographic-trends/#:;:text5The%20Gig%20Economy%3A%20Research%20and%20Policy%20Implications%20of,and%20the%20Aspen%20Institute%E2%80%99s%20Future%20of%20Work%20Initiative

#Gig responsibly: The rise of NextGen work. (2017). *Manpower Group.* Retrieved from https://www.manpowergroup.com/wps/wcm/connect/cf010c08-826a-4f00-bd27-70a63144083d/manpowergroup-next-GEN-work.pdf?MOD=AJPERES. Accessed on September 18, 2020.

Global human capital trends 2016. (2016). New York, NY: Deloitte University Press.

Gobble, M. A. M. (2017). Defining the sharing economy. *Research-Technology Management, 60*(2), 59–61. doi:10.1080/08956308.2017.1276393

Gore, A. (2013). *Al Gore the future.* New York, NY: Random House.

GrubHub form 10-K. (2018). SEC. Retrieved from https://www.sec.gov/Archives/edgar/data/1594109/000156459019005487/grub-10k_20181231.htm

Guttmann, A. (2020). U.S. YouTube net advertising revenues 2018-2022. *Stat.* Retrieved from https://www-statista-com.ezproxy.rollins.edu/statistics/289660/youtube-us-net-advertising-revenues/

Hagel, J., Schwartz, J., & Bersin, J. (2017, July). Navigating the future of work. *Deloitte Review*, (21). Retrieved from https://www2.deloitte.com/za/en/pages/human-capital/articles/navigating-the-future-of-work.html

Hagel, J., Schwartz, J., & Bersin, J. (2019). Redefining work for new value: The next opportunity. *MIT Sloan Management Review*. Retrieved from https://mitsmr.com/2OFAAa8

Harris, S. D., & Krueger, A. B. (2015, December). A proposal for modernizing labor laws for twenty-first-century work: The "independent worker. Discussion Paper 2015-10. The Hamilton Project. Retrieved from https://www.hamilton-project.org/assets/files/modernizing_labor_laws_for_twenty_first_century_work_krueger_harris.pdf. Accessed on September 10, 2020.

Helling, B. (2020). How much does Instacart pay in 2020? Instacart's pay structure revealed. *Ridester.com*. Retrieved from https://www.ridester.com/how-much-do-instacart-drivers-make/

Household debt remains high. (2020, March 9). Peter G. Peterson Foundation. Retrieved from https://www.pgpf.org/chart-archive/0062_household-debt

Hunt, A., & Samman, E. (2019, January). *Gender and the gig economy: Critical steps for evidence-based policy*. Working Paper 546. Overseas Development Institute, London. Retrieved from https://www.odi.org/publications/11272-gender-and-gig-economy-critical-steps-evidence-based-policy

IHS Markit. (2017). Franchise business economic outlook for 2018. International Franchise Association Franchise Education and Research Foundation.

Jin, L. (2019, October 8). The passion economy and the future of work. Andressen Horowitz. Retrieved from https://a16z.com/2019/10/08/passion-economy/. Accessed on September 18, 2020.

Just eat buys Canadian-based skip the dishes for $110 million. (2016). *CTV News*. Retrieved from https://www.ctvnews.ca/business/just-eat-buys-canadian-based-skipthedishes-for-110m-1.3204999

Katz, L. F., & Krueger, A. B. (2016, September). *The rise and nature of alternative work arrangements in the United States, 1995-2015*. Cambridge, MA: National Bureau of Economic Research. Retrieved from http://www.nber.org/papers/w22667

Key, A. (2019). Amazon takes bite of Deliveroo in £450m funding round. *Yahoo Finance*. Retrieved from https://uk.finance.yahoo.com/news/amazon-takes-bite-deliveroo-450-061951253.html?guccounter=1&guce_referrer=''' aHR0cHM6Ly9lbi53aWtpcGVkaWEuEub3JnL3dpa2kvRGVsaXZlcm9v& guce_referrer_sig=AQAAAG-ur7vTX40_DV8oohoqF_xYKUDr0MYNW_ fuRNp7rq2zqJqFGGO3Lmjmz8fUxMXHWkdabbfuhPGKyeKibmnQPKTjlXf 3jTKh72CSvHQpZoej6Mlj8NzWTUf4tcu9EftHD_wdZ7nx08Y3hkgsBv-yjiVxUhTcI86Hc5K0qUa2qncE

Kharpal, A. (2016). Taxi app rival Didi Chuxing to buy Uber's China business in $35 billion deal. *CNBC*. Retrieved from https://www.cnbc.com/2016/08/01/ chinas-didi-chuxing-to-acquire-ubers-chinese-operations-wsj.html

Kile, C. (2020). HomeAdvisor vs. Angie's list vs. Houzz vs. Porch vs. Thumbtack vs. Yelp vs. Bark. Adapt Digital Solutions. Retrieved from https://www. adaptdigitalsolutions.com/blog/homeadvisor-vs-angieslist-vs-houzz-vs-porch-vs-thumbtack-vs-yelp-vs-bark/#contractor-con

Lifestyle category. (2020). Fiverr. Retrieved from https://www.fiverr.com/cate-gories/lifestyle

Lyft. (2020). Find your city. *Lyft*. Retrieved from https://www.lyft.com/rider/ cities

Marino, J. (2020). Uber needs grubhub to keep growing – these charts explain why. *Forbes*. Retrieved from https://www.forbes.com/sites/jonmarino/2020/05/ 13/uber-needs-grubhub-to-keep-growingthese-charts-explain-why/ #3cca08ff696d

Market share of the leading ride-hailing companies in the United States from September 2017 to April 2020. (2020). *Statista*. Retrieved from https:// www.statista.com/statistics/910704/market-share-of-rideshare-companies-united-states/

Mastercard gig economy industry outlook and needs assessment. (2019, May). Mastercard and Kaiser Associates.

Mitic, I. (2020). Gig economy statistics 2020: The new normal in the workplace. *Fortunly*. Retrieved from https://fortunly.com/statistics/gig-economy-statistics

Mohan, A., & Sen, S. (2019). Ola valued at $10 billion in ongoing funding round. *MoneyControl*. Retrieved from https://www.moneycontrol.com/news/business/companies/ola-valued-at-10-billion-in-ongoing-funding-round-4584971.html

Monahan, K., Schwartz, J., & Schleeter, T. (2018). Decoding millennials in the gig economy. *Deloitte Insights*. Retrieved from https://www2.deloitte.com/content/dam/insights/us/articles/4569_Decoding-millennials/DI_Decoding-millennials.pdf

Morehouse, W., Speiser, S., & Taylor, K. (2000, March). The universal capitalism movement in the United States. *Review of Social Economy, 58*(1), 63–80. doi:10.1080/003467600363110

National tracking poll #180825 August 16–19, 2018 (p. 38). (August 2018). Morning Consult. Retrieved from https://morningconsult.com/wp-content/uploads/2018/09/180825_crosstabs_BRANDS_v1_DK-3.pdf. Accessed on September 18, 2020.

New study shows what consumers crave in a food delivery service. (2019). U.S. Foods. Retrieved from https://www.usfoods.com/our-services/business-trends/2019-food-delivery-statistics.html

Oyer, P. (2016, November 30). The independent workforce in America: The economics of an increasingly flexible labor market. Upwork. Retrieved from https://www.upwork.com/i/us-independent-workforce/

Oyer, P. (2020, January). The Gig Economy: Non-traditional employment is a great opportunity for many, but it won't replace traditional employment. *IZA World of Labor*. Retrieved from https://wol.iza.org/articles/the-gig-economy/long

Ozimek, A. (2019, November 14). *Report: Freelancing and the economy in 2019*. Upwork. Press Release.

P2P lending market – forecast (2020-2025). (2019). Industry ARC. Retrieved from https://www.industryarc.com/Report/19177/P2P-Lending-Market

Personal savings rate 1960-2018. (2018). Federal Reserve Economic Data. St. Louis Fed. PowerPoint Presentation.

Peterson, R. A., & Ferrell, O. C. (2005). *Business ethics.* Armonk, NY: M.E. Sharpe, Inc.

Peterson, R. A., & Wotruba, T. R. (1996). What is direct selling? – definition, perspectives, and research agenda. *Journal of Personal Selling and Sales Management, 16*(4), 1–16.

Peterson, R. A. (2018). Professional and personal benefits of a direct selling experience. Direct Selling Education Foundation. Retrieved from https://dsef.org/wp-content/uploads/2018/07/Professional-Personal-Benefits-Report.pdf#:~:text=PROFESSIONAL%20AND%20PERSONAL%20BENEFITS%20OF%20A%20DIRECT%20SELLING,selling%20experience%20suggests%20a%20variety%20of%20managerial%20implications

PYMNTS.com. (2018, August). New data: 58 percent of gig workers don't hold full-time jobs – and don't want to. *PYMNTS.com.* Retrieved from https://www.pymnts.com/gig-economy/2018/hyperwallet-tilr-digital-marketplace/. Accessed on September 18, 2020.

Quarterly report on household debt and credit: Q2 2020. (2020, August). Federal Reserve Bank of New York - Center for Microeconomic Data. Retrieved from https://www.newyorkfed.org/medialibrary/interactives/householdcredit/data/pdf/HHDC_2020Q2.pdf. Accessed on September 20, 2020.

Ransbotham, S., Kiron, D., Gerbert, P., & Reeves, M. (2017). Reshaping business with artificial intelligence: Closing the gap between ambition and action. *MIT Sloan Management Review.* Retrieved from https://image-src.bcg.com/Images/Reshaping%20Business%20with%20Artificial%20Intelligence_tcm9-177882.pdf

Redefining entrepreneurship: Etsy's sellers' economic impact. (2013). *Etsy.* Retrieved from https://blog.etsy.com/news/2013/redefining-entrepreneurship-etsy-sellers-economic-impact/

Reilly, C. (2020). Technology trends that will disrupt the future of work in 2020. *Forbes.* Retrieved from https://www.forbes.com/sites/forbestechcouncil/2020/01/03/technology-trends-that-will-disrupt-the-future-of-work-in-2020/#20d98d936abe

Report on the economic well-being of U.S. Households in 2018. (2019, May). Board of Governors of the Federal Reserve.

Robles, B., & McGee, M. (2016). Exploring online and offline informal work: Findings from the enterprising and informal work activities (EIWA) survey. Finance and Economics Discussion Series 2016-089. Washington, DC: Board of Governors of the Federal Reserve System doi:10.17016/FEDS.2016.089

Roy, A. (2018). Delivery start-up Postmates expanding to 100 new cities and going deeper with Chipotle. *CNBC*. Retrieved from https://www.cnbc.com/2018/07/09/postmates-adds-100-new-cities-goes-deeper-with-chipotle.html

Sandberg, S. (2013). *Lean in: Women, work, and the will to lead*. New York, NY: Alfred A. Knopf.

Scott, R. (2020). Introducing offsite ads: A new risk-free way to advertise. *Etsy News*. Retrieved from https://blog.etsy.com/news/2020/introducing-offsite-ads-a-new-risk-free-way-to-advertise/

Shopify. (2020b). Shopify releases 2019 sustainability report and economic impact report. Shopify. Retrieved from https://news.shopify.com/shopify-releases-2019-sustainability-report-and-economic-impact-report

Shopify. (2020a). Shopify announces fourth-quarter and full-year 2019 financial results. Shopify. Retrieved from https://news.shopify.com/shopify-announces-fourth-quarter-and-full-year-2019-financial-results

Sim, D. (2020). The Covid-19 crisis is hurting Asia's gig economy workers and they want the government to help. *South China Morning Post*. Retrieved from https://www.scmp.com/week-asia/economics/article/3075125/coronavirus-bites-southeast-asias-gig-workers-eye-government

Skip the Dishes pulling out of U.S. market after making deal with rival company. (2020). *CBC News*. Retrieved from https://www.cbc.ca/news/canada/manitoba/skip-the-dishes-us-market-1.5085749

Smith Meeks, J. (2017). *Gracious leadership*. Westlake, OH: Smart Business Network.

Smith, I. (2019). The FT 1000: Third annual list of Europe's fastest-growing companies. *The Financial Times*. Retrieved from https://www.ft.com/content/238174d2-3139-11e9-8744-e7016697f225

Solomon, M. R., Marshall, G. W., & Stuart, E. W. (2018). *Marketing: Real people, real choices* (9th ed.). Hoboken, NJ: Pearson.

Steward, S. (2018, November 2). Annual freelancing in America survey addresses size and needs of independent workforce. *Gig Economy Data Hub.* Retrieved from https://www.gigeconomydata.org/blog/freelancing-america-2018. Accessed on August 26, 2020.

Sundararajan, A. (2017). *The sharing economy.* Cambridge, MA; London: The MIT Press.

The future of gig work is female. (2017). HyperWallet.

The gig economy – marketplace-Edison research poll. (2018, December). Edison Research & Marketplace.

The gig economy and alternative work arrangements. (2018). Gallup Inc.

The gig economy: Opportunities, challenges, and employer strategies. 17th Annual U.S. Employee Benefit Trends Study 2019. (2019). *MetLife.*

The new science of distributed workforce productivity growth. White paper. (2019). Rallyware Inc.

The state of independence in America 2019: The changing nature of the American workforce. (2019). MBO Partners. Retrieved from https://s29814.pcdn.co/wp-content/uploads/2019/06/MBO-SOI-2019.pdf. Accessed on September 18, 2020.

Top 100 gig economy jobs like Uber. (2019, April 23). Hurdlr. Retrieved from https://www.hurdlr.com/blog/on-demand-economy-gigs. Accessed August 26, 2020.

U.S. Bureau of Economic Analysis. (2020, September 9). Personal saving rate [PSAVERT]. Federal Reserve Bank of St. Louis. Retrieved from https://fred.stlouisfed.org/series/PSAVERT

Uber. (2017). Sustainability on the go with uberGREEN. Uber. Retrieved from https://www.uber.com/en-CH/blog/zurich/454743/

Ultimate Gig. (2019). Dallas, TX: Ideas & Design Group.

Upwork. (2019, September). Freelancing in America: 2019. Slide 15. Upwork & Freelancers' Union. Retrieved from https://www.slideshare.net/upwork/freelancing-in-america-2019/1. Accessed on September 10, 2020.

Vaynerchuk, G. (2011). *The thank you economy.* New York, NY: HarperCollins Publishers.

Warriors partner with Uber Eats to launch 'golden giveback'. (2020). NBA. Retrieved from https://www.nba.com/warriors/news/uber-eats-golden-giveback-20200624

What is the gig economy? (2018, March 22). *Deputy.com*. Retrieved from https://www.deputy.com/blog/gig-economy-jobs-the-ultimate-list. Accessed on August 26, 2020.

Women as levers of change: Unleashing the power of women to transform male-dominated industries. (2018). FP Analytics. Retrieved from https://womenasleversofchange.com/

Yildirmaz, A., Goldar, M., & Klein, S. (2020, February). *Illuminating the shadow workforce: Insights into the gig workforce in businesses*. ADP Research Institute.

Zenger, J., & Folkman, J. (2019, June 25). Research: Women score higher than men in most leadership skills. *Harvard Business Review*. Retrieved from https://hbr.org/2019/06/research-women-score-higher-than-men-in-most-leadership-skills

https://ipropertymanagement.com/research/airbnb-statistics

https://kajabi.com/about-us.

https://news.airbnb.com

https://news.shopify.com/company-info

https://www.buzzfeednews.com/article/allysonlaquian/can-you-make-real-money-on-a-dog-walking-app

https://www.etsy.com/press?ref=ftr

https://www.fundingcircle.com/us/about/

https://www.lendingclub.com/

https://www.prosper.com/about

https://www.wealthyaffiliate.com

INDEX